Pan Study Aids

KV-374-486

German

D. F. Shotter

Pan Books London and Sydney
in association with **Heinemann Educational Books**

First published 1981 by Pan Books Ltd,
Cavaye Place, London SW10 9PG
in association with Heinemann Educational Books Ltd
2 3 4 5 6 7 8 9
ISBN 0 330 26474 5
© D. F. Shotter 1981
Printed and bound in Great Britain by
Richard Clay (The Chaucer Press) Ltd, Bungay, Suffolk

Pan Study Aids
Titles published in this series

Accounts and Book-keeping
Biology
British Government and Politics
Chemistry
Commerce
Economics
Effective Study Skills
English Language
French
Geography 1   *Physical and Human*
Geography 2   *British Isles, Western Europe, North America*
German
History 1   *British*
History 2   *European*
Human Biology
Maths
Physics
Spanish

Advanced Biology
Advanced Chemistry
Advanced Mathematics
Advanced Physics

Brodie's Notes on English Literature
This long established series published in Pan Study Aids now
contains more than 150 titles. Each volume covers one of the
major works of English literature regularly set for examinations.

Illustrations by M. Brierley

Contents

Acknowledgements

The publishers are grateful to the following Exam Boards, whose addresses are listed on pages 7 and 8, for permission to reproduce questions from examination papers:

Associated Examining Board, University of Cambridge Local Examinations Syndicate, Joint Matriculation Board, University of London Schools Examination Department, Oxford and Cambridge Schools Examination Board, Oxford Delegacy of Local Examinations, Southern Universities Joint Board, Welsh Joint Education Committee.

The suggested answers to past examination questions are the work of the author and not of the examination boards concerned.

The publishers are also grateful to Heinemann Educational Books for permission to reproduce material from *Deutscher Sprachkurs*.

To the student

How this book can help you

This is not a course book. It has been designed to complement the work you will have done at school, at evening class or during your private study.

It aims to help you with your revision by suggesting *what* you should revise and *how* you should revise most efficiently. There are regular opportunities for you to test yourself on vocabulary and grammar. Hints on the techniques of revision are carefully explained and advice on essay writing, translation from and into German, comprehensions, oral tests and dictation is given together with appropriate practice materials. Suggested answers are given for the exercises and many of the tests so that you will be able to check your progress.

How to use the study aid
More detailed advice on how to approach the individual skills is given at the beginning of the major sections of the book but you may find the following general hints useful.

1 Remember that to be successful at O level you must have a wide and accurate vocabulary and a good knowledge of German grammar.
2 Don't just stare at the pages and hope that the information will sink in. Make your revision positive. Always have a notebook handy and keep an accurate record of what you revise. Do a *little* at a time but *often*! Test yourself in writing.
3 Read through the grammar section carefully and learn it as thoroughly as possible. Persevere with those sections you may find difficult.

4 Make a careful note of the vocabulary you don't know. The successful linguist will bother to look up and check genders and plurals of nouns, principal parts of verbs, etc. Revise the vocabulary frequently. Don't just leave it to 'rot' in your notebook.

5 Try to work your way through all of the book. You will find that the units overlap and complement each other.

6 If you have a cassette recorder, use it to help you with your revision.

7 When you have done the exercises and tests, use the answer key as a new set of exercises. The original questions will become your new answer key.

8 *Hals- und Beinbruch!*

The Exam Boards

The addresses given below are those from which copies of syllabuses and past examination papers may be ordered. The abbreviations (AEB, etc.) are those used in this book to identify actual questions.

Associated Examining Board,   (AEB)
Wellington House,
Aldershot, Hants GU11 1BQ

Unversity of Cambridge Local Examinations Syndicate,   (CAM)
Syndicate Buildings, 17 Harvey Road,
Cambridge CB1 2EU

Joint Matriculation Board   (JMB)
(Agent) John Sherratt and Son Ltd,
78 Park Road
Altrincham, Cheshire WA14 5QQ

University of London School Examinations Department,   (LOND)
66–72 Gower Street,
London WC1E 6EE

Oxford and Cambridge Schools Examination Board,   (O & C)
10 Trumpington Street,
Cambridge CB2 1QB

Oxford Delegacy of Local Examinations,   (OX)
Ewert Place,
Summertown,
Oxford OX2 7BZ

Southern Universities Joint Board,   (SUJB)
Cotham Road, Bristol BS6 6DD

Welsh Joint Education Committee,   (WEL)
245 Western Avenue,
Cardiff CF5 2YX

1 Revising grammar

In the same way as a motor mechanic needs a car manual to help him understand the way a car works, the language student needs something similar to help him understand how a language works. This is called grammar.

The grammar that follows is very basic and you should try to understand and learn all of it. You should consider it a bare minimum for the examination. It has been divided up into small units so that you can work intensively for a short time on a single topic and then test yourself. You can do this by writing out from memory the section you have been revising and by doing the practice sentences. You don't have to work in any particular order of units but keep a record of *what* and *how* you revise.

It is, however, a good idea to start with the glossary of grammar terms. Try to understand and remember the grammatical terminology. In the long run it should help you to understand better how German works.

Glossary of grammar terms

Parts of speech
Words can be divided up into several different groups called parts of speech. These include: nouns, articles, adjectives, pronouns, verbs, adverbs, prepositions and conjunctions.

Nouns are names of persons (e.g. Churchill, Herr Schmidt), places (Munich, Germany) and things. You can often tell if a word is a noun by seeing if it makes sense when preceded by *the* or *a* (*the* man; *a* car).

Articles: *The* is known as *the definite article* and *a* is called *the indefinite article*.

Adjectives describe nouns (e.g. words like *red*, *large*, *beautiful*. They frequently come between an article and a noun (a *red* book; the *large* house).

Pronouns are words that are used in place of nouns (I, you, he, she, it, we, they).

Verbs are words that denote actions or a state of being (e.g. the woman *was reading*; he *is* happy).

Verbs are usually accompanied by a noun or pronoun (e.g. the woman/he) called the *subject*. This tells you *who* or *what* does the action indicated by the verb.

Adverbs modify verbs (e.g. quickly, sadly, often, now).

Prepositions are used in phrases and are followed by a noun or pronoun. Many are to do with position (in, on, under, above, etc.).

Other prepositions include *with*, *during*, etc.

Conjunctions are used to join words, phrases, clauses or sentences (words like *and*, *but*, *or*).

Objects

Objects are the nouns or pronouns that are acted upon or affected by the verb. There are two types – the direct object and the indirect object.

The direct object   He (subject) visited (verb) *his uncle* (direct object). Ask yourself the question, '*Whom* did he visit?'

(Your answer is the direct object.)

He (subject) bought (verb) *a book* (direct object). Ask yourself the question, '*What* did he buy?' (Your answer is the direct object.)

The indirect object   An indirect object usually has the word *to* or *for* in front of it.

He (subject) bought (verb) a book (direct object) for *his son* (indirect object). Ask yourself the question, '*For whom* did he buy the book?'

(Your answer is the indirect object.)

He (subject) sent (verb) the letter (direct object) to *his brother* (indirect object). Ask yourself the question, '*To whom* did he send the letter?'
(Your answer is the indirect object.)

The words *to* and *for* do not always occur in the sentence, however, but you can easily rephrase it to enable you to identify the indirect object:

He bought his son a book (Rephrase as above.)
He sent his brother a letter. (Rephrase as above.)

Gender

All nouns in German have a gender. This could be masculine, feminine or neuter.

The three forms of the definite article are *der* (masculine), *die* (feminine) and *das* (neuter).

You must learn the gender of each noun as you meet it.

A noun may be preceded, however, not only by the definite or indefinite articles but also by a number of other words. You should learn the grammatical names for them (the three genders are given):

The definite article	(the) der/die/das
The demonstrative adjectives	(this) dieser/diese/dieses
	(that) jener/jene/jenes
	(each/every) jeder/jede/jedes
The interrogative adjective	(which?) welcher/welche/welches
The indefinite article	(a/an) ein/eine/ein
The negative of the indefinite article	(not a/an) kein/keine/kein
The possesssive adjectives	(my) mein/meine/mein

Here are some examples for a masculine noun (*der Garten*):

the garden	der Garten	definite article
this garden that garden each/every garden	dieser Garten jener Garten jeder Garten }	demonstrative adjectives
which garden?	welcher Garten?	interrogative adjective
a garden	ein Garten	indefinite article
not a garden	kein Garten	indefinite article (negative)

my garden	mein Garten	
your garden (familiar sg.)	dein Garten	
your garden (polite sg.)	Ihr Garten	
his garden	sein Garten	
her garden	ihr Garten	possessive adjectives
its garden	sein Garten	
our garden	unser Garten	
your garden (familiar pl.)	euer Garten	
your garden (polite pl.)	Ihr Garten	
their garden	ihr Garten	

Possession

In English, possession may be indicated by the possessive adjectives (see above *my* garden, *their* garden, etc.) or when there are two nouns by using an apostrophe *s* or by putting the word *of* in front of the noun that is the owner or possessor:

the man's car = the car of the man
the woman's cat = the cat of the woman

German also has possessive adjectives (see above, *mein* Garten, *ihr* Garten, etc.) but when you have two nouns, one of which is the owner or possessor of the other, always think of them in terms of the *of* construction: *of the man/of the woman*.

An introduction to case

You have seen in this glossary that nouns and pronouns have different functions in a sentence. They can be a subject, a direct object, show possession (of) or be an indirect object.

Compare the following sentences in English and German:

The man (subject) is reading.
Der Mann (subject) liest.

I saw *the man* (direct object).
Ich sah *den Mann* (direct object);

I saw the man's car (the car *of the man*) (possession (of)).
Ich sah das Auto *des Mannes* possession (of)).

I gave it to *the man* (indirect) object
Ich gab es *dem Mann* (indirect object).

Whereas English uses *the* man in each sentence, German has four different forms for the definite article: *der* Mann (subject), *den* Mann (direct object), *des* Mannes (possession (of)), *dem* Mann (indirect object).

You should, therefore, think of nouns and pronouns in German as existing on four levels. In grammar, each level is called a *case* and each case has a particular name: the nominative, the accusative, the genitive and the dative.

You might find it helpful to think of this as four floors of a house. Each floor has a name and is used for a particular purpose.

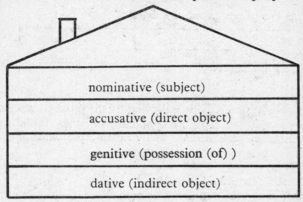

nominative (subject)

accusative (direct object)

genitive (possession (of))

dative (indirect object)

Der, den, des and *dem* are the masculine singular forms of the definite article. There are also corresponding forms in the four cases for the feminine and neuter as well as for the plural. Here is the complete table for the definite article. Learn it by heart and make sure you can write it out from memory.

The articles and limiting adjectives

The definite article

the	singular			plural
	masc.	fem.	neut.	all genders
nom.	der	die	das	die
acc.	den	die	das	die
gen.	des	der	des	der
dat.	dem	der	dem	den

Here are the tables for some other words that can precede a noun. Learn them by heart too and test yourself.

The indefinite article

a/an	singular		
	masc.	fem.	neut.
nom.	ein	eine	ein
acc.	einen	eine	ein
gen.	eines	einer	eines
dat.	einem	einer	einem

The negative of the indefinite article

not a/an	singular			plural
	masc.	fem.	neut.	all genders
nom.	kein	keine	kein	keine
acc.	keinen	keine	kein	keine
gen.	keines	keiner	keines	keiner
dat.	keinem	keiner	keinem	keinen

The possessive adjectives

our	singular			plural
	masc.	fem.	neut.	all genders
nom.	unser	unsere	unser	unsere
acc.	unseren	unsere	unser	unsere
gen.	unseres	unserer	unseres	unserer
dat.	unserem	unserer	unserem	unseren

and

my	mein	meine	mein	meine
your	dein	deine	dein	deine
your	Ihr	Ihre	Ihr	Ihre
his	sein	seine	sein	seine
her	ihr	ihre	ihr	ihre
its	sein	seine	sein	seine
your	euer	eure*	euer	eure*
your	Ihr	Ihre	Ihr	Ihre
their	ihr	ihre	ihr	ihre

* Note that the 'e' is left out when an ending is added

The demonstrative adjectives

this	singular			plural
(these)	masc.	fem.	neut.	all genders
nom.	dieser	diese	dieses	diese
acc.	diesen	diese	dieses	diese
gen.	dieses	dieser	dieses	dieser
dat.	diesem	dieser	diesem	diesen

Similarly:

jener	jene	jenes (that)	jene (pl.) (those)
jeder	jede	jedes (each/every)	(no pl.)
solcher	solche	solches (such a)	solche (pl.) (such)
mancher	manche	manches (many a)	manche (pl.) (many)

The interrogative adjective

which	singular			plural
	masc.	fem.	neut.	all genders
nom.	welcher	welche	welches	welche
acc.	welchen	welche	welches	welche
gen.	welches	welcher	welches	welcher
dat.	welchem	welcher	welchem	welchen

You should revise the notes on p. 109.

Translate into German 1 Which man lives in that house? **2** Her husband has a motorbike but he hasn't got a car. **3** She bought her son a raincoat. **4** His brother has no friends. **5** Her sister's house hasn't got a bathroom. **6** He was reading his brother's newspaper. **7** The children's teacher was wearing a skirt and a blouse **8** His uncle sent his son's friend a letter.

Pronouns

Personal pronouns
When you are talking to members of your family, close friends, young children and animals, you should use the *du* form for *you* in the singular and the *ihr* form in the plural. Otherwise the *Sie* form for *you* should be used.

The genitive forms are rarely used in modern German so you don't need to know them at this stage.

	nominative	accusative	dative
singular	ich (I) du (you) Sie (you) er (he/it) sie (she/it) es (it)	mich (me) dich (you) Sie (you) ihn (him/it) sie (she/it) es (it)	mir (me) dir (you) Ihnen (you) ihm (him) ihr (her) ihm (it)
plural	wir (we) ihr (you) Sie (you) sie (they)	uns (us) euch (you) Sie (you) sie (them)	uns (us) euch (you) Ihnen (you) ihnen (them)

Translate into German 1 They saw me. 2 I saw them. 3 She saw him. 4 He saw us. 5 Did she see her?
(Note: the preposition *mit* is always followed by the dative case.)
6 She went with us. 7 I went with him. 8 We went with her. 9 Did you (three forms) go with me? 10 They went with you (three forms).

Interrogative pronouns
You should revise the notes on p. 107.

nom.	wer (who)	was (what)
acc.	wen (whom)	was (what)
gen.	wessen (whose)	
dat.	wem (whom)	

With prepositions use *wo-* (*wor-* before vowels):
Womit schält sie die Kartoffeln? (What does she peel the potatoes with?)
Worauf wartet er? (What is he waiting for?)
Also: woran? worüber? worin? wodurch? etc.

Relative pronouns

A relative pronoun in English is the word *who, whom, whose* or *which* when it refers back to the noun in the same sentence. It agrees in gender and number (i.e. singular or plural) with that noun, but its case is determined by the part it plays in its own clause.

Er ist der Mann, *dessen* Frau in München arbeitet. (He is the man *whose* wife works in Munich.)
(*der Mann* is the *nominative* masculine singular. *Dessen* is the *genitive* masculine singular and refers back to *der Mann*.) (whose wife = the wife of whom, i.e. the man.)

Note that the forms of the relative pronoun are the same as those of the definite article with the exception of the genitive (sg. and pl.) and the dative plural. The verb in a relative clause is at the end of that clause.

| | singular | | | plural |
	masc.	fem.	neut.	all genders
nom.	der	die	das	die
acc.	den	die	das	die
gen.	dessen	deren	dessen	deren
dat.	dem	der	dem	denen

Translate into German 1 The man who is smoking a pipe is wearing sunglasses. **2** The woman whose husband is reading the newspaper is writing a letter. **3** Did you visit your brother who lives in Cologne? **4** The children whose father is washing the car are playing in the garden. **5** The friend to whom he sent a postcard lived in Vienna. **6** The friend with whom she went to the pictures was called Sally. **7** The friend with whom she went to the theatre was called John. **8** The girls with whom she went to France worked in her office.

The complement

Nouns and pronouns that come after the following verbs must be in the nominative case:
sein (to be); werden (to become); bleiben (to remain); heißen (to be called).
The noun or pronoun that follows is called the *complement*. It refers back to the subject.

Er war *der Mann* (He was the man.)
Er war *sein junger Bruder*. (He was his young brother.)
Note: the indefinite article is omitted in German with professions unless there is an adjective present:
Er ist Arzt (He is *a* doctor.)
Er ist *ein guter* Arzt. (He is a good doctor.)

Use of the articles

German and English sometimes differ in their use of the articles.

1 German often prefers to use the definite article in place of the possessive adjective with parts of the body and clothes when it is obvious to whom they belong:
Er steckte *die* Hand in *die* Tasche. (He put *his* hand in *his* pocket.)
2 The definite article is used when a proper noun is preceded by an adjective:
der kleine Karl (little Karl);
das schöne Deutschland (beautiful Germany).
3 You should learn the following phrases by heart where usage differs:
vor *dem* Frühstück/Mittagessen/Abendessen (before breakfast/lunch/supper);
nach *dem* Frühstück/Mittagessen/Abendessen (after breakfast/lunch/supper);
bei*m* Frühstück/Mittagessen/Abendessen (at breakfast/lunch/supper);
nach *der* Arbeit/nach *der* Schule (after work/after school);
mit leiser Stimme (in *a* quiet voice);
Er hat Kopfschmerzen. (He has *a* headache.)
Er hat Fieber. (He has *a* temperature.)
Er hat Besuch. (He has *a* visitor (visitors).

Translate into German 1 He is my brother. 2 She became a doctor. 3 He is a teacher. 4 He is a good teacher. 5 Beautiful France. 6 Little Rainer is older than little Anna. 7 He spoke in a loud voice. 8 He put his pipe into his mouth. 9 Are you going to Garmisch before or after lunch? 10 He always reads the newspaper at breakfast. 11 I've got a temperature. 12 Have you got a headache?

Nouns

Declension (i.e. what happens to the noun in the four grammatical cases)

1 All feminine nouns remain the same in the singular.
2 Most masculine and neuter nouns add -*s* or -*es* in the genitive singular (des Zimmer*s*/des Schrank*es*).
3 Most nouns add -*n* in the dative plural if the plural doesn't already end in -*n* (mit den Kinder*n*/gegenüber den Häuser*n* etc.).

Gender

You should always learn each noun together with its definite article. The following notes may be helpful:

(a) Masculine nouns

Names of the days, months, seasons: der Montag; der Mai; der Sommer, etc.

Nouns ending in -*er* (when they refer to a person); der Bäcker; der Arbeiter, etc.

(b) Feminine nouns

Most nouns ending in -*e* (except those with the prefix *Ge-* or those denoting males – der Junge, der Matrose): die Garage; die Rose; die Flasche, etc.

Nouns ending in -*heit*, -*keit*, -*schaft*, -*ung* and -*in* (female professions): die Kindheit (childhood); die Freundlichkeit (friendliness); die Mannschaft (team); die Hoffnung (hope); die Schauspielerin (actress).

(c) Neuter nouns

Nouns ending in -*chen* or -*lein*: das Mädchen, das Fräulein, etc.

Infinitives used as nouns: das Fahren (driving), etc.

Names of towns and most countries: Bonn ist die Hauptstadt der BRD. *Es* liegt am Rhein. Das schöne Deutschland. But: *die* Schweiz.

Collective nouns in *Ge-*: das Gebirge (range of mountains); das Gewitter (storm).

Plurals

The only sure way of mastering plurals is to learn the plural form of each noun as you meet it. You may, however, find the following observations helpful:

(a) Masculine nouns

Most masculine nouns ending in *-er, -en* or *-el* have the same form in the plural as in the singular:

der Lehrer (-) teacher   der Sessel (-) armchair
der Wagen (-) car

A few add an umlaut in the plural. You should know the following:

der Apfel (⁻) apple   der Laden (⁻) shop
der Bruder (⁻) brother   der Schwager (⁻) brother-in-
                                  law
der Garten (⁻) garden   der Vater (⁻) father
der Hafen (⁻) harbour   der Vogel (⁻) bird

Most monosyllabic masculine nouns (e.g. *Tisch*) and their compounds (e.g. *Schreibtisch*) form their plural by adding *-e* or *⁻e*. Those containing the vowels *-i* or *-e* in their stem add *-e*:

der Berg (-e) mountain   der Stein (-e) stone
der Tisch (-e) table

Those containing the vowels *-a, -o,* or *-u* in their stem usually add *⁻e*:

der Arzt (⁻e) doctor   der Hut (⁻) hat
der Stock (⁻e) stick   der Baum (⁻) tree

You should learn the following common monosyllabic masculine nouns (with their stem vowel, *-a, -o, -u*) that are exceptions in so far as they form their plural in *-e*:

der Arm (-e) arm   der Pfad (-e) path
der Dom (-e) cathedral   der Ruf (-e) shout, call
der Hund (-e) dog   der Schuh (-e) shoe
der Ort (-e) place   der Tag (-e) day

A very few masculine nouns form their plural by adding *⁻er* or *-er*. Remember the following sentence:

The *spirit* of *God*, the *riches* and the *error* of *man*, the *mouth* and the *body* of the *worm* that lives in the *shrub* on the *edge* of the *forest*.

der Geist (-er) spirit   der Leib (-er) body
der Gott (⁻er) God   der Wurm (⁻er) worm
der Reichtum (⁻er) riches   der Strauch (⁻er) shrub
der Irrtum (⁻er) error   der Rand (⁻er) edge
der Mann (⁻er) man   der Wald (⁻er) forest
der Mund (⁻er) mouth

Weak masculine nouns add *-n* or *-en* in the accusative, genitive and dative singular as well as in the plural.

You should know the following common weak masculine nouns:

der Affe (-n) monkey	der Löwe (-n) lion
der Junge (-n) boy	der Matrose (-n) sailor
der Knabe (-n) boy	der Neffe (-n) nephew
der Kunde (-n) customer	der Nachbar (-n) neighbour
der Elefant (en) elephant	der Held (-en) hero
der Soldat (-en) soldier	der Herr (-en) gentleman
der Student (-en) student	der Mensch (-en) human being

Most masculine nouns ending in *-e* that denote nationality are weak masculines:

der Franzose (-n) Frenchman   der Russe (-n) Russian

Note: *der Deutsche* is an exception. It is declined like an adjective.

(b) Feminine nouns

Most feminine nouns form their plural by adding *-n* or *-en*:

die Küche (-n) kitchen   die Uhr (-en) clock

A few feminine nouns add ⸚e in the plural. You should know the following:

die Bank (⸚e) bench	die Nacht (⸚e) night
die Gans (⸚e) goose	die Stadt (⸚e) town
die Hand (⸚e) hand	die Wand (⸚e) wall
die Kuh (⸚e) cow	die Wurst (⸚e) sausage
die Maus (⸚e) mouse	

Feminine counterparts of male professions and nationalities form their plural by adding *-nen*:

die Sekretärin (-nen) secretary
die Französin (-nen) Frenchwoman

The following two feminine nouns add an umlaut in the plural:

die Mutter (⸚) mother   die Tochter (⸚) daughter

(c) Neuter nouns

Most neuter nouns ending in -er, -en or -el have the same form in the plural as in the singular:

das Zimmer (-) room   das Viertel (-) quarter
das Mädchen (-) girl

You should, also, note the following neuter nouns that add either -er or -̈er:

das Bild (-er) picture
das Brett (-er) board, shelf
das Ei (-er) egg
das Feld (-er) field

das Kind (-er) child
das Kleid (-er) dress
das Lied (-er) song

das Blatt (-̈er) leaf
das Buch (-̈er) book
das Dach (-̈er) roof
das Dorf (-̈er) village
das Glas (-̈er) glass

das Haus (-̈er) house
das Loch (-̈er) hole
das Rad (-̈er) wheel, bike
das Schloß (-̈sser) castle
das Tal (-̈er) valley

A few neuter nouns and their compounds add -n or -en in the plural:

das Auge (-n) eye
das Bett (-en) bed
das Ende (-n) end

das Hemd (-en) shirt
das Leid (-en) sorrow
das Ohr (-en) ear

Note also: das Doppelbett (-en); das Einzelbett (-en); das Wochenende (-n); das Sporthemd (-en).

A few neuter nouns ending in -um change this to -en in the plural:
das Gymnasium (Gymnasien) grammar school
das Museum (Museen) museum

The following neuter nouns add -s in the plural:

das Auto (-s) car
das Büro (-s) office
das Hotel (-s) hotel
das Kino (-s) cinema

das Kotelett (-s) cutlet, chop
das Radio (-s) radio
das Taxi (-s) taxi

Adjectives

An adjective in German must have an ending
(a) if it is followed by a noun:
   der neue Tisch/ein neuer Tisch/auf einem neuen Tisch;
(b) or if a noun is understood:
   Er hat einen alten Tisch, aber ich habe einen neuen ('Tisch'
   understood, i.e. 'a new one').
It doesn't have an ending if it stands by itself:
   Der Tisch ist neu.

Adjectival endings

The ending you use will depend not only on the gender, number
(singular or plural) or case of the noun you are describing but also
on the article or other limiting word (if any) that precedes it. There
are three different groups of adjectival endings and you must learn
not only the endings themselves but also which articles or other
limiting words that cause that group to be used.

Group 1

After *der, dieser, jener, jeder, solcher, mancher* and *welcher* (also after
alle in the plural):

	singular							

	masc.			fem.			neut.	
nom.	*der* junge	Mann	*die* junge		Frau	*das* junge		Mädchen
acc.	*den*	-en Mann	*die*	-e	Frau	*das*	-e	Mädchen
gen.	*des*	-en Mannes	*der*	-en	Frau	*des*	-en	Mädchens
dat.	*dem*	-en Mann	*der*	-en	Frau	*dem*	-en	Mädchen

plural
all genders

nom.	*die* jungen Männer (Frauen) (Mädchen)
acc.	*die* jungen Männer (Frauen) (Mädchen)
gen.	*der* jungen Männer (Frauen) (Mädchen)
dat.	*den* jungen Männern (Frauen) (Mädchen)

Group 2

After *ein* (sg. only), *kein, mein, dein, sein*, etc. (i.e. after the possessive adjectives):

singular		
	masc.	fem.	neut.
nom.	*ein* jung*er* Schüler	*eine* jung*e* Schülerin	*ein* jung*es* Kind
acc.	*einen* -en Schüler	*eine* -e Schülerin	*ein* -es Kind
gen.	*eines* -en Schülers	*einer* -en Schülerin	*eines* -en Kindes
dat.	*einem* -en Schüler	*einer* -en Schülerin	*einem* -en Kind

plural
all genders
nom. *meine* jung*en* Schüler (Schülerinnen) (Kinder)
acc. *meine* jung*en* Schüler (Schülerinnen) (Kinder)
gen. *meiner* jung*en* Schüler (Schülerinnen) (Kinder)
dat. *meinen* jung*en* Schülern (Schülerinnen) (Kindern)

Group 3

This group is used:

(a) if the adjective stands alone before a noun (e.g. 'good wine', 'black ink', 'red pencils');

(b) in the plural when the adjective is preceded by a number (2, 3, 4, etc.), ein paar (a few), einige (several), etliche (several), manche (many), mehrere (several), viele (many) or wenige (few):

singular			plural
masc.	fem.	neut.	all genders
nom. kalt*er* Wein	kalt*e* Milch	kalt*es* Bier	kalt*e* Getränke
acc. kalt*en* Wein	kalt*e* Milch	kalt*es* Bier	kalt*e* Getränke
gen. kalt*en* Weins	kalt*er* Milch	kalt*en* Biers	kalt*er* Getränke
dat. kalt*em* Wein	kalt*er* Milch	kalt*em* Bier	kalt*en* Getränken

Translate into German 1 This young man has a pretty wife. 2 His small daughter has a brown dog, a black cat and two white mice. 3 Which new film did you see? 4 Her young brother ran out of his new school and got into her small car. 5 Our young doctor lives in a small house. 6 Does his young brother's friend work in this large factory? 7 His new neighbour likes to drink cold beer, cold milk and hot coffee. 8 These young children live in those old houses.

Basic adjectives

Make certain you know the following list of adjectives. (They are arranged in boxes, so you can study a box at a time.)

(un) glücklich	(un) lucky, (un)happy (un)fortunate)	sauber	clean
		schmutzig	dirty
		reich	rich
traurig	sad	arm	poor
besorgt	worried	groß	large, big, tall
verlegen	embarrassed		
böse (auf + acc.)	angry (with)	klein	small, little
		lang	long
zornig (auf + acc.)	angry (with)	kurz	short
		hoch	high, tall
stolz (auf + acc.)	proud (of)	niedrig	low
enttäuscht	disappointed		
erleichtert	relieved		
froh	happy		
munter	merry, cheerful	tief	deep
langweilig	boring	seicht	shallow
unterhaltend	entertaining	laut	loud
(un)zufrieden	(dis)satisfied	leise	quiet, soft
heiß	hot	ruhig	quiet, peaceful
kalt	cold		
warm	warm	naß	wet
kühl	cool	trocken	dry
eisig	icy	dunkel	dark
regnerisch	rainy	hell	light, bright
		verblüfft	puzzled
sonnig	sunny	überrascht	surprised
neblig	foggy, misty	erstaunt	astounded
gut	good	intelligent	intelligent
schlecht	bad	klug	clever
schlimm	bad	geschickt	skilled, clever
herrlich	marvellous	ungeschickt	clumsy
(un)angenehm	(un)pleasant	(un)begabt	(un)talented
wunderbar	wonderful	dumm	stupid
sonderbar	strange	stumm	dumb
gefährlich	dangerous	taub	deaf

letzt	last	ledig	single, unmarried
nächst	next	verlobt	engaged
(un)freundlich	(un)friendly	verheiratet	married
(un)sicher	(un)safe	geschieden	divorced
(un)fähig	(in)capable	(un)gehorsam	(dis)obedient
zerbrochen	shattered	müde	tired
zerrissen	torn (to shreds)	träge	weary
voll	full	trübe	gloomy
leer	empty	fertig	ready, finished
(un)beliebt	(un)popular	(un)nötig	(un)necessary

früh	early	alt	old
spät	late	jung	young
ausgezeichnet	excellent	neu	new
hervorragend	excellent	nagelneu	brand new
nett	nice	krank	ill, sick
schön	beautiful	gesund	healthy, well
hübsch	pretty	tot	dead
reizend	charming	lebendig	living
häßlich	ugly	offen	open
(un)möglich	(im)possible	geschlossen	closed

hölzern	wooden	schnell	quick, fast
steinern	stone, stony	rasch	rapid
ledern	leather	langsam	slow
hart	hard	glatt	smooth
weich	soft	fett	oily
bequem	comfortable	lockig	curly
unbequem	uncomfortable	scharf	sharp
schwer	heavy, difficult	stumpf	blunt
leicht	light, easy	rund	round
einfach	simple	viereckig	square
kräftig	powerful	(un)interessant	(un)interesting

dick	fat	vernünftig	sensible
dünn	thin	blöde	stupid
schlank	slim	albern	silly
teuer	dear, expensive	verrückt	mad
billig	cheap	blaß	pale
preiswert	reasonable (a bargain)	bleich	pale
		betrunken	drunk
fleißig	hardworking	nüchtern	sober
faul	lazy	(un)erwartet	(un)expected
(un)freundlich	(un)friendly	seltsam	strange
grausam	cruel	lächerlich	ridiculous

richtig	correct	scheu	shy
falsch	false, wrong	feige	cowardly
echt	genuine	tapfer	brave
(un)geduldig	(im)patient	mutig	courageous
breit	wide	schwach	weak
weit	far	stark	strong
eng	narrow, confined	winzig	tiny
		riesig	huge, gigantic
schmal	narrow		
vorsichtig	careful, cautious	wertvoll	valuable
		wertlos	worthless
(un)ehrlich	(dis)honest		

(un)pünktlich	(un)punctual	(un)wichtig	(un)important
seltsam	strange	aufgeregt	excited
merkwürdig	remarkable	aufregend	exciting
artig	good, well-behaved	mager	lean, skinny
		beleibt	portly, stout
unartig	naughty	(un)empfind-lich	(in)sensitive
lustig	amusing		
komisch	funny	schrecklich	awful
tragisch	tragic	furchtbar	frightful, terrible
sorgfältig	careful	neidisch (auf + *acc.*)	envious (of)
einsam	lonely		
		eifersüchtig (auf + *acc.*)	jealous (of)

The comparison of adjectives and adverbs

1   Many adjectives can be used as adverbs:
Die Frau ist *schön* (The woman is *beautiful* (adjective).
Die Frau singt *schön* (The woman sings *beautifully* (adverb).
Similarly: gut (well); schlecht (badly); schnell (quickly); langsam (slowly), etc.

2   Learn the grammatical names for the three forms of comparison:
quick (positive)/quicker (comparitive)/quickest (superlative).

3   Look at the following pair of sentences; the first is comparing *adjectives*, the second *adverbs*:

(a) Der *schnelle* Zug fährt um sieben Uhr, der *schnellere* Zug (fährt) um acht Uhr und der *schnellste* Zug (fährt) um neun Uhr ab. (The *fast* train leaves at seven, the *faster* train leaves at eight and the *fastest* train leaves at nine o'clock.)

(b) Dieser Zug fährt *schnell,* der fährt *schneller,* aber der dort drüben fährt *am schnellsten.* (This train goes *fast,* that one goes *faster* but that one over there goes *fastest.*)

4   (a) The comparative of both adjectives and adverbs is formed by adding -*er* to the positive form.

(b) The superlative of adverbs is formed by adding -*(e)sten* to the positive form and putting *am* in front:

positive	comparative	superlative
schön	schöner	am schönsten
schnell	schneller	am schnellsten

Irregular comparisons:

positive	comparative	superlative
bald (soon)	eher (sooner)	am ehesten (soonest)
früh (early)	früher (earlier)	am frühsten (earliest)
gut (well) } wohl (well) }	besser (better)	am besten (best)
oft (often)	öfter (more often)	am öftesten (most often)
häufig (frequently)	häufiger (more frequently)	am häufigsten (most frequently)
viel (a lot)	mehr (more)	am meisten (most of all)
wenig (not much) {	weniger (less) minder (less)	am wenigsten (least of all) mindestens (least of all)

Note:

Ich spiele *gern* Tennis, ich spiele *lieber* Rugby, aber *am liebsten*
spiele ich Fußball. (I like playing tennis, I prefer playing rugby
but most of all I like playing football.)

(c) The superlative of adjectives is formed by adding -*(e)st* to
the positive form.

Comparative and superlative adjectives take the same endings as their positive forms (see p. 23).

Note:

(a) Most adjectives of one syllable add an umlaut in the comparative and superlative (if their stem vowel contains -*a*, -
o or -*u*):

alt/älter/ältest
jung/jünger/jüngst

Exceptions: bunt (bright); falsch (false); froh (glad); lahm
(lame); laut (loud); naß (wet); rund (round); schlank (slim).

(b) Irregular comparisons:

positive	comparative	superlative
hoch (tall)	höher	der höchste
nah (near)	näher	der nächste
gut (good)	besser	der beste
viel (a lot)	mehr	die meisten (pl.)

You should learn the following phrases by heart:

so groß wie (as big as);
größer als (bigger than);
immer größer (bigger and bigger);
je größer, desto besser (the bigger, the better).

Translate into German 1 This young man is my elder brother.
2 He came by a quicker train. **3** My father is older than my
mother. **4** She is taller than her sister but not so tall as her
brother. **5** Are you younger than me? **6** He climbed higher and
higher. **7** He is the smallest boy in his class. **8** The more he played,
the better he became. **9** He was his best friend. **10** Karl runs fast,
Achim runs faster but Rainer runs the fastest. **11** Can you sing as
well as your sister? **12** He speaks Spanish well, German better and
French best of all. **13** He eats more than me but not as much as his
brother. **14** He likes smoking cigarettes, he prefers to smoke cigars
but most of all he likes smoking a pipe.

Basic adverbs (and other 'little words')

Remember that the 'little words' are very important. You can lose a lot of marks unnecessarily if you don't know them!

ganz	quite	entweder	either . . . or
ziemlich	fairly	oder	
sehr	very	weder . . .	neither . . . nor
höchst	extremely	noch	
äußerst	extremely	dabei	thereby (in so doing)
zuerst	first of all	im voraus	in advance
dann	then	inzwischen	meanwhile
anschließend	then	unterdessen	meanwhile
schließlich	finally	übrigens	by the way
endlich	at last	immerhin	all the same, anyhow
		zusammen	together
		zwar	indeed

nur	only	dennoch	yet
bloß	only, merely	aber	however
nun	now	jedoch	however
jetzt	now	rechtzeitig	in good time
damals	at that time	manchmal	sometimes
gelegentlich	occasionally	nie(mals)	never
besonders	especially	je	ever, each
sonst	otherwise	sofort	immediately
umsonst	in vain	gleich (darauf)	immediately (afterwards)
angeblich	apparently	bald (darauf)	soon (afterwards)

vergebens	in vain	sogar	even
vergeblich	in vain	vielleicht	perhaps
auch	also	plötzlich	suddenly
also	therefore	auf einmal	suddenly
deshalb	therefore	fast	almost
diesmal	this time	beinahe	almost
erst dann	only then	wohl	probably
genau	exactly	wahrscheinlich	probably
ungefähr	approximately	wirklich	really
etwa	about	eigentlich	actually

etwas	something	mindestens	at least
nichts	nothing	wenigstens	at least
gar nicht	not at all	gewöhnlich	usually
überhaupt nicht	not at all	normalerweise	usually
		vorher	previously
doch	certainly, yes (as contradiction)	danach	afterwards
		sowieso	in any case
		kaum	scarcely, hardly
noch	still, another (+ noun)	gründlich	thoroughly
		sicher	certainly
noch nicht	not yet	völlig	completely
noch einmal	once again		
unbedingt	at all costs		
zufällig	by chance		

jedenfalls	in any case	selbstverständlich	of course
nämlich	namely, you see	natürlich	of course
neulich	recently	bergauf	uphill
dafür	instead of that	bergab	downhill
tatsächlich	really, indeed	leider	unfortunately
dauernd	continuously	(un)glücklicherweise	(un)fortunately
oft	often	ab und zu	from time to time
öfters	often		
häufig	frequently	dann und wann	from time to time
selten	rarely		
		auf und ab	up and down
		hin und her	to and fro

Prepositions

You must know the following prepositions:

1 With the dative only

aus	out of, from	seit	since, for (time)
von	from, of	gegenüber	opposite
zu	to, at	mit	with
nach	to, after, according to	außer	except, besides
bei	at (cf. French *chez*)		

2 With the accusative only

bis	as far as, to, until	gegen	against, towards, about
durch	through, by means of	ohne	without
entlang	along	um	around, at
für	for, on behalf of		

3 With the genitive only

(an)statt	instead of	trotz	in spite of
außerhalb	outside	unweit	not far from
innerhalb	inside, within	um . . . willen	for the sake of
diesseits	on this side of	während	during
jenseits	on that side of	wegen	because of

4 With the accusative and dative

in	in, into	neben	near, next to
an	on (vertical), to, at	zwischen	between
auf	on (horizontal), on to	über	over, across, about
vor	in front of, ago	unter	under, among
hinter	behind		

The *accusative* is used if there is movement *to* a place:
  Er ging in *den* Garten (*into* the garden)
The *dative* is used if there is *no* movement towards:
  Er spielte *im* Garten. (*in* the garden)

Note:
  (a) Contraction of certain prepositions takes place with the definite article:

  zum = zu dem   am = an dem
  zur = zu der   ans = an das
  im = in dem   beim = bei dem
  ins = in das

  (a) *entlang* comes after the noun (die Straße entlang);
  (c) *nach* means *according to*; when it follows the noun (meiner Meinung nach/in my opinion);

(d) *gegenüber* usually comes in front of a noun (gegenüber dem Haus) and after a pronoun (ihm gegenüber).

Translate into German
(a) 1 in spite of the rain.   2 instead of his brother.   3 opposite the town hall.   4 at his brother's (house).   5 with his father.
6 around the garden.   7 after breakfast.   8 in the morning.
9 during the spring.   10 for his mother's sake.   11 out of the garden.   12 from the town.   13 except for her dog.   14 along the road.   15 to the airport.   16 because of the snow.   17 without his coat.   18 through the kitchen.   19 for his uncle.   20 on this side of the mountain.   21 within an hour.   22 not far from the village.
(b) 1 He was sitting in an armchair.   2 He sat down in an armchair.   3 She hung the mirror on the wall.   4 The mirror was hanging on the wall.   5 She lay down on the bed.   6 She was lying on the bed.   7 He put the money in his pocket.   8 The money was in his pocket.   9 The post office was between the cinema and the supermarket.   10 He sat down next to the man.

Measurements and quantity

1) Use the accusative case to show distance:
   Er wohnt *einen Kilometer* von hier entfernt.
2) Masculine and neuter nouns denoting measurements use the singular form for the plural. Feminine nouns (with the exception of *die Mark*) use the normal plural:

zwei Pfund Äpfel	drei Paar Schuhe
zwei Kilo	vierzig Pfennig
hundert Gramm	drei Mark
vier Kilometer	drei Pfund (£3)

But: zwei Flaschen Bier; drei Tassen Kaffee; vier Meilen, etc.

Translate into German   1 I'd like 250 grammes of ham, half a pound of cherries and five kilos of potatoes, please.   2 That costs thirty-three marks.   3 I'd like three cups of tea and two bottles of coke, please.   4 He wanted two pounds of oranges.   5 They live a kilometre from the town centre.

Expressions of time

These are very important and you should make sure that you can answer all the questions at the end of this section.

1 Expressions of *definite time* are in the *accusative*:
letzten Sonntag (last Sunday); nächste Woche (next week); jedes Jahr (every year).

2 Expressions of *indefinite time* are in the *genitive*:
eines Morgens (one morning); eines Tages (one day).
Note: eines Nachts.
If there is an adjective, it is better to use *an + the dative*:
an einem kalten Dezembermorgen (on a cold December morning).

3 *Time started in the past and uncompleted:*
Use *seit* + the dative. Watch the tense!
Er *arbeitet* (present) hier *seit einem Jahr*. (He *has been working* (perfect) here *for* a year.)
Er *arbeitete* (imperfect) hier *seit einem Jahr*. (He *had been working* (pluperfect) here *for* a year.)

4 *With prepositions:*

um 9 Uhr (at 9 o'clock)
am Sonntag (on Sunday)
im Mai (in May)
im Frühling (in spring)
früh am Morgen (early in the morning
spät am Abend (late in the evening

bis Freitag (by Friday)
von Montag bis Freitag (from Monday till Friday)
jeden Tag außer Sonntag (every day except for Sunday)
zu Weihnachten (at Christmas); zu Ostern (at Easter); zu Pfingsten (at Whitsun); vor einem Monat (a month ago)

5 *Other expressions of time:*

heute (today)
morgen (tomorrow)

gestern (yesterday)
vorgestern (the day before yesterday)

übermorgen (the day after tomorrow)

samstags (on Saturdays)

einmal/zweimal in der Woche (once/twice a week).

heute morgen (this morning)
morgen nachmittag (tomorrow afternoon)
gestern abend (last night)
morgens (in the mornings)
nachmittags (in the afternoons)
abends (in the evenings)
am Morgen, etc. (in the morning, etc.)
morgen früh (tomorrow morning)

Translate into German

(a) **1** at 3.30. **2** on Tuesday. **3** in autumn. **4** at Christmas.
5 in January. **6** last night. **7** early in the morning. **8** one day
last week. **9** one foggy November morning. **10** in the evenings.
11 at the weekend. **12** during the afternoon. **13** this afternoon.
14 on the sixteenth of February. **15** two days ago. **16** a month
ago. **17** next Thursday. **18** one Saturday. **19** once a week.
20 every month.

(b) **1** a quarter of an hour later. **2** half an hour later. **3** an hour
later. **4** an hour and a half later. **5** two hours later.

(c) **1** suddenly. **2** at first. **3** shortly afterwards. **4** soon
afterwards. **5** then. **6** shortly before. **7** finally. **8** at last. **9** a
few minutes later. **10** after a few minutes.

Conjunctions

Conjunctions are used to join sentences or clauses, or words in the
same sentence or clause. You must be very careful with the word
order when you use them.
There are two types of conjunction:

1 Coordinating conjunctions

The following *coordinating conjunctions* link main clauses (i.e.
clauses that are of equal importance and convey the main information of the sentence) and *do not affect the word order*:

aber	but	sondern	but (as a contrast)
denn	for (i.e. because)	und	and
oder	or		

2 Subordinating conjunctions

The following conjunctions introduce subordinate clauses (i.e.
clauses that do *not* convey the main information of the sentence
but tell *when, why, how* etc. actions take place). The verb is sent
to the end of the clause.

(a) *Temporal* (time)

als	when (one occasion in the past)	solange	as long as
		nachdem	after
wenn	when(ever), if	bevor ⎱	
während	while	ehe ⎰	before
bis	until	seitdem	since
sobald	as soon as		
sooft	as often as		

(b) *Cause, purpose result*

weil	because	damit	so that
da	as, since	so daß	so that, with the result that

(c) *Miscellaneous*

daß	that	obwohl ⎫	
ob	if (whether)	obgleich ⎬	although
falls	in case	obschon ⎭	
		als ob ⎱	as if
		als wenn ⎰	

(d) *Interrogative words used as subordinating conjunctions*

wo	where	wie	how
wohin	where . . . to	wann	when
woher	where . . . from	warum	why

Verbs

Tense

The tense of a verb is the form taken by that verb to indicate *when* an action, state or happening takes place (i.e. = time).

The finite verb

The finite verb is the *main verb* of a clause or sentence. It has *person*, *number* and *tense*.

The persons and numbers are as follows:

1st person sg.	ich (I)	1st person pl.	wir (we)
2nd person sg. (familiar)	du (you)	2nd person pl. (familiar)	ihr (you)
2nd person sg. (polite)	Sie (you)	2nd person pl. (polite)	Sie (you)
3rd person sg.	er (he, it) sie (she, it) es (it)	3rd person pl.	sie (they)

A noun in the singular is always 3rd person singular:
Der Mann (3rd person sg.) spielt Tennis.
A noun in the plural (or two or more nouns) always 3rd person plural:
Die Männer (3rd person pl.) spielen Tennis.
Der Mann und die Frau (3rd person pl.) spielen Tennis.
'ich' + noun as subjects are always 1st person plural:
Mein Bruder und ich (1st person pl.) spielen Tennis.

The infinitive
The infinitive is the simplest form of the verb. It is the form you will find in a dictionary or vocabulary where *in English* it is usually preceded by the word *to*. The infinitive in German always ends in *-en* or *-n*:
spiel*en* (to play) erwider*n* (to reply)

The past participle
The past participle is that part of the verb that is used to help form some past tenses:
Er hat *gespielt*. (He has *played*.)/Er hat *getrunken*. (He has *drunk*.)
Most past participles in German (but by no means all) begin with *ge-*. Regular verbs (weak verbs) end their past participle with *-t* and most irregular verbs (strong verbs) end it with *-en*:
*ge*spiel*t* is weak/*ge*trunk*en* is strong.

The principal parts
You should learn the principal parts of every verb you meet to enable you to form the tenses. The four parts are: the infinitive; the 3rd person singular present tense; the 3rd person singular imperfect tense; the past participle:

Weak verbs (regular) spielen (to play)
spielen   spielt   spielte   gespielt

Strong verbs (irregular) tragen (to wear, carry)
tragen   trägt   trug   getragen

You will find verb lists at the end of the book together with further details.

The formation and use of tenses

1 There are *eight* tenses in German that you should know. You should learn the alternative forms in English and realize that there is only *the one form* for each tense (with the exception of the conditional perfect) in German. Think carefully about these alternatives when you are translating from and into German.

Present: er spielt (he plays/he is playing/he does play).
Imperfect: er spielte (he played/he was playing/he used to play).
Future: er wird spielen (he will play/he will be playing/he is going to play).
Conditional: er würde spielen (he would play/he would be playing).
Perfect: er hat gespielt (he played/he has played/he has been playing/he did play).
Pluperfect: er hatte gespielt (he had played/he had been playing).
Future perfect: er wird gespielt haben (he will have played/he will have been playing);
Conditional perfect: er würde gespielt haben (he would have played/he would have been playing).

2 A close look at these tenses shows that there are two types – *simple* and *compound*.
Simple tenses are formed solely from the verb itself and compound tenses need to bring in another verb to help with their formation. These other verbs are called *auxiliary verbs*. There are three auxiliary verbs which as well as helping in tense formation also exist in their own right:
haben (to have);   sein (to be) and werden (to become).

haben

present		imperfect	
ich habe	wir haben	ich hatte	wir hatten
du hast	ihr habt	du hattest	ihr hattet
Sie haben	Sie haben	Sie hatten	Sie hatten
er ⎫		er ⎫	
sie ⎬ hat	sie haben	sie ⎬ hatte	sie hatten
es ⎭		es ⎭	

sein

	present		imperfect	
ich bin	wir sind		ich war	wir waren
du bist	ihr seid		du warst	ihr wart
Sie sind	Sie sind		Sie waren	Sie waren
er ⎫			er ⎫	
sie ⎬ ist	sie sind		sie ⎬ war	sie waren
es ⎭			es ⎭	

werden

	present		imperfect	
ich werde	wir werden		ich wurde	wir wurden
du wirst	ihr werdet		du wurdest	ihr wurdet
Sie werden	Sie werden		Sie wurden	Sie wurden
er ⎫			er ⎫	
sie ⎬ wird	sie werden		sie ⎬ wurde	sie wurden
es ⎭			es ⎭	

3 There are two simple tenses – the present and the imperfect.

The present
You must be very careful with strong verbs as many of them change
their stem vowel in the *du* and *er*, *sie* and *es* forms, e.g. fahren (du
fährst/er fährt); lesen (du liest/er liest).

You will see from the second of the principal parts if there is a
change in the stem vowel (see verb list). Apart from this, strong
and weak verbs have the same endings.

Formation: add the following endings to the stem (e.g. *spiel-*):

	singular			plural	
ich	-e	(spiele)	wir	-en	(spielen)
du	-st	(spielst)	ihr	-t	(spielt)
Sie	-en	(spielen)	Sie	-en	(spielen)
er/sie/es	-t	(spielt)	sie	-en	(spielen)

Translate into German 1 She is eating an apple. 2 What do you
(3 forms) drink in the evenings? 3 They're watching television.
4 Is he standing or sitting? 5 He is getting into the car. 6 He
gets dressed in his bedroom. 7 Does she sing well? 8 They go
to the pictures once a week.

The imperfect

Note that the *ich* and *er*, *sie* and *es* forms are identical.

(a) *Weak verbs*

Add the following endings to the stem (e.g. *spiel-*):

	singular			plural	
ich	-te	(spiel*te*)	wir	-ten	(spiel*ten*)
du	-test	(spiel*test*)	ihr	-tet	(spiel*tet*)
Sie	-ten	(spiel*ten*)	Sie	-ten	(spiel*ten*)
er/sie/es	-te	(spiel*te*)	sie	-ten	(spiel*ten*)

(b) *Strong verbs*

Formed from the third of the principal parts (see verb list) which becomes the new stem. To this add the following endings (e.g. *trank-*):

	singular			plural	
ich	-	(trank)	wir	-en	(trank*en*)
du	-st	(trank*st*)	ihr	-t	(trank*t*)
Sie	-en	(trank*en*)	Sie	-en	(trank*en*)
er/sie/es	-	(trank)	sie	-en	(trank*en*)

Translate to German 1 She was laying the table. 2 They used to live in Cologne. 3 She went into the supermarket and bought a pound of apples. 4 He was reading a book when the phone rang. 5 She would (i.e. she used to) visit her grandfather on Sundays. 6 She used to work in a travel office. 7 They were running along the street. 8 He was lying in bed.

4 The other six tenses are compound tenses.

The future and conditional use parts of the auxiliary verb *werden* and the infinitive.

The future

Formation: use the present tense of *werden* (see p. 39) and the infinitive of the verb. The infinitive is at the end of the clause or sentence:

Er wird mit seiner Frau in die Stadt *fahren*.

Note that the present tense is often used in German with a future implication as it is in English:

Kommst du heute abend? (Are you coming tonight?)

Morgen fährt er nach Deutschland. (He is going to Germany tomorrow.)

Translate into German 1 I shall do my homework tonight.
2 He will be getting up soon. 3 Are they coming this afternoon?
4 We shall be going to the pictures on Saturday. 5 Will you (3
forms) visit me in hospital?

The conditional

Formation: use the following forms of *werden* and the infinitive of
the verb:

   ich würde/du würdest/Sie würden/er, sie, es würde
   wir würden/ihr würdet/Sie würden/sie würden

As in the future, the infinitive is at the end of the clause or sentence.
   Er würde nach Amerika *fahren*.
Note that the conditional tense is usually linked with a conditional
clause introduced by *wenn* (if). If the conditional clause comes first,
add the word *so* and invert the verb.
Wenn ich reich wäre, würde ich einen Rolls-Royce kaufen.
   (If I were rich, I would buy a Rolls-Royce.)

Translate into German 1 We would go to Munich. 2 They
would buy a larger house. 3 I would go by air. 4 What would
you do (3 forms)? 5 She would stay in bed until eleven o'clock.

The perfect and pluperfect use parts of the auxiliary verbs *haben*
and *sein* and the past participle.

The perfect tense

Formation: use the *present* tense of *haben* or *sein* (see p. 38) and the
past participle. The past participle is at the end of the clause or
sentence.
   Er hat seinen Bruder gestern abend *gesehen*.
   Er ist in die Stadt *gegangen*.

The pluperfect tense

Formation: use the *imperfect* tense of *haben* or *sein* (see p. 38) and
the past participle. As in the perfect tense, the past participle is at
the end of the clause or sentence.
   Er hatte seinen Bruder gestern abend *gesehen*.
   Er war in die Stadt *gegangen*.
You must make a great effort to learn those verbs that go with *sein*
and make certain that you use them correctly in all parts of the
examination. They are indicated in the verb table by an asterisk (*).
Here is a list of some of the more common ones.

Verbs + sein

- *Intransitive verbs of motion* (an *intransitive* verb is a verb that can't be followed by a direct object. A *transitive* verb is one that can): aufstehen (to get/stand up); eilen (to hurry); fahren (to go); folgen (to follow); gehen (to go); klettern (to climb); kommen (to come); laufen (to run); reisen (to travel); reiten (to ride) springen (to jump); steigen (to climb); stürzen (to rush); umziehen (to move house); verreisen (to go away).

- *Intransitive verbs showing a change of state:* aufwachen (to wake up); einschlafen (to fall asleep); erscheinen (to appear); frieren (to freeze); kentern (to capsize); schmelzen (to melt); sterben (to die); verschwinden (to disappear); wachsen (to grow); werden (to become).

- *Miscellaneous verbs:* begegnen (to meet by chance); bleiben (to remain); einfallen (to occur); gelingen (to succeed); geschehen (to happen); sein (to be); vorkommen (to happen).

Points to watch

(i) A few of the verbs above can also be used transitively (i.e. with a direct object). They then form their perfect and pluperfect tenses with *haben* and the past participle.

Compare the following pairs of sentences:

Perfect: Er *ist* zum Bahnhof gefahren. (He drove to the station.)
Er *hat* seinen Wagen (d.o.) zum Bahnhof gefahren. (He drove his car to the station.)

Pluperfect: Er *war* durch den Wald geritten. (He had ridden through the forest.)
Er *hatte* das Pferd (d.o.) durch den Wald geritten. (He had ridden the horse through the forest.)

(ii) '*eben*'/'*gerade*' + *perfect or pluperfect:*
Sie ist *eben* (*gerade*) in die Stadt gegangen. (She has *just* gone into town.)
Er hatte *eben* (*gerade*) den Rasen gemäht. (He had *just* cut the grass.)

(iii) Verbs with separable prefixes sandwich the *ge-* between the prefix and the verb:
Sie sind neulich um*ge*zogen. (They have moved recently.)
Der Zug war ab*ge*fahren. (The train had gone.)

(iv) *Inseparable prefixes*
A number of verbs have inseparable prefixes (i.e. they do not add the prefix '*ge-*' in the past participle). The most common of these are: *be; emp-; ent-; er-; ge-; ver-; miß-; zer-*:

beginnen (to begin)   gefallen (to please)
empfangen (to receive)   verstehen (to understand)
entkommen (to escape)   mißverstehen (to
                                  misunderstand)
erzählen (to relate)   zerstören (to destroy)

Translate into German
(a) *Perfect*: **1** We got up early. **2** When did you have breakfast (3 forms)? **3** He has just left the house. **4** Why did you (3 forms) go to Germany? **5** Have you (3 forms) written the letter? **6** He has become a doctor. **7** Did she buy the coat? **8** His father died two days ago. **9** They have gone away. **10** Did the rowing boat capsize?
(b) *Pluperfect*: **1** He had fallen asleep in the armchair. **2** Why had they stayed at home? **3** We had just seen the film. **4** What had happened there? **5** He had been playing football. **6** After the sailing boat had capsized. **7** When she had made the beds. **8** Because she had missed the train. **9** She had just got dressed. **10** Why had they been watching television?

The future perfect and conditional perfect tenses use two auxiliary verbs in their formation as do their English counterparts.

The future perfect
This is a combination of the future and the perfect tenses.

Formation: use the present tense of *werden* + *past participle* + either *haben* or *sein*:
    Er wird schon *gegessen haben*. (He will already have eaten.)
    Er wird schon *gegangen sein*. (He will already have gone.)
You should be able to recognize this tense but it is doubtful if you will have to use it.

The conditional perfect
This is a combination of the conditional and perfect tenses.

Formation: use the forms of *würde* + *past participle* + either *haben* or *sein*:

> *Er würde es gekauft haben*. (He would have bought it.)
> *Er würde nach Amerika gefahren sein*. (He would have gone to America.)

You should be able to recognize these forms if you meet them. In practice, however, modern German prefers to use shorter forms:

> würde haben = hätte
> würde sein = wäre

You are, therefore, more likely to meet:

> *Er hätte es gekauft*. (He would have bought it.)
> *Er wäre nach Amerika gefahren*. (He would have gone to America.)

Translate into English 1 Wir hätten Tennis gespielt, wenn es nicht geregnet hätte. 2 Wirst du schon gegessen haben? 3 Er hätte sich ein Auto gekauft, wenn er reicher gewesen wäre. 4 Was hätten Sie gemacht, wenn Sie nicht zu Hause geblieben wären? 5 Er wird ihn schon gesehen haben. 6 Das wäre nicht geschehen, wenn die Polizei früher gekommen wäre.

Modal verbs
There are six modal verbs:

wollen (to want to)	sollen (to ought to/should)
müssen (to have to)	dürfen (to be allowed to/may/ can)
können (to be able to)	mögen (to like)

Points to watch
(i) These verbs are irregular in the present tense. (Note that the *ich* and *er, sie* and *es* forms are the same.)
(ii) They are followed by an infinitive (without *zu*) which is at the end of the clause or sentence:

> *Er wollte einen Ausflug machen*. (He wanted to go on a trip.)

wollen (to want to)

present		imperfect	
ich will	wir wollen	ich wollte	wir wollten
du willst	ihr wollt	du wolltest	ihr wolltet
Sie wollen	Sie wollen	Sie wollten	Sie wollten
er ⎫		er ⎫	
sie ⎬ will	sie wollen	sie ⎬ wollte	sie wollten
es ⎭		es ⎭	

Similarly:

present	imperfect
ich muß	ich mußte
ich kann	ich konnte
ich soll	ich sollte
ich darf	ich durfte
ich mag	ich mochte

(iii) After the infinitive of another verb, you must use the infinitive of the modal verb instead of the past participle in the perfect and pluperfect tenses:

Er hat es gewollt. (He wanted it.)

But: Er *hat* in die Stadt gehen *wollen*. (He wanted to go into the town.)

You should note the unusual word order in a subordinate clause:

Weil er in die Stadt *hat* gehen wollen. (Because he wanted to go into the town.)

(iv) There are two infinitives together (without *zu*) in the future and conditional tenses:

Er *wird* den Brief *schreiben müssen*. (He will have to write the letter.)

Er *würde* es *kaufen können*. (He would be able to buy it.)

Watch out again for the unusual word order in a subordinate clause:

Weil er den Brief *wird* schreiben müssen. (Because he will have to write the letter.)

The following exercise contains some tricky sentences. Check your answers carefully.

Translate into English 1 Wir werden uns beeilen müssen, sonst werden wir zu Fuß gehen müssen. 2 Er konnte gestern abend nicht kommen. 3 Er könnte morgen abend kommen. 4 Er mußte einen Brief schreiben. 5 Er hatte einen Brief zu schreiben. 6 Er hatte einen Brief geschrieben. 7 Morgen wird sie zur Arbeit gehen müssen. 8 Das Bier soll sehr gut sein. 9 Er hätte das nicht machen sollen. 10 Darf ich noch eine Tasse Tee haben, bitte?

Reflexive verbs

There are two types of construction.

1 The pronoun is the direct object (acc.):

ich wasche mich	wir waschen uns
du wäschst dich	ihr wascht euch
Sie waschen sich	Sie waschen sich
er, sie, es wäscht sich	sie waschen sich

2 The pronoun is a dative of possession:

ich putze mir die Zähne	wir putzen uns die Zähne
du putzt dir die Zähne	ihr putzt euch die Zähne
Sie putzen sich die Zähne	Sie putzen sich die Zähne
er, sie, es putzt sich die Zähne	sie putzen sich die Zähne

Reflexive verbs are conjugated with *haben*. (Don't confuse them with reflexive verbs in French!)

Translate into German 1 We felt tired. 2 Did you (3 forms) remember the photos? 3 After she had washed, she got changed. 4 I went upstairs to have a rest. 5 Did you (3 forms) wash your hands and face?

The imperative

The imperative is the form of the verb you use when giving commands. The usual forms for both strong and weak verbs are as follows:

Mach(e) (*du* form)   Mach(e) die Fenster auf!
                      (Open the windows!)
Macht (*ihr* form)   Macht die Fenster auf!
                      (Open the windows!)
Machen Sie (*Sie* form sg. & pl.)   Machen Sie die Fenster auf!
                      (Open the windows!)

1 Most strong verbs do not show any irregularity in the *du* form of
  the imperative. The exceptions are those with the stem vowel -*e*.
  They change the -*e* to -*ie* or -*i* (i.e. as they would in the *du* form
  of the present tense).
  G*i*b mir das Buch! (from *geben*)
  N*i*mm das Geld! (from *nehmen*)
  L*i*es die Zeitung! (from *lesen*)
2 The imperatives of *sein* are irregular:
  Sei/seid/seien Sie vorsichtig! (Be careful!)
3 Note the more polite form of the imperative that is more a sugges-
  tion than a command:
  Wollen wir Karten spielen? (Let's play cards.)
4 You must have an exclamation mark after an imperative!

Translate into German   1 Shut that door (3 forms).   2 Let's go
to the pictures.   3 Send him a postcard (3 forms).   4 Be punctual
(3 forms).   5 Read this novel (3 forms).

Verbs with the dative
Some verbs are always followed by the dative. You should know
this basic list:

antworten (to answer)   gelingen (to succeed, manage)
befehlen (to order, command)   gleichen (to resemble)
begegnen (to meet by chance)   helfen (to help)
danken (to thank)   sich nähern (to approach)
dienen (to serve)   passen (to suit)
drohen (to threaten)   raten (to advise)
einfallen (to occur)   trauen (to trust)
erlauben (to allow)   schmecken (to like (food))
folgen (to follow)   verzeihen (to forgive)
gefallen (to please)   zuhören (to listen to)
gehorchen (to obey)   zusehen (to watch)
gehören (to belong to)

Einfallen, gefallen, gelingen, passen and *schmecken* are used imper-
sonally. An *impersonal* verb is used almost exclusively in the 3rd

person singular often with the subject *es*. A few may also be used in the 3rd person plural:

Es fiel mir ein. (It occured to me.)
Die Bücher haben mir gut gefallen. (I enjoyed the books.)
Es gelang mir, meinen Aufsatz zu schreiben. (I managed to write my essay.)
Das Essen hat mir geschmeckt. (I enjoyed the meal.)

Note also: Es tut mir leid. (I'm sorry).
           Es tut mit weh. (It hurts me.)
           Es geht mir gut. (I'm well.)
           Es ist mir warm (kalt). (I'm warm (cold).)

Translate into German 1 The car belonged to his brother.
2 He thanked his sons. 3 Has she forgiven you (3 forms)?
4 After they had helped their father, they followed him into the house. 5 She allowed her daughter to go to the party. 6 The train was approaching the station.

Verbs with prepositions
Many verbs in German are used with prepositions that often differ from their English counterparts. You should know the following basic list:

denken an + *acc.* (to think of)

sich erinnern an + *acc.* (to remember)

sich freuen auf + *acc.* (to look forward to)

sich freuen über + *acc.* (to be pleased about)

warten auf + *acc.* (to wait for)

sich verlassen auf + *acc.* (to rely on)

halten für + *acc.* (to consider)

sich interessieren für + *acc.* (to be interested in)

sprechen über + *acc.* (to talk about)

lachen über + *acc.* (to laugh about)

sich ärgen über + *acc.* (to be annoyed about)

bitten um + *acc.* (to ask for)

Angst haben vor + *dat.* (to be afraid of)

Translate into German 1 Did you remember his birthday?
2 He was looking forward to the holidays. 3 He was waiting for the train. 4 He had to rely on his friend. 5 He asked for another bottle of wine. 6 He was afraid of the dog.

Translation of the English present participle
The present participle in German is formed by adding -d to the
infinitive: fahrend (travelling), folgend (following, etc.). It is used
mainly as an adjective:
die folgende Geschichte (the following story)
English uses the present participle in all sorts of ways. The following
German sentences and phrases can all be translated by an English
present participle. Check carefully with the key and note the constructions carefully.

Translate into English 1 Sie hörte ihn singen. 2 Sie sahen uns
kommen. 3 ohne einen Augenblick zu zögern. 4 anstatt ins
Theater zu gehen. 5 Bevor ich mich anziehe, wasche ich mich.
6 Sie lag im Garten und sonnte sich. 7 Der Mann, der die
Zeitung liest, hat einen Schnurrbart. 8 Er verließ das Haus, ohne
daß ich ihn bemerkte. 9 Er kam die Straße entlang gelaufen.
10 Ich hörte, wie er den Rasen mähte. 11 Ich trinke gern
Bier. Was trinkst du am liebsten? 12 Es ist herrlich, durch den
Wald zu wandern.

The passive
1 All the verb forms you have met so far have been in what is called
the *active voice* (i.e. the subject either *is* something or *does* something to someone or something):
    Der Einbrecher nahm den Ring. (The burglar took the ring.)
2 In the *passive voice* the subject has something done to it *by* someone or something *(the agent)*:
    Der Ring wurde von dem Einbrecher genommen. (The ring
    was taken by the burglar.)
Note that the direct object of the active is the subject of the
passive (i.e. *den* Ring becomes *der* Ring).
It is unlikely that you will have to use the passive yourself but
you should be able to recognize it.

Formation: the passive is formed from the appropriate tense of
werden + the past participle:

Present: Er wird genommen. (It is being taken.)
Imperfect: Er wurde genommen. (It was taken.)
Future: Er wird genommen werden. (It will be taken.)
Conditional: Er würde genommen werden. (It would be taken.)
Perfect: Er ist genommen worden. (It has been taken.)
Pluperfect: Er war genommen worden. (It had been taken.)

Future Perfect: Er wird genommen worden sein. (It will have been taken.)
Conditional Perfect: Er würde genommen worden sein. (It would have been taken.)

Note that the past participle of *werden* (geworden) is shortened to *worden*.

By (the agent) is usually translated by *von* for people (von dem Einbrecher) and *durch* (by means of) for things (durch ein Seil – by means of a rope). Sometimes *mit* is used (e.g. mit einem Messer – with a knife).

The passive can often be avoided by using the pronoun *man* with the active:

Man spricht deutsch. (German is spoken.)

Translate into English 1 Der Dom wurde im dreizehnten Jahrhundert erbaut. 2 Nachdem die Jungen gerettet worden waren, wurden sie ins Krankenhaus gebracht. 3 Die Diebe sind von der Polizei verhaftet worden. 4 Du wirst leicht gesehen werden. 5 Die Teller sind von der Frau zerbrochen worden. 6 Er wurde mit einer Schere ermordet.

The subjunctive

Formation: the endings for all tenses are the same for all types of verbs except in the 1st and 3rd persons singular Present of *sein*:

    singular: -e   -est -en -e
    plural: -en -et -en -en

Present: Add the above endings to the stem of the infinitive:
ich gebe, du gebest, Sie geben, er/sie/es gebe, wir geben, ihr gebet, Sie geben, sie geben.

Imperfect: Add the above endings to the stem of the ordinary imperfect of both weak and strong verbs. Add an umlaut if possible to the stem of strong verbs:
ich gäbe, du gäbest, Sie gäben, er/sie/es gäbe, wir gäben, ihr gäbet, Sie gäben, sie gäben.

The present subjunctive forms of *haben* and *sein* are used with the past participle to form the *perfect subjunctive* and the imperfect subjunctive forms of those verbs are used with the past participle to form the *pluperfect subjunctive*:

present subjunctive		imperfect subjunctive	
ich habe	wir haben	ich hätte	wir hätten
du habest	ihr habet	du hättest	ihr hättet
Sie haben	Sie haben	Sie hätten	Sie hätten
er ⎱		er ⎱	
sie ⎰ habe	sie haben	sie ⎰ hätte	sie hätten
es ⎰		es ⎰	
ich sei	wir seien	ich wäre	wir wären
du seiest	ihr seiet	du wärest	ihr wäret
Sie seien	Sie seien	Sie wären	Sie wären
er ⎱		er ⎱	
sie ⎰ sei	sie seien	sie ⎰ wäre	sie wären
es ⎰		es ⎰	

e.g. Er habe/hätte gegessen; er sei/wäre gegangen.

Usage
1 In indirect speech (e.g. *Er sagte, daß* . . . He said that . . ./*Er fragte, ob* . . . He asked if . . .
   The tense of the subjunctive is that of the original statement: He said that he *was* a doctor. = Er sagte, daß er Arzt *sei*. (Present subjunctive. The actual words were: ‚Ich *bin* Arzt.')
2 After *als ob* (as if) The pluperfect subjunctive is frequently used in this construction.

Translate into English 1 Er sagte, er sei arm. 2 Er fragte, ob ich in Deutschland gewesen sei. 3 Sie sagte, daß sie schon gegessen habe. 4 Er fragte, ob sie den Film gesehen habe. 5 Es schien, als ob es geregnet hätte. 6 Es schien, als hätte er das wertvolle Bild gestohlen.

2 Revising vocabulary and useful constructions

The following twenty themes have been devised for you to practise and revise vocabulary and structures within a context.

The German text on the left-hand page is of the type you will be expected to produce in an essay. The questions and exercises on the right-hand page expand and complement the theme.

Suggested method of working

1 Read through the German and English sentences at least three times.
2 Study each sentence carefully and look out especially for:
   (a) The subject and possibly the direct and indirect objects. What cases are they in?
   (b) The tense used.
   (c) Different word order. Ask yourself why.
   (d) Prepositions. What case follows them? Why?
3 Cover up the English sentences, look carefully at the German ones and see how much you can translate into English.
4 Now cover up the German sentences, look carefully at the English ones and see how much you can translate into German.
5 Test yourself on the vocabulary in each of the twelve sections. (a dictionary will be helpful):
   (a) Write down all the nouns with their gender and plural.
   (b) Find the infinitive of each verb and write down the principal parts.
   (c) Write down all the adjectives. Do you know their opposites if they have one?
   (d) Keep a separate list of all the little words (like *sogar, gleich,*

jedoch, etc.) that occur and learn them. Several marks can be lost if you don't know them.

6 You can now tackle the questions and exercises following the sentences.

Comprehension The questions are based on the text on the left-hand page. Remember that you can't just pick the answers straight from the text. You will have to think!

The sentences for translation into German These contain the vocabulary of the text of the left-hand page but use different structures. The changes you will have to make are very similar to those needed in the comprehension.

The sentences for translation into English These will sometimes contain words you don't know. You will have to make intelligent guesses here just as you will have to in the exam.

1 Ende gut, alles gut

1 An einem Nachmittag in der letzten Woche spielten Uwe und seine zwei Freunde Fußball im Garten.

2 Sie amüsierten sich gut, als Uwe plötzlich den Ball sehr hart schoß.

3 Anstatt ein Tor zu schießen, wurde es Uwe jedoch klar, daß er den Ball durch eines der Fenster des Nachbarhauses geschossen hatte.

4 Herr Schulze, Uwes Nachbar, der den Rasen gemäht hatte, während die Jungen Fußball spielten, hörte das Glas zerbrechen.

5 Er war sehr böse auf die Jungen, die herbeikamen, um sich zu entschuldigen.

6 Sie fegten das zerbrochene Glas zusammen, holten Geld von Uwes Mutter und gingen dann zum Glaser, um eine neue Scheibe zu kaufen.

7 Eine halbe Stunde später kehrten sie mit der neuen Scheibe zurück.

8 Glücklicherweise waren die Jungen alle praktisch veranlagt, und deshalb gelang es ihnen, die neue Scheibe einzusetzen.

9 Herr Schulze war überrascht und erfreut, als er sah, was die Jungen gemacht hatten.

All's well that ends well

1 One afternoon last week Uwe and his two friends were playing football in the garden.

2 They were enjoying themselves when suddenly Uwe kicked the ball very hard.

3 Instead of scoring a goal, however, Uwe realized that he had kicked the ball through one of the windows of the house next door.

4 Herr Schulze, Uwe's neighbour, who had been mowing the lawn while the boys were playing football, heard the glass breaking.

5 He was very angry with the boys who came round to apologize.

6 They swept up the broken glass, fetched some money from Uwe's mother and then went to the glazier's in order to buy a new pane of glass.

7 Half an hour later they returned with the new pane of glass.

8 Fortunately all the boys were practical and, therefore, they managed to put in the new pane.

9 Herr Schulze was surprised and delighted when he saw what the boys had done.

10 Er lud die Jungen ein, in sein Haus zu kommen.

10 He invited the boys to come into his house.

11 Frau Schulze brachte ihnen je ein Stück Kuchen und Limonade.

11 Frau Schulze brought them each a piece of cake and some lemonade.

A Comprehension

1 Mit wem spielte Uwe Fußball im Garten?
2 Wo wohnte Herr Schulze?
3 Warum war er böse auf die Jungen?·
4 Was machten die Jungen beim Glaser?
5 Was machten die Jungen mit der neuen Scheibe, als sie Herrn Schulzes Haus erreicht hatten? ·
6 Wem brachte Frau Schulze den Kuchen und die Limonade?

B Translate into German

1 Last Tuesday afternoon the boys went into the garden to play football.   2 One of the boys broke a window.   3 They heard him cutting the grass.   4 He was angry with them because they had broken the window.   5 After they had swept up the glass, they fetched some money.   6 They went to the glazier's where they bought a new pane of glass.   7 The boy managed to put in the new pane because he was practical.   8 The boys were surprised when Herr Schulze invited them into his house.   9 The boys thanked Herr and Frau Schulze for the lemonade and cake that they had offered them.   10 The following day Uwe had to cut the lawn in his own garden.

C Translate into English

1 Anstatt weiterzuspielen, beschlossen die drei Jungen, gleich zum Glaser zu gehen.   2 Sie sahen den Nachbarn mit seiner Frau sprechen.   3 „Sei nicht böse auf ihn!" sagte Frau Schulze. 4 „Wollen wir mal versuchen, eine neue Scheibe zu kaufen?" schlug Uwe vor.   5 „Glaubt ihr, daß es uns gelungen wird, die Scheibe einzusetzen?"   6 Paßt auf, sonst zerbrecht ihr auch die neue Scheibe!' sagte Uwe.   7 „Na, Jungens, habt ihr Durst? Kommt mal rein!" sagte Herr Schulze.   8 Da es (ihnen) sehr heiß war, freuten sie sich, als der Nachbar sie einlud, etwas zu trinken, aber sie waren etwas verlegen.

2 Ein Banküberfall

1 Letzten Freitag überfielen drei maskierte Männer die Bank in der Hauptstraße.

2 Sie hatten den Überfall sorgfältig geplant.

3 Zwei der Männer trugen das Geld in Säcken aus der Bank, während der andere im Fluchtauto blieb.

4 Nachdem sie das Geld in den Kofferraum des Autos gelegt hatten, stiegen sie ein und fuhren so schnell wie möglich zu einem einsamen Bauernhof.

5 Sie hatten vorher beschlossen, sich dort zwei oder drei Wochen aufzuhalten.

6 Es war Pech für die Räuber, daß es einem Autofahrer gelang, ihnen zu folgen, ohne daß sie es bemerkten.

7 Er rief die Polizei an, um sie zu informieren, wo die Räuber waren.

8 Kurz darauf kamen mehrere Polizeiwagen am Bauernhof an.

9 Sie umstellten das Gebäude und überredeten die Räuber herauszukommen.

10 Die Polizisten verhafteten sie und fuhren sie zur Polizeiwache.

A bank robbery

1 Last Friday three masked men robbed the bank in the high street.

2 They had planned the raid carefully.

3 Two of the men carried the money in sacks out of the bank while the other stayed in the getaway car.

4 After they had put the money into the boot of the car, they got in and drove as quickly as possible to a remote farmhouse.

5 They had previously decided to stay there for two or three weeks.

6 It was bad luck for the thieves that a motorist managed to follow them without them noticing.

7 He phoned the police to inform them where the thieves were.

8 Shortly afterwards several police cars arrived at the farmhouse.

9 They surrounded the building and persuaded the thieves to come out.

10 The policemen arrested them and drove them to the police station.

11 Der Autofahrer bekam eine Belohnung von 10 000 DM.	11 The motorist received a reward of 10,000 Dm.
12 Er beschloß, das Geld auf der Bank in der Haupstraße einzuzahlen.	12 He decided to pay the money in the bank in the high street.

A Comprehension

1 Was wollten die drei maskierten Männer machen?
2 Wo war das Geld, als sie zum einsamen Bauernhof fuhren?
3 Wem folgte der Autofahrer?
4 Woher wußte die Polizei, wo die Räuber sich aufhalten wollten?
5 Was machte der Autofahrer mit dem Geld, das er als Belohnung bekam?

B Translate into German

1 The three masked men intended to rob the bank in the high street. 2 The robbery had been carefully planned by the three masked men. 3 One of the men stayed in the car and the other two went into the bank. 4 They put the money into sacks and carried them out of the bank. 5 After they had got into the car again, they drove off as quickly as possible. 6 They wanted to stay at a remote farmhouse. 7 After the motorist had followed the men, he phoned the police. 8 After the police had surrounded the farm, they managed to persuade the thieves to come out. 9 They were arrested and driven to the police station. 10 The money was paid into the bank by the motorist.

C Translate into English

1 Die arme Bankangestellte hatte Angst vor den zwei maskierten Männern, die plötzlich in die Bank gestürzt waren. 2 Sie hatte weder Zeit noch Gelegenheit, sich gegen die Räuber zu wehren. 3 ,,Mach schnell! Gib das Geld her!'' sagte einer der Männer barsch. 4 Die Frau hinter dem Schalter sah sie mit großen Augen an. 5 Die Räuber hatten jedoch gar nicht bemerkt, daß jemand ihnen gefolgt war. 6 Als sie am Bauernhof angelangt waren, lachten sie sich tot. 7 ,,Wir haben's geschafft'', sagte der große Mann mit dem grauen Bart. 8 ,,Ihr habt Pech gehabt'', sagte der Polizist. ,,Jetzt werdet ihr keine Banken mehr überfallen können!''

3 Vollbad

1 Es war Sonntagabend um etwa sieben Uhr, und Herr Braun aß mit seinen beiden Töchtern im Eßzimmer zu Abend.

2 Seine Frau war oben im Badezimmer und badete ihren dreijährigen Sohn Hansi.

3 Es machte ihm viel Spaß mit seinen Schiffen und seiner Gummiente in der Badewanne zu spielen.

4 Plötzlich klingelte das Telefon. Es war Frau Schulze, Frau Brauns Schwester.

5 Frau Braun ging nach unten, um mit ihrer Schwester zu sprechen.

6 Während seine Mutter telefonierte, drehte Hansi den Hahn auf.

7 Da Frau Braun lange nichts von ihrer Schwester gehört hatte, interessierte es sie sehr, alle ihre . Neuigkeiten zu hören.

8 Herr Braun und die Mädchen beendeten gerade ihr Essen, als sie plötzlich bemerkten, daß Wasser durch die Decke tropfte.

9 Sie stürzten die Treppe hinauf, um festzustellen, was los war.

10 Als sie ins Badezimmer kamen, sahen sie wie Hansi in der Badewanne stand und weinte.

The overflowing bath

1 It was Sunday evening at about seven o'clock and Herr Braun was having supper in the dining room with his two daughters.

2 His wife was upstairs in the bathroom giving her three-year-old son Hansi a bath.

3 He was very happy playing with his boats and rubber duck in the bath.

4 Suddenly the phone rang. It was Frau Schulze, Frau Braun's sister.

5 Frau Braun went downstairs to talk to her sister.

6 While his mother was phoning, Hansi turned the tap on.

7 As Frau Braun hadn't heard from her sister for a long time, she was very interested to hear all her news.

8 Herr Braun and the girls were just finishing their meal when suddenly they noticed water dripping through the ceiling.

9 They rushed upstairs to see what was the matter.

10 When they went into the bathroom they saw Hansi standing in the bath crying.

11 Die Badewanne war übergelaufen, und der Boden schwamm im Wasser.

11 The bath had overflowed and the floor was swimming with water.

12 Frau Braun wird ihren Sohn nie wieder allein in der Badewanne lassen!

12 Frau Braun won't leave her son alone in the bath again!

A Comprehension

1 Wer war Hansi?

2 Wie war Frau Schulze mit Frau Braun verwandt?

3 Unter welchen Umständen wäre Frau Braun nicht plötzlich nach unten gegangen?

4 Warum tropfte Wasser durch die Decke des Eßzimmers?

5 Was fanden Herr Braun und seine Töchter, als sie ins Badezimmer stürzten?

B Translate into German

1 It was Saturday morning. 2 The two daughters were having breakfast with their father. 3 His wife went upstairs into the bathroom to bath her little son. 4 Suddenly she heard the phone ringing in the hall. 5 While the little boy was turning the tap on, his mother was talking to her sister. 6 After they had noticed that water was dripping through the ceiling, they rushed upstairs. 7 They saw that the bath had overflowed and that Hansi was standing up in the bath crying. 8 Herr Braun was angry with his wife and his little son. 9 He would not have turned the tap on, if his mother hadn't left him alone. 10 Frau Braun ought not to have left her son alone!

C Translate into English

1 „Inge", rief Herr Braun nach oben. ‚Deine Schwester ist am Apparat.' 2 „Also, sei brav!" sagte Frau Braun zu ihrem kleinen Sohn. „Ich komme gleich zurück." 3 Sie hätte mit ihrer Schwester nicht so lange sprechen sollen. 4 Ohne einen Augenblick zu zögern, stürzten die beiden Mädchen nach oben. 5 Es war ihnen klar, was passiert war. 6 Wären sie nicht gleich die Treppe hinaufgestürzt, dann wäre der Unfall noch schlimmer gewesen. 7 Ob der Junge wohl den Hahn wieder aufdreht, wenn die Mutter nicht da ist? 8 „Das hättest du nicht machen sollen!" sagte er zornig.

4 Episode am Strand

1 Letzten August verbrachte
die Familie Meyer ihre
Sommerferien am Meer.

2 An einem heißen,
sonnigen Tag saßen sie am
Strand.

3 Herr und Frau Meyer
hatten Liegestühle
mitgebracht; sie saßen
darin und lasen.

4 Von Zeit zu Zeit sahen sie
auf und betrachteten die
anderen Leute um sie
herum.

5 Sie betrachteten auch ihre
fünfjährige Tochter
Jutta, die Sandburgen
baute, und ihren
siebenjährigen Sohn
Hans, der mit einem
Schiff in einer Pfütze
spielte.

6 Die ganze Familie sonnte
sich gern, und ab und zu
rieben sie sich mit
Sonnencreme ein, damit
sie keinen Sonnenbrand
bekamen.

7 Es war ein herrlicher Tag,
und alle amüsierten sich.

8 Einmal, als Frau Meyer
von ihrem Buch aufsah,
bemerkte sie, daß Hans
nicht mehr da war.

9 Ihr kleiner Sohn war
verschwunden.

10 Sie waren sehr besorgt.

11 Sie suchten überall, und
plötzlich sah Jutta ihn mit
einem kleinen Hund in
der Ferne spielen.

Episode on the beach

1 Last August the Meyer
family spent their summer
holidays by the sea.

2 One hot, sunny day they
were sitting on the beach.

3 Herr and Frau Meyer had
brought deck chairs with
them; they were sitting
reading.

4 From time to time they
looked up and watched the
other people around them.

5 They also watched their
five-year-old daughter
Jutta who was building
sandcastles and their
seven-year-old son Hans
who was playing with a
toy boat in a small pool.

6 The whole family liked to
sunbathe and every so
often they rubbed in sun
tan cream so that they
didn't get sunburnt.

7 It was a marvellous day
and they were all enjoying
themselves.

8 Once when Frau Meyer
looked up from her book,
she noticed that Hans was
no longer there.

9 Their little son had
disappeared.

10 They were very worried.

11 They looked everywhere
and suddenly Jutta saw
him playing with a little
dog in the distance.

12 Sie waren sehr erleichtert, und Herr Meyer ging, um ihn zurückzuholen.	12 They were very relieved and Herr Meyer went to fetch him back.

A Comprehension

1 Wie war das Wetter, als die Familie Meyer am Strand war?
2 Worin saßen Herr und Frau Meyer, während sie lasen?
3 Was machten Jutta und Hans am Strand?
4 Warum waren Herr und Frau Meyer besorgt?
5 Was machte Hans, als Jutta ihn in der Ferne sah?

B Translate into German

1 During the summer the Meyer family drove to the seaside to spend two weeks in a small hotel that was next to the beach.
2 They sat down on the deck chairs that they had brought with them. 3 Their little son helped his younger sister to build sandcastles. 4 After they had sunbathed for half an hour, they ran into the sea to swim. 5 'Pass me the suntan cream,' she said. 'I don't want to get sunburnt.' 6 While their mother was reading the newspaper, the two young children were playing with their little boats. 7 As it was a hot, sunny day, they were all enjoying themselves on the beach. 8 She was very worried when she noticed that her little son had disappeared. 9 Where had he gone to? 10 She was so relieved when she saw him and a little black dog in the distance.

C Translate into English

1 ,,Wollen wir jetzt baden, oder möchtest du lieber deinen Roman weiterlesen?" fragte sie mit leiser Stimme. 2 ,,Eigentlich hab' ich gar keinen Hunger, aber ich hätte gern ein Eis. Holst du mir eins?" 3 ,,Wollen wir einen kleinen Spaziergang zum alten Leuchtturm machen?" fragte er auf einmal. 4 In dem Augenblick hatte sie keine Lust, da sie eben dabei war, sich mit Sonnencreme einzureiben. 5 ,,Was machen wir heute nachmittag? Ich möchte gern eine Fahrt mit einem kleinen Motorboot um die Bucht machen. Wie wär's?" 6 ,,Paßt gut auf!" sagte sie zu Hans. ,,Das Wasser kann plötzlich sehr tief werden." 7 ,,Wo ist Hansi? Ich kann ihn nirgendwo sehen. Ich hätte ihn doch nicht allein hingehen lassen sollen!" 8 ,,Mach dir keine Sorgen! Ich sehe ihn dort drüben in der Ferne."

5 Ein kleiner Junge wird vor dem Ertrinken gerettet

1 Letzten Sonntagnachmittag machten Karl-Heinz und Ulla einen Spaziergang am Fluß.

2 Es war ein herrlicher Tag. und die Sonne schien hell.

3 Plötzlich sahen sie einen kleinen Jungen, der mit seiner jüngeren Schwester am gegenüberliegenden Ufer gespielt hatte, in den Fluß fallen.

4 Es war klar, daß der Junge nicht schwimmen konnte.

5 Er zappelte im Wasser herum und ertrank fast.

6 Das kleine Mädchen rief um Hilfe.

7 Ohne einen Augenblick zu zögern, hob Karl-Heinz einen großen Ast auf, den er zufällig in der Nähe sah, und warf ihn ins Wasser.

8 Es gelang dem Jungen, sich an dem Ast festzuhalten, und er trieb auf eine niedrige hölzerne Brücke zu.

9 Karl-Heinz und Ulla liefen so schnell wie möglich zur Brücke.

10 Es gelang ihnen, den Jungen aus dem Wasser zu ziehen.

11 Das Mädchen, das geweint hatte, war erleichtert, als sie sah, daß ihr Bruder in Sicherheit war.

A little boy is saved from drowning

1 Last Sunday afternoon Karl-Heinz and Ulla were going for a walk by the river.

2 It was a lovely day and the sun was shining brightly.

3 Suddenly they saw a little boy who had been playing with his younger sister on the opposite bank fall into the river.

4 It was obvious that the boy couldn't swim

5 He was thrashing about in the water and was almost drowning.

6 The little girl shouted for help.

7 Without hesitating a moment, Karl-Heinz picked up a large branch that he happened to see nearby, and threw it into the water.

8 The boy managed to hold on to the branch and drifted towards a low wooden bridge.

9 Karl-Heinz and Ulla ran to the bridge as quickly as possible.

10 They managed to pull the boy out of the water.

11 The girl, who had been crying, was relieved when she saw that her brother was safe.

12 Karl-Heinz und Ulla brachten die zwei Kinder nach Hause.	12 Karl-Heinz and Ulla took the two children home.

A Comprehension

1 Wer spielte auf dem gegenüberliegenden Ufer, während Karl-Heinz und Ulla einen Spaziergang am Fluß machten?

2 Was geschah plötzlich mit dem kleinen Jungen?

3 Woher wußten Karl-Heinz und Ulla, daß der Junge nicht schwimmen konnte?

4 Wo standen Karl-Heinz und Ulla, als sie den Jungen aus dem Wasser zogen?

5 Wann brachten Karl-Heinz und Ulla die Kinder nach Hause?

B Translate into German

1 After lunch they decided to go for a walk by the river as the sun was shining brightly. 2 A little girl was playing with her elder brother on the opposite bank. 3 Suddenly he fell into the water and began thrashing about in the river as he couldn't swim.
4 Fortunately they saw what had happened. 5 He managed to pick up a large branch which he threw into the river. 6 After the man had picked up the branch, he carried it to the river to throw it into the water. 7 They stood on the low, wooden bridge and pulled the boy, who was holding on to the branch, out of the river. 8 The little girl stopped crying when she saw that her brother was safe. 9 They took the boy whom they had rescued and his sister who had been crying home. 10 The children's parents were relieved to see their son and daughter and thanked the young couple.

C Translate into English

1 Der Junge hätte ertrinken können, hätte das junge Paar ihn nicht gesehen. 2 „Mach doch schnell, sonst ertrinkt der Kleine!" rief sie. 3 Sie liefen auf das kleine Mädchen zu, um es zu trösten. 4 Obwohl es ein herrlicher Tag war, war es noch glitschig am Flußufer, und der Junge rutschte aus und fiel ins Wasser. 5 Hätte er nicht schwimmen können, so wäre der Unfall noch schlimmer gewesen. 5 Wenn der Ast nicht da gewesen wäre, so hätte der junge Mann wohl selbst ins Wasser springen müssen. 8 Der Vater hätte böse auf seinen Sohn sein sollen, aber er konnte nicht umhin zu lächeln, als er den traurigen, nassen Jungen ansah. 8 „Geh sofort nach oben, dusch dich und zieh dich um, sonst erkältest du dich!" sagte die Mutter.

6 Ein ‚Terrorist' wird beinahe verhaftet

1 Vorige Woche ging Herr Becker in ein Spielwarengeschäft, um seinem Sohn ein Geschenk zu kaufen.

2 Einige Minuten später kam er mit einem langen Paket unter dem Arm aus dem Geschäft.

3 Er ging in eine Gaststätte, um ein Glas Bier zu trinken.

4 Der Kellner bemerkte, daß im Paket des Mannes ein Gewehr war.

5 Er (der Kellner) hatte gerade in der Zeitung gelesen, daß die Polizei einen Terroristen suchte.

6 Er brachte dem Mann sein Bier, und dann rief er die Polizei an.

7 Nachdem Herr Becker das Bier getrunken hatte, verließ er die Gaststätte.

8 Die Polizei kam gerade an der Gaststätte an, als er in sein Auto stieg.

9 Sie folgten Herrn Becker zu seinem Haus.

10 Herr Becker ging ins Haus und gab seinem Sohn, der als Cowboy verkleidet war, das Gewehr.

11 Die Polizisten stiegen aus ihrem Wagen aus und klopften an die Haustür von Herrn Becker.

A 'terrorist' is nearly arrested

1 Last week Herr Becker went into a toy shop to buy his son a present.

2 A few minutes later he came out of the shop with a long parcel under his arm.

3 He went into a restaurant to drink a glass of beer.

4 The waiter noticed that there was a rifle in the man's parcel.

5 He (the waiter) had just been reading in the newspaper that the police were looking for a terrorist.

6 He brought the man his beer and then phoned the police.

7 After Herr Becker had drunk the beer, he left the restaurant.

8 The police arrived at the restaurant just as he was getting into his car.

9 They followed Herr Becker to his house.

10 Herr Becker went into the house and gave his son, who was dressed as a cowboy, the rifle.

11 The police got out of their car and knocked on Herr Becker's front door.

| 12 Sie waren sehr erstaunt, als sie den kleinen Jungen mit dem Gewehr sahen. | 12 They were very surprised when they saw the little boy with the rifle. |

A Comprehension
1 Wo kaufte Herr Becker seinem Sohn das Geschenk?
2 Was wollte Herr Becker in der Gaststätte machen?
3 Wann rief der Kellner die Polizei an?
4 Wie fuhr Herr Becker nach Hause?
5 Wann klopften die Polizisten an die Haustür von Herrn Becker?
6 Wer hatte das Gewehr, als die Polizisten in Herrn Beckers Haus waren?

B Translate into German
1 Last week Herr Becker bought his son a marvellous present in a toy shop. 2 Shortly afterwards he left the shop and decided to go into a restaurant because he was thirsty. 3 The waiter came up to him and he (the latter) ordered a glass of beer. 4 As soon as he had brought the man his beer, the waiter decided to phone the police. 5 After he had left the restaurant, he got into his car. 6 The police arrived a few minutes later and followed his car. 7 The little boy thanked his father when he gave him the rifle. 8 After the two policemen had got out of their car, they knocked on the man's front door. 9 He was surprised to see the policemen at the front door. 10 The policemen smiled when they saw Herr Becker's son playing with the rifle.

C Translate into English
1 Er wollte seinem Sohn etwas Ungewöhnliches zum Geburtstag kaufen. 2 Das nagelneue Gewehr solle für ihn eine große Überraschung sein. 3 ,,Stimmt es so?" sagte der Verkäufer, nachdem der Mann das Geschenk bezahlt hatte. ,,Ja, in Ordnung", erwiderte er. 4 Der Kellner wurde höchst mißtrauisch und hielt den Mann für einen gefährlichen Terroristen. 5 Er dachte einen Augenblick nach, was er machen sollte. 6 Es bestand nur eine Möglichkeit – er mußte sofort die Polizei verständigen. 7 Er wußte, daß er sich immer auf die Polzei verlassen konnte und war erleichtert, als er sie gegenüber der Gaststätte erblickte. 8 ,,Na so was," sagte einer der Polizisten, als er den als Cowboy verkleideten Jungen mit dem Gewehr spielen sah.

7 Pilze zum Mittagessen

1 Rainer, seine Verlobte
   Gisela und ihre zwei
   Freunde Peter und Helga
   verbrachten eine Woche
   auf dem Lande.

2 Sie hatten eine schöne
   Hütte am Rande eines
   Waldes gemietet.

3 Eines Morgens nach dem
   Frühstück beschlossen
   sie, einen Spaziergang im
   Wald zu machen.

4 Nachdem sie einige Zeit
   gegangen waren, bemerkte
   Helga plötzlich einige
   Pilze, die im Schatten
   einer großen Eiche
   wuchsen.

5 Sie entschieden sich, sie
   zu sammeln und sie zum
   Mittagessen zu kochen.

6 Als sie zur Hütte
   zurückkamen, halfen sie
   alle, das Essen zu
   bereiten.

7 Während Gisela die
   Kartoffeln schälte, wusch
   Rainer die Pilze.

8 Helga schob das Fleisch in
   den Ofen, während Peter
   den Tisch deckte.

9 Bald war das Essen fertig,
   und nachdem Rainer eine
   Flasche Wein geöffnet
   hatte, setzten sie sich an
   den Tisch, um das Essen
   zu genießen.

10 Leider fühlten sie sich am
   Nachmittag alle sehr
   krank.

Mushrooms for lunch

1 Rainer, his fiancée Gisela
   and their two friends Peter
   and Helga were spending a
   week in the country.

2 They had rented a
   pleasant cottage on the
   edge of a forest.

3 One morning after
   breakfast they decided to
   go for a walk in the forest.

4 After they had been
   walking for some time,
   Helga suddenly noticed
   some mushrooms growing
   in the shade of a large oak
   tree.

5 They decided to pick them
   and cook them for lunch.

6 When they got back to the
   cottage they all helped to
   prepare the meal.

7 While Gisela was peeling
   the potatoes, Rainer
   washed the mushrooms.

8 Helga put the meat in the
   oven while Peter laid the
   table.

9 Soon the meal was ready
   and after Rainer had
   opened a bottle of wine,
   they sat down at the table
   to enjoy the meal.

10 Unfortunately in the
   afternoon they all felt very
   ill.

11 Peter konnte gerade noch mit dem Krankenhaus telefonieren, damit man einen Krankenwagen schickte.	11 Peter was just able to phone the hospital for an ambulance.
12 Sie mußten alle die Nacht im Krankenhaus verbringen.	12 They all had to spend the night in hospital.

A Comprehension
1 Wo wohnten Rainer, Gisela und ihre Freunde auf dem Lande?
2 Was hatten sie gemacht, bevor sie die Hütte verließen, um den Spaziergang im Wald zu machen?
3 Was machten sie mit den Pilzen, nachdem sie sie gesehen hatten?
4 Was machte Rainer, kurz bevor sie sich an den Tisch setzten?
5 Wo brachte der Krankenwagen die Freunde hin?
6 Warum mußten die Freunde die Nacht im Krankenhaus verbringen?

B Translate into German
1 Last August Rainer spent a week in the country with his fiancée and two friends. 2 The pleasant cottage was in the vicinity of a large forest. 3 'Let's go for a walk in the forest,' Rainer suggested after breakfast. 4 They picked the mushrooms that were growing under the large oak tree. 5 Gisela went into the kitchen to peel the potatoes. 6 After Rainer had washed the mushrooms, Peter laid the table in the dining room. 7 They sat at the table enjoying the meal and drinking the wine that Rainer had opened. 8 After lunch they all began to feel ill. 9 Peter managed to phone the hospital. 10 The ambulance drove them to the hospital where they had to spend the night.

C Translate into English
1 „Mir gefällt's hier," sagte Gisela. „Die Hütte liegt ja herrlich so dicht am Wald." 2 „Wollen wir nach dem Frühstück spazierengehen, oder geht ihr lieber einkaufen?" fragte Helga.
3 „Seht mal die schönen Pilze, die da drüben wachsen!"
4 „Ob die giftig sind?" fragte Gisela ihre Verlobten.
5 „Keineswegs. Du brauchst dir keine Sorgen zu machen," antwortete Rainer . 6 Es was Pech, daß er sich geirrt hatte.
7 Der Arzt bestand darauf, daß sie nicht gleich nach Hause durften, und daß sie die Nacht im Krankenhaus verbringen mußten. 8 Sie hätten die Pilze nicht essen sollen!

8 Die Geburtstagsparty

The birthday party

1 Vor zwei Tagen hatte Karl seinen siebten Geburtstag. Es war der dritte Mai.

1 Two days ago Karl had his seventh birthday. It was the third of May.

2 Er wachte früh auf und wartete auf den Briefträger, der ihm einige Karten und Päckchen brachte.

2 He woke up early and waited for the postman who brought him several cards and some parcels.

3 Beim Frühstück gaben seine Eltern ihm ihr Geschenk, ein neues Fahrrad.

3 At breakfast his parents gave him their present, a new bike.

4 Er freute sich sehr, besonders weil er am Nachmittag eine Geburtstagsparty haben sollte.

4 He was very happy especially as he was to have a birthday party in the afternoon.

5 Während er sich die Zähne nach dem Frühstück putzte, bemerkte er jedoch leider, daß ihm einer seiner Zähne weh tat.

5 Unfortunately, however, while he was cleaning his teeth after breakfast, he noticed that one of his teeth was hurting.

6 Deshalb beschloß seine Mutter, mit ihm zum Zahnarzt zu gehen.

6 His mother decided, therefore, to take him to the dentist's.

7 Da der Zahn faul war, beschloß der Zahnarzt, ihn sofort zu ziehen.

7 As the tooth was bad, the dentist decided to take it out straight away.

8 Karl freute sich nicht mehr; in der Tat fühlte er sich sehr elend, als er nach Hause kam.

8 Karl was no longer happy; in fact he felt very miserable when he arrived home.

9 Eine Stunde später kamen Karls Freunde an.

9 An hour later Karl's friends arrived.

10 Es gelang ihm gerade noch, zu lächeln und ihnen für ihre Karten und Geschenke zu danken.

10 He just managed to smile and thank the for their cards and presents.

11 Karls Mutter hatte zum Geburtstag einen schönen Kaffeetisch vorbereitet.

11 Karl's mother had prepared a lovely birthday tea.

12 Während seine Freunde aßen, tranken und sich amüsierten, saß Karl ruhig und traurig da, weil sein Mund ihm immer noch weh tat.	12 While his friends were eating, drinking and enjoying themselves, Karl sat there quietly and sadly because his mouth was still hurting.

A Comprehension
1 An welchem Tag wurde Karl sieben Jahre alt?
2 Wer brachte ihm Karten und Päckchen früh am Morgen?
3 Was machte Karl, als er bemerkte, daß ihm einer seiner Zähne weh tat?
4 Was machte der Zahnarzt mit dem faulen Zahn?
5 Wann dankte Karl seinen Freunden?

B Translate into German
1 Karl was excited because it was his birthday. 2 He hoped that the postman would bring him some cards and parcels. 3 He wanted to try out the new bicycle that his parents had given him for his birthday. 4 After breakfast he went upstairs so that he could clean his teeth. 5 Unfortunately he had to go to the dentist's because he had toothache. 6 He felt ill when the dentist had taken out his bad tooth. 7 Instead of looking forward to his party, he felt miserable. 8 He thanked his friends for the presents that they had given him. 9 He didn't want to eat anything. 10 Instead of playing with his friends, poor Karl had to sit quietly in an armchair.

C Translate into English
1 Karl wußte gar nicht im voraus, was er zum Geburtstag bekommen sollte. 2 Seit Tagen freute er sich auf seine Geburtstagsparty. 3 „Guck mal, Mutti, was der Briefträger mir gebracht hat!" sagte er aufgeregt. 4 „Tut dir der Zahn wirklich weh?" fragte die Mutter. 5 „Wir müssen unbedingt zum Zahnarzt" sagte sie. „Muß das sein?" erwiderte der kleine Karl traurig. 6 „Es tut uns wirklich leid, daß es dir nicht gut geht," sagten sie. 7 Er hätte versuchen sollen, ein Glas Orangensaft zu trinken. 8 Es war schade, daß er weder trinken noch essen durfte.

9 Das Horoskop

1 Frau Mainzer saß in der Küche und las ihr Horoskop.

2 Sie freute sich, als sie las, daß sie einen erfolgreichen Tag haben sollte.

3 Als sie die Zeitung gelesen hatte, mußte sie ihre Hausarbeit beginnen.

4 Zuerst wusch sie ab, und gerade als sie im Begriff war, die Teller in einen Schrank zu stellen, rutschte sie aus und ließ sie fallen.

5 Nachdem sie die zerbrochenen Teller aufgefegt hatte, steckte sie die schmutzige Wäsche in die Waschmaschine.

6 Eine Stunde später ging sie in den Garten, um die nasse Wäsche auf die Leine zu hängen.

7 Leider begann es kurz darauf zu regnen, und sie mußte die ganze Wäsche ins Haus zurücktragen.

8 Anschließend begann sie, das Mittagessen zu kochen, und danach stellte sie es in den Ofen.

9 Eine halbe Stunde später läutete das Telefon. Es war eine alte Freundin, von der sie lange nichts gehört hatte.

10 Sie plauderten schon seit einer dreiviertel Stunde, als sie plötzlich roch, daß etwas angebrannt war.

The horoscope

1 Frau Mainzer was sitting in the kitchen reading her horoscope.

2 She was delighted when she read that she was going to have a successful day.

3 When she had read the newspaper she had to begin her housework.

4 First she did the washing up and just as she was about to put the plates into a cupboard, she slipped and dropped them.

5 After she had swept up the broken plates, she put the dirty washing into the washing machine.

6 An hour later she went into the garden to hang the wet clothes on the washing line.

7 Unfortunately it began to rain shortly afterwards and she had to carry all the clothes back into the house.

8 She then began to get the lunch and afterwards she put it into the oven.

9 Half an hour later the phone rang. It was an old friend from whom she hadn't heard for a long time.

10 They had been talking for three quarters of an hour when she suddenly smelled something burning.

11 Sie stürzte in die Küche und sah Rauch aus dem Ofen kommen.	11 She rushed into the kitchen and saw smoke coming out of the oven.
12 Sie schwor, daß sie von diesem Augenblick an nie wieder das Horoskop lesen würde!	12 From that moment on, she swore that she would never read the horoscope again!

A Comprehension

1 Wann wollte Frau Mainzer die Teller in den Schrank stellen?
2 Warum ließ sie die Teller fallen?
3 Wo war die Leine?
4 Warum mußte sie die ganze Wäsche ins Haus zurücktragen?
5 Unter welchen Umständen hätte sie wohl das Mittagessen nicht anbrennen lassen?

B Translate into German

1 Frau Mainzer picked up the newspaper to read her horoscope.
2 After she had read that her day was to be successful, she began her housework. 3 She dropped the plates that she was about to put into the cupboard because she slipped. 4 She had to sweep up the plates that she had just broken. 5 She took the clean clothes out of the washing machine and hung them on the washing line. 6 She was annoyed when it began to rain as she had to take the washing that was hanging on the line back into the house.
7 Just as she was about to lay the table, the phone rang in the hall. 8 She chatted for three quarters of an hour with the friend who had phoned her. 9 As soon as she smelled that something was burning, she rushed out of the hall to see what was the matter. 10 She hoped that the next day would be better for her.

C Translate into English

1 Sie blätterte durch die Zeitung, und als sie das Horoskop fand, fing sie an, es eifrig zu lesen. 2 Sie glaubte seit Jahren an die Sternzeichen. 3 „Ich kann doch nicht den ganzen Tag herumsitzen," dachte sie sich. 4 Sie hatte sich gerade an die Arbeit gemacht, als sie auf einmal ausrutschte und das eben abgewaschene Geschirr fallen ließ. 5 „Ach, du meine Güte," sagte sie sich. „Jetzt fängt's an zu regnen." 6 „Nun muß ich aber wirklich gehen," sagte sie zu ihrer Freundin. „Ich glaube, daß in der Küche etwas angebrannt ist." 7 „Ich rufe dich nächste Woche an. Auf Wiederhören." 8 Am Abend erzählte sie ihrem Mann alles, was während des Tages passiert war.

10 Die verpaßte Fähre

The missed ferry

1 Die Familie Robinson hatte deutsche Freunde, die in Bonn wohnten.

1 The Robinson family had German friends who lived in Bonn.

2 Letzten Juli besuchten die Robinsons ihre deutschen Freunde.

2 Last July the Robinsons went to visit their German friends.

3 Sie beluden das Auto am Abend vor der Abfahrt, damit sie sich früh auf den Weg machen konnten.

3 They loaded the car the night before they were due to leave so that they could set off early.

4 Am folgenden Morgen verließen sie das Haus rechtzeitig und begannen die Fahrt nach Dover.

4 The following morning they left the house in good time and began the drive to Dover.

5 Ihre Fähre sollte um 14.00 Uhr abfahren.

5 Their ferry was due to leave at two o'clock.

6 Als sie etwa 30 km vor Dover waren, stoppte der Verkehr auf der Autobahn.

6 When they were about 30 kilometers from Dover, the traffic on the motorway came to a halt.

7 Es hatte einen schweren Unfall gegeben, und die Straße war blockiert.

7 There had been a serious accident and the road was blocked.

8 Die Verkehrsschlange wurde immer länger.

8 The queue of traffic got longer and longer.

9 Der Reihe nach kamen mehrere Polizeiwagen, ein Krankenwagen und ein Abschleppwagen an der Unglücksstelle an.

9 In turn several police cars, an ambulance and a breakdown van arrived at the scene of the accident.

10 Erst nach etwa anderthalb Stunden konnten die Robinsons ihre Fahrt fortsetzen.

10 Only after about an hour and a half were the Robinsons able to continue their journey.

11 Sie kamen um etwa 14.00 Uhr in Dover an.

11 They arrived in Dover at about two o'clock.

12 Natürlich hatten sie ihre Fähre verpaßt, und sie mußten auf die nächste warten.

12 Of course they had missed their ferry and they had to wait for the next one.

A Comprehension

1 Wer wohnte in Bonn?
2 Was konnten die Robinsons machen, weil sie das Auto am Abend vor der Abfahrt beladen hatten?
3 Warum wollten die Robinsons lange vor 14.00 Uhr in Dover sein?
4 Was mußten die Robinsons wegen des Unfalls machen?
5 Unter welchen Umständen wären die Robinsons rechtzeitig in Dover angekommen?

B Translate into German

1 Last Summer the Robinson family drove to Bonn to visit their German friends. 2 As they had to set off early in the morning, they loaded the car the previous evening. 3 They wanted to be in Dover by one o'clock. 4 They didn't want to miss the ferry that was due to leave at two o'clock. 5 Suddenly Mr Robinson had to stop because there had been a serious accident. 6 They could see an ambulance and a breakdown van in the distance. 7 They had to wait almost an hour and a half before they could continue their journey. 8 The accident had happened about 30 kilometres from Dover. 9 When they arrived in Dover the ferry had already left. 10 They talked about the accident while they waited for the next ferry.

C Translate into English

1 ,,Ihr sollt gleich ins Bett gehen," sagte Mr Robinson zu seinen zwei Kindern. ,,Morgen haben wir einen langen Tag vor uns."
2 ,,Um Gottes willen, was ist da passiert?" fragte Mrs Robinson ihren Mann. 3 ,,Es muß ein schwerer Unfall passiert sein," erwiderte er. 4 ,,Hoffentlich ist niemand schwer verletzt."
5 ,,Wir werden sicher lange warten müssen," fügte er hinzu.
6 ,,Wir hätten doch früher abfahren sollen," sagte er traurig.
7 ,,Jetzt schaffen wir es nicht mehr. Die Fähre wird sicher schon abgefahren sein, wenn wir in Dover ankommen." 8 Mrs Robinson meinte, daß sie anrufen sollten, um ihren Freunden Bescheid zu sagen, daß sie später ankommen würden.

11 Ein Unfall beim Schlittschuhlaufen

A skating accident

1 Es hatte die ganze Nacht hindurch geschneit.

1 It had been snowing all night long.

2 Dieter telefonierte mit seinem Freund Achim, um herauszufinden, ob er zum Spielen kommen könne.

2 Dieter phoned his friend Achim to see if he could play.

3 Eine halbe Stunde später kam Achim mit seinem Schlitten und seinen Schlittschuhen an.

3 Achim arrived with his sledge and skates half an hour later.

4 Die zwei Jungen beschlossen, einen Schneemann im Garten zu bauen.

4 The two boys decided to build a snowman in the garden.

5 Als sie ihn fertig gebaut hatten, bewarfen sie ihn mit Schneebällen.

5 When they had finished it, they pelted it with snowballs.

6 Dann holten sie ihre Schlittschuhe und rodelten den Hügel hinunter bis zu einem kleinen See, der nicht weit von Dieters Haus entfernt lag.

6 Then they fetched their skates and tobogganed downhill to a small lake that was not far from Dieter's house.

7 Der See war zugefroren, und sie begannen Schlittschuh zu laufen. Es machte Spaß.

7 The lake was frozen and they began to skate. It was fun.

8 Plötzlich jedoch brach das Eis, und der arme Achim fiel ins eisige Wasser.

8 Suddenly, however, the ice broke and poor Achim fell into the icy water.

9 Glücklicherweise waren noch andere Leute am See.

9 Fortunately there were other people at the lake.

10 Ohne Zeit zu verlieren, lief ein Mann zu seinem Auto und holte ein Seil aus dem Kofferraum.

10 Without losing a moment, a man ran to his car and fetched a rope out of the boot.

11 Er warf es Achim schnell zu, und es gelang ihm, ihn aus dem Wasser zu ziehen.

11 He threw it quickly to Achim and managed to pull him out of the water.

| 12 Achim was sehr dankbar, und es war ihm klar, daß es viel schlimmer hätte ausgehen können. | 12 Achim was very grateful and he realized that it could have been much worse. |

A Comprehension
1 Was brachte Achim mit, als er Dieter besuchte?
2 Wozu gingen die zwei Jungen in den Garten?
3 Wo wollten die Jungen Schlittschuh laufen?
4 Unter welchen Umständen wäre Achim nicht ins Wasser gefallen?
5 Wann lief der Mann zu seinem Wagen?
6 Womit zog der Mann Achim aus dem Wasser?

B Translate into German
1 Dieter was pleased when he saw that it had been snowing all night long.   2 Achim fetched his skates from his bedroom and his sledge from the shed.   3 They went into the garden to build a large snowman.   4 They sat down on the sledge so that they could toboggan down the hill.   5 They put on their skates and walked on to the ice.   6 It was fun skating on the frozen lake.
7 Suddenly Dieter saw poor Achim fall into the icy water.
8 Fortunately a man saw what had happened.   9 He pulled him out of the water with the rope that had been in the boot of his car.   10 Achim was very relieved and thanked the man.

C Translate into English
1 ,,Schau mal den Schnee an, Mutti! Darf Achim zu uns kommen?"   2 ,,Wollen wir einen Schneemann bauen?" schlug er vor.   3 Dieter verschwand im Haus und kehrte nach einem Augenblick mit einer Mohrrübe für die Nase und zwei Knöpfen für die Augen zurück.   4 Sie setzten ihm auch einen Hut auf den Kopf und banden ihm einen Schal um den Hals.   5 ,,Seid vorsichtig und macht keinen Blödsinn!" sagte die Mutter, bevor die Jungen losgingen.   6 ,,Bleib ruhig!" rief der Mann dem armen Achim zu. ,,Ich werfe dir das Seil zu."   7 ,,Ach, Gott sei Dank," seufzte Achim. ,,Ohne Ihre Hilfe wäre ich sicher ertrunken."   8 Der Mann sah den zitternden Jungen und dessen Freund an. ,,Kommt! Ich bringe euch nach Hause, sonst erkältet ihr euch!"

12 Der neue Couchtisch

1 Uwes Lieblingsfach in der Schule war Werken.

2 Seit einigen Wochen hatte er an einem Couchtisch gebastelt, den er seinen Eltern als Geschenk geben wollte.

3 Letzten Montag machte er ihn endlich fertig und sah ihn stolz an.

4 Nach seiner letzten Stunde ging er zum Werkraum, um den Tisch zu holen.

5 Er mußte ihn zur Bushaltestelle tragen und auf den nächsten Bus warten.

6 Nach einer Viertelstunde kam der Bus an.

7 Leider erlaubte der Fahrer ihm nicht, mit dem Tisch in den Bus einzusteigen.

8 Deswegen mußte Uwe den Tisch nach Hause tragen.

9 Nachdem er etwa vier Kilometer am Flußufer entlang gegangen war, mußte er einen steilen Hügel hinaufsteigen.

10 Als er oben ankam, fühlte er sich sehr müde und beschloß sich auf den Tisch zu setzen, um sich auszuruhen.

11 Leider brach der Tisch zusammen, und Uwe fiel zu Boden.

12 Er weinte beinahe, weil er so enttäuscht war.

The new coffee table

1 Uwe's favourite lesson at school was woodwork.

2 He had been making a coffee table for several weeks which he wanted to give to his parents as a present.

3 Last Monday he finally finished it and looked at it proudly.

4 After his last lesson he went to the woodwork room to fetch the table.

5 He had to carry it to the bus stop and wait for the next bus.

6 After a quarter of an hour the bus arrived.

7 Unfortunately, the driver wouldn't allow him to get on the bus with the table.

8 Therefore Uwe had to carry the table home.

9 After he had walked about four kilometres along the river bank, he had to walk up a steep hill.

10 When he arrived at the top, he felt very tired and decided to sit down on the table to rest.

11 Unfortunately the table collapsed and Uwe fell to the ground.

12 He almost wept because he was so disappointed.

A Comprehension

1 Was wollte Uwe mit dem Couchtisch machen, als er ihn fertig gebastelt hatte?
2 Was machte Uwe, als er die Haltestelle erreicht hatte?
3 Woher wissen Sie, daß der Fahrer unfreundlich war?
4 Was mußte Uwe also mit dem Tisch machen, nachdem der Bus abgefahren war?
5 Wann setzte er sich auf den Tisch und warum?

B Translate into German

1 Uwe wanted to give his parents the coffee table that he had made at school. 2 He was very proud of his coffee table. 3 Last Monday he fetched it from the woodwork room. 4 As he wanted to surprise his parents, he decided to carry the table home. 5 He wasn't allowed to get on the bus with the table. 6 He was angry with the driver. 7 After he had walked up the steep hill, he sat down on the coffee table because he felt tired. 8 If he hadn't sat down on the table, it wouldn't have collapsed. 9 He could have cried. 10 He hoped he could repair the table.

C Translate into English

1 „Der Tisch sieht wirklich gut aus," sagte der Lehrer. „Deine Eltern werden sich bestimmt darüber freuen." 2 Es tut mir leid,' sagte der Fahrer. „Mit dem Ding da darfst du nicht einsteigen!" 3 „Er hätte freundlicher sein können," dachte Uwe. 4 Je weiter er ging, desto schwerer schien der Tisch zu werden. 5 Vielleicht hätte Uwe seinen Lehrer bitten sollen, ihn mit dem Tisch nach Hause zu fahren. 6 Er hatte schon eine gute Strecke hinter sich, als er beschloß, sich einen Augenblick auszuruhen. 7 „Ach, verdammt," fluchte er, „Das hätte ich nicht machen sollen." 8 „Das macht nichts," sagten die Eltern, als sie den zusammengebrochenen Tisch sahen. „Du wirst ihn sicher reparieren können."

13 Ein Zufall

1 Frau Gauglitz wohnte mit ihrem Mann und ihren zwei Kindern, Bernd und Anna in Köln.

2 Sie freute sich auf den folgenden Freitag, da es ihr Geburtstag war.

3 Bernd und Anna beschlossen, ihrer Mutter Geschenke zu kaufen.

4 Sie gingen nach oben in ihre Schlafzimmer und machten ihre Spardosen auf, um Geld herauszunehmen.

5 Dann machten sie sich auf den Weg zu den Läden.

6 Zuerst gingen sie in ein Warenhaus, um zu sehen, was sie kaufen konnten.

7 Anna schlug vor, daß sie ihrer Mutter einen neuen Pullover kaufen sollten, und Bernd war damit einverstanden.

8 Danach gingen sie zur Blumenhandlung, um ein paar Blumen zu kaufen.

9 Zufälligerweise kaufte Herr Gauglitz seiner Frau den gleichen Pullover wie Bernd und Anna.

10 Am Freitag war Frau Gauglitz entzückt, als sie sah, daß sie Geschenke bekommen hatte.

11 Ihr Mann war jedoch enttäuscht, als er den anderen Pullover sah.

A coincidence

1 Frau Gauglitz lived with her husband and her two children, Bernd and Anna in Cologne.

2 She was looking forward to the following Friday as it was her birthday.

3 Bernd and Anna decided to buy their mother presents.

4 They went upstairs to their bedrooms and opened their money boxes in order to get some money.

5 Then they set off for the shops.

6 First they went into a department store to see what they could buy.

7 Anna suggested that they should buy their mother a new sweater and Bernd agreed.

8 Afterwards they went to the florist's to buy some flowers.

9 By chance Herr Gauglitz bought his wife the same sort of pullover as Bernd and Anna.

10 On Friday Frau Gauglitz was delighted when she saw that she had got some presents.

11 Her husband was, however, disappointed when he saw the other pullover.

12 Am nächsten Tag ging er zum Geschäft zurück und tauschte seinen Pullover gegen eine Handtasche um.

12 The next day he went back to the shop and changed his sweater for a handbag.

A Comprehension
1 Wer waren Bernd und Anna?
2 Was hatten die Kinder gemacht, ehe sie weggingen?
3 Wo genau war das Geld gewesen?
4 Wann gingen sie zur Blumenhandlung?
5 Was mußte Herr Gauglitz am nächsten Tag machen?

B Translate into German
1 Herr Gauglitz lived with his wife and his two children in a small detached house. 2 The children wanted to buy their mother presents because it was her birthday on Friday. 3 Anna took some money out of the money box that was standing on the dressing table in her bedroom. 4 Her brother went into his bedroom to fetch some money. 5 After they had bought their mother a new sweater in a department store, they went to a florist's to buy her some flowers. 6 Herr Gauglitz didn't know what his children had bought. 7 The next day Herr Gauglitz had to go back with the sweater to the shop where he changed it for a handbag. 8 When he got home he gave it (the handbag) to his wife. 9 Fortunately she liked it. 10 Now she had a lovely new handbag, a new, red sweater and some beautiful flowers.

C Translate into English
1 „Weißt du was Mutti zum Geburtstag möchte?" fragte Bernd seine Schwester. 2 „Eigentlich nicht," erwiderte sie. „Wollen wir nach dem Frühstück in die Stadt gehen und ihr etwas kaufen?" 3 Das konnten sie machen, da sie schulfrei hatten. 4 Sie holten ihr Geld und eilten zur Bushaltestelle, da sie ziemlich weit von der Stadtmitte wohnten. 5 Als sie in einem großen Warenhaus waren, erinnerte Anna sich plötzlich an den schönen Pullover, den die Mutter neulich gesehen hatte, und der ihr gut gefallen hatte. 6 „Sollen wir ihn kaufen?" fragte Bernd. „Ich glaub' schon. Er ist wirklich preiswert," antwortete Anna. 7 Der Vater war völlig verblüfft, als er sah, was die Kinder der Mutter geschenkt hatten. 8 Frau Gauglitz lächelte ihren Mann an. „Das macht nichts, Liebling. Morgen kannst du ihn umtauschen. Übrigens, ich hätte gern eine neue Handtasche."

14 Der Kinobesuch

Going to the pictures

1 Letzten Samstag-
nachmittag saß Rita in
ihrem Schlafzimmer,
hörte Schallplatten
und las eine Illustrierte.

1 Last Saturday afternoon
Rita was sitting in her
bedroom, listening to
records and reading a
magazine.

2 Plötzlich klingelte das
Telefon im Flur.

2 Suddenly the phone rang
in the hall.

3 Sie lief nach unten, um zu
sehen, wer es war.

3 She ran downstairs to see
who it was.

4 Es war ihr Freund Robert,
und er lud sie ein, am
Abend mit ihm ins Kino
zu gehen.

4 It was her friend Robert
and he invited her to go to
the pictures with him that
evening.

5 Sie machten aus, sich um
7.30 Uhr vor dem Kino zu
treffen.

5 They arranged to meet in
front of the cinema at
7.30.

6 Später an jenem
Nachmittag wusch sie sich
das Haar und zog ein
neues Kleid an.

6 Later that afternoon she
washed her hair and put
on a new dress.

7 Nach dem Abendessen
verließ sie das Haus und
ging zur Bushaltestelle,
um den Bus zur
Stadtmitte zu nehmen.

7 After supper she left the
house and walked to the
bus stop to catch the bus
to the town centre.

8 Bald war sie vor dem
Kino, aber Robert war
nicht da.

8 Soon she was in front of
the cinema but Robert
wasn't there.

9 Zehn Minuten später war
Robert immer noch nicht
angekommen, und Rita
begann sich unruhig und
verlegen zu fühlen.

9 Ten minutes later Robert
still hadn't arrived and
Rita began to feel worried
and embarrassed.

10 Sie beschloß, noch eine
Viertelstunde zu warten,
und als Robert dann
immer noch nicht
gekommen war, nahm sie
den Bus nach Hause.

10 She decided to wait
another quarter of an hour
and then, when Robert
still hadn't come, she
caught the bus home.

11 Sie weinte fast, als sie zu Hause ankam, und sie sagte ihrer Mutter, daß sie sehr böse auf Robert sei.	11 She was almost crying when she arrived home and she told her mother that she was very angry with Robert.

A Comprehension

1 Wann genau letzten Samstag klingelte das Telefon?

2 Was wollten Rita und Robert am Samstagabend machen?

3 Was hatte Rita gemacht, bevor sie das Haus verließ?

4 Womit fuhr Rita in die Stadtmitte?

5 Warum fühlte sich Rita unruhig und verlegen?

6 Unter welchen Umständen wäre Rita nicht gleich nach Hause gefahren?

B Translate into German

1 After lunch Rita went upstairs into her bedroom. 2 She wanted to listen to the record that she had bought that morning. 3 She had just sat down to read her magazine when the phone rang in the hall. 4 She was very pleased when Robert invited her to go to the pictures as she liked him a lot. 5 She put on the new dress that she had got for her birthday. 6 When she arrived at the cinema, Robert wasn't there. 7 The longer she waited the more embarrassed she felt. 8 After half an hour she decided to go home. 9 She was very angry with her friend. 10 She told her mother what had happened.

C Translate into English

1 „Rita," rief die Mutter. „Stell bitte den Plattenspieler leiser! Mußt du die Platten immer so laut spielen?" 2 „Hast du Lust heute abend ins Kino zu gehen?" fragte er. „Gerne," erwiderte sie. 3 „Bringt Robert dich gleich nach dem Film nach Hause?" fragte die Mutter. „Ja, klar, Mutti." 4 „Das Kleid steht dir gut. Du siehst wirklich nett aus," sagte sie. 5 „Tschüß, Mutti. Ich muß mich beeilen," rief sie, als sie die Haustür zumachte. 6 Sie hatte das Gefühl, daß die anderen Menschen sie komisch ansahen, was aber nicht stimmte. 7 Obwohl sie den Film gern hätte sehen wollen, hatte sie keine Lust, allein hinzugehen. 8 Robert rief später an, um sich bei ihr zu entschuldigen.

15 Ein Brand

1 Herr Krause war ein junger Geschäftsmann, der in München wohnte.

2 Er arbeitete oft zu Hause, und sein Arbeitszimmer war oben im ersten Stock.

3 Eines Winterabends arbeitete er an seinem Schreibtsich in seinem Arbeitszimmer, als das Telefon klingelte.

4 Es war seine Frau, und sie wollte, daß er sie vom Haus einer Freundin abholte.

5 Er ging, um das Auto zu holen, aber er vergaß die Lampe auf seinem Schreibtisch auszumachen.

6 Während er weg war, sprang seine Katze Mitzi auf den Schreibtisch und stieß die Lampe um.

7 Nach einigen Minuten begannen die Papiere auf dem Tisch zu brennen.

8 Bald stand der Tisch in Flammen, und Rauch begann aus dem Fenster seines Zimmers zu dringen.

9 Glücklicherweise sah ein Nachbar den Rauch und rief schnell die Feuerwehran.

10 Kurz darauf kam der Feuerwehrwagen an, und die Feuerwehrleute hatten den Brand bald unter Kontrolle.

A fire

1 Herr Krause was a young businessman who lived in Munich.

2 He often worked at home and his study was upstairs on the first floor.

3 One winter evening he was working at his desk in his study when the phone rang.

4 It was his wife and she wanted him to fetch her from a friend's house.

5 He went to fetch the car but he forgot to turn off the lamp on his desk.

6 While he was gone, his cat, Mitzi, jumped on to his desk and knocked over the lamp.

7 After a few minutes the papers on the desk began to burn.

8 Soon the desk was alight and smoke began to pour from the window of his room.

9 Fortunately a neighbour saw the smoke and quickly phoned the fire brigade.

10 Shortly afterwards the fire engine arrived and the firemen soon had the fire under control.

11 Es gelang einem der
Feuerwehrleute, die Katze
zu retten.

11 One of the firemen
managed to rescue the cat.

12 Als Herr Krause und seine
Frau nach Hause kamen,
waren sie entsetzt über
das, was geschehen war.

12 When Herr Krause and
his wife returned home,
they were horrified about
what had happened.

A Comprehension

1 Zu welcher Jahreszeit fand diese Episode statt?

2 Was sollte Herr Krause nach dem Telefongespräch mit seiner
Frau machen?

3 Unter welchen Umständen wäre der Brand nicht geschehen?

4 Wann rief der Nachbar die Feuerwehr an?

5 Wer rettete die Katze?

6 Warum waren Herr und Frau Krause entsetzt, als sie nach Hause
kamen?

B Translate into German

1 Herr Krause was a businessman. 2 Last Tuesday evening he
had just sat down at his desk when the phone rang. 3 His wife
asked him to fetch her. 4 She was at a friend's house.
5 Unfortunately he didn't turn off the lamp. 6 After the cat had
jumped on to the desk and knocked over the lamp, the papers
began to burn. 7 The neighbour phoned the fire brigade as soon
as he saw the smoke. 8 The fire was soon under control. 9 Herr
Krause saw one of the firemen with the cat. 10 Herr Krause
should have turned the lamp off.

C Translate into English

1 Letzten Dienstagabend mußte Herr Krause besonders fleißig
arbeiten, denn am anderen Morgen sollte er geschäftlich nach
Hamburg fliegen. 2 Er arbeitete schon seit zweieinhalb Stunden,
als seine Frau anrief. 3 Sie sagte, sie sei bei ihrer Freundin, und
sie wollte wissen, ob er sie abholen könne. 4 ,,Ja, ich komme
gleich," sagte er. 5 Er ärgerte sich jedoch etwas, weil er gerade
dabei war, einen wichtigen Brief zu schreiben. 3 Da er immer
noch an den Brief dachte, verließ er sein Arbeitszimmer ohne die
Lampe auszumachen. 7 ,,Schnell, schau mal hin, Ilse!" sagte der
Nachbar zu seiner Frau. ,,Brennt es bei Krauses?" 8 ,,Du hast
recht. Ruf schnell die Feuerwehr an!"

16 Von der Flut eingeholt

Cut off by the tide

1 Karl und Uwe waren Brüder und wohnten in Travemünde, einem angenehmen Badeort an der Ostsee.

1 Karl and Uwe were brothers and lived in Travemünde, a pleasant resort on the Baltic.

2 Eines Tages schwänzten sie die Schule und verbrachten den Tag am Strand, statt in die Schule zu gehen.

2 One day they played truant and spent the day on the beach instead of going to school.

3 Sie verließen das Haus zur gewohnten Zeit, damit ihre Eltern nicht argwöhnisch werden würden.

3 They left the house at the usual time so that their parents wouldn't be suspicious.

4 Sie nahmen den Bus, und zwanzig Minuten später erreichten sie den Strand.

4 They caught the bus and twenty minutes later they reached the beach.

5 Es war ein heißer Tag, und sie beschlossen, gleich ins Wasser zu gehen.

5 It was a hot day and they decided to go into the water straight away.

6 Danach sonnten sie sich bevor sie picknickten.

6 Afterwards they sunbathed before they picknicked.

7 Nach dem Imbiß beschlossen sie, auf einige Felsen zu klettern.

7 After their snack they decided to climb some rocks.

8 Es machte Spaß, aber leider bemerkten sie nicht, daß die Flut schnell hereinkam.

8 It was fun but unfortunately they didn't notice that the tide was coming in quickly.

9 Zu ihrem großen Entsetzen wurde ihnen klar, daß sie durch die Flut vom Land abge-schnitten worden waren.

9 To their great horror, they realized that they had been cut off by the tide.

10 Sie schrien um Hilfe und winkten mit ihren Hemden.

10 They shouted for help and waved their shirts.

11 Ein junges Ehepaar hörte sie und verständigte sofort die Küstenwacht.

11 A young couple heard them and informed the coastguard station straight away.

| 12 Als der Hubschrauber kam, wurde ein Seil herabgelassen, und sie wurden gerettet. | 12 When the helicopter came, a rope was lowered and they were rescued. |

A Comprehension

1 Was für ein Badeort ist Travemünde?

2 Was hätten Karl und Uwe machen sollen, anstatt den Tag am Strand zu verbringen?

3 Unter welchen Umständen wären ihre Eltern argwöhnisch geworden?

4 Wo standen die beiden Jungen, als sie um Hilfe schrien?

5 Was mußten die Hubschrauber piloten machen, bevor die Jungen in Sicherheit gebracht werden konnten?

B Translate into German

1 Last Wednesday Karl and Uwe played truant from school. 2 It was a marvellous day and they decided to go to the beach.
3 Their parents weren't at all suspicious as the boys left the house at the usual time. 4 It was much nicer on the beach then at school. 5 Karl swam in the warm sea while Uwe sunbathed next to some rocks. 6 Then Karl suggested that they should climb the rocks. 7 They hadn't noticed that the tide had come in quickly.
8 At first they didn't know what to do. 9 After the young couple had heard their shouts, they informed the coastguard station.
10 The boys were relieved when they saw the helicopter that was to rescue them.

C Translate into English

1 ,,Ich habe gar keine Lust, heute in die Schule zu gehen," sagte Karl. 2 ,,Ich auch nicht," erwiderte Uwe. ,,Wie wär's, wenn wir die Schule schwänzten?" 3 ,,Beeilt euch, Jungen, sonst verpaßt ihr den Schulbus!" rief die Mutter. 4 Es war das erste Mal, daß die beiden Brüder ihre Eltern auf diese Weise betrogen hatten. 5 ,,Es ist jetzt halb elf," sagte Karl. ,,Wäre ich in der Schule gewesen, so hätte ich Geschichte." ,,Und ich Erdkunde," fügte sein jüngerer Bruder hinzu. 6 Plötzlich erblickte Uwe zwei Menschen in der Ferne. 7 ,,Schau mal hin!" rief er. ,,Zieh dir schnell das Hemd aus und winke damit! Vielleicht sehen sie uns." 8 Obwohl die Jungen Angst hatten vor dem, was die Eltern sagen würden, gefiel ihnen der Flug im Hubschrauber sehr.

17 In der Jugendherberge

1 Letztes Wochenende
gingen Georg und sein
Freund Peter im Harz
wandern.

2 Sie wollten zur Jugend-
herberge in Goslar
wandern.

3 Kurz nach dem
Frühstück machten sie
sich auf den Weg.

4 Sie trugen feste Schuhe
und hatten je einen
Rucksack auf dem
Rücken.

5 Sie hatten beschlossen,
Schlafsäcke in der
Jugendherberge zu leihen.

6 Sie hatten Essen, eine
Landkarte und Anoraks,
falls es regnen sollte.

7 Nachdem sie drei Stunden
lang gewandert waren,
beschlossen sie, im Wald
eine Pause zu machen und
da zu essen.

8 Nach dem Picknick
machten sie sich wieder
auf den Weg und
erreichten die Jugend-
herberge am späten
Nachmittag.

9 Der Herbergsvater war
sehr freundlich und zeigte
ihnen ihre Betten im
Schlafsaal im ersten Stock.

10 Sie beschlossen, sich die
Stadt anzusehen, bevor sie
in der Jugendherberge das
Abendessen einnehmen
wollten.

11 Nach dem Abendessen
spielten sie Tischtennis im
Spielraum.

Youth hostelling

1 Last weekend Georg and
his friend Peter went
hiking in the Harz
mountains.

2 They wanted to hike to
the youth hostel in Goslar.

3 They set off shortly after
breakfast.

4 They wore stout shoes and
each had a rucksack on his
back.

5 They had decided to hire
sleeping bags in the youth
hostel.

6 They had food, a map and
anoraks with them in case
it rained.

7 After they had hiked for
three hours, they decided
to stop for lunch in the
forest.

8 After their picnic, they set
off again and reached the
youth hostel late in the
afternoon.

9 The warden was very
friendly and showed them
their beds in the dormi-
tory on the first floor.

10 They decided to have a
look round the town
before having supper in
the youth hostel.

11 After supper they played
table tennis in the games
room.

12 Am folgenden Morgen halfen sie der Herbergsmutter beim Putzen und Aufräumen des Tagesraumes.	12 The following morning, they helped the warden's wife to clean and tidy the common room.

A Comprehension

1 Wo hatten die Jungen ihr Essen und ihre Anoraks?

2 Was würden die Jungen mit den Anoraks machen, falls es regnen sollte?

3 Wohin führte der Herbergsvater die Jungen führen, um ihnen ihre Betten zu zeigen?

4 Was machten die Jungen, kurz bevor sie das Abendessen in der Jugendherberge einnehmen wollten?

5 Wobei halfen die Jungen der Herbergsmutter am folgenden Tag?

B Translate into German

1 Last weekend Georg hiked to Goslar with his friend Peter.

2 They put on their stoutest shoes and set off with their rucksacks on their backs. 3 They didn't have sleeping bags with them as they wanted to hire them in the youth hostel. 4 If it had rained, they would have put on their anoraks. 5 After three hours they sat down on the grass to eat. 6 They had written to the warden in advance to reserve two beds. 7 After the warden had shown them their dormitory, they looked round the town. 8 After supper they went into the games room to play table tennis. 9 The other young people in the youth hostel were very friendly. 10 While Peter helped the warden's wife to clean the games room, George helped the warden to tidy up the common room.

C Translate into English

1 ,,Machen wir jetzt Pause?" fragte George atemlos. ,,Nein, noch nicht. Mir wär's lieber, wenn wir noch ein paar Kilometer zurücklegten." 2 ,,Ist es nicht herrlich hier oben auf dem Hügel? Schau dir mal die Landschaft an!" sagte Peter. 3 ,,Ich kann nicht weiter," sagte Georg. ,,Ich muß mich einen Augenblick ausruhen." 4 ,,Ich glaube, wir haben uns verirrt," sagte Peter. ,,Wir hätten uns die Landkarte früher ansehen sollen!" 5 Sie bogen nach links ein und gingen bergauf durch einen dichten Wald. 6 Die beiden Jungen zogen es vor, ihr Abendessen in der Jugendherberge einzunehmen, statt in eine Imbißstube zu gehen. 7 Sie schliefen gleich ein, da sie so müde waren. 8 Wäre das Wetter schlecht gewesen, dann wären sie wohl mit dem Zug nach Hause gefahren.

18 Auf dem Campingplatz

1 Vorige Woche kaufte Herr Ahrens ein Zelt.

2 Niemand in der Familie hatte vorher gezeltet, und sie beschlossen, es am folgenden Wochenende auszuprobieren.

3 Am Freitagabend machten sie sich auf den Weg und fuhren zu einem Campingplatz, der leider nicht sehr modern war.

4 Sie meldeten sich bei dem Bauern an, und er zeigte ihnen, wo sie ihr Zelt aufbauen konnten.

5 Der Himmel war bewölkt, als die Kinder ihrem Vater halfen, das Zelt aufzubauen.

6 Nachdem sie Abendbrot gegessen hatten, legten sie sich in ihre Schlafsäcke.

7 Kurz darauf begann es heftig zu regnen.

8 Zu ihrem großen Erstaunen tropfte der Regen durch das Zelt, da es nicht wasserdicht war.

9 Sie brachten ihre Sachen so schnell wie möglich ins Auto und liefen dann zum Bauernhof.

10 Der Bauer war sehr freundlich und schlug vor, daß sie in seiner Scheune übernachten sollten.

11 Als Herr Ahrens das Zelt ins Geschäft zurückbrachte, beschwerte er sich bei dem Verkäufer.

On the campsite

1 Last week Herr Ahrens bought a tent.

2 No one in the family had camped before and they decided to try it out the following weekend.

3 On the Friday evening they set off and drove to a campsite that unfortunately wasn't very modern.

4 They reported to the farmer and he showed them where they could pitch their tent.

5 The sky was overcast when the children helped their father to put up the tent.

6 After they had eaten their supper, they slipped into their sleeping bags.

7 Shortly afterwards it began to rain heavily.

8 To their great surprise the rain dripped through the tent as it wasn't waterproof.

9 They put their things into the car as quickly as possible and then ran to the farmhouse.

10 The farmer was very friendly and suggested that they should spend the night in his barn.

11 When Herr Ahrens took the tent back to the shop, he complained to the salesman.

A Comprehension

1 Was wollte die Familie am folgenden Wochenende mit dem neuen Zelt machen?
2 Wer zeigte ihnen, wo sie das Zelt aufbauen konnten?
3 Was machten sie, bevor sie sich in ihre Schlafsäcke legten?
4 Was fühlten sie durch das Zelt tropfen, als sie in ihren Schlafsäcken lagen?
5 Wann liefen sie zum Bauernhof?
6 Warum brachte Herr Ahrens das Zelt ins Geschäft zurück?

B Translate into German

1 Last Monday Herr Ahrens returned home with a new tent.
2 As his family had never been camping before, they wanted to try out the new tent as soon as possible. 3 Last Friday evening they reached the campsite one and a half hours after they had set off. 4 Unfortunately it was not a modern campsite. 5 After they had put up the tent, they ate their supper in the tent as the sky was overcast. 6 They had just slipped into their sleeping bags when it began to rain. 7 Suddenly they felt the rain dripping through the tent. 8 As they were getting very wet, they decided to run to the farmhouse after they had put their things into the car. 9 The friendly farmer showed them his barn where they could spend the night. 10 The following Monday Herr Ahrens was very angry when he went into the shop to complain to the salesman.

C Translate into English

1 ,,Kommt mit, Kinder, ich habe etwas Interessantes für euch im Kofferraum," sagte Herr Ahrens, als er nach Hause kam.
2 Die beiden Kinder konnten sich gar nicht vorstellen, was ihr Vater am Vormittag gekauft hatte. 3 Sobald die Kinder das Zelt sahen, wollten sie es gleich im Garten aufbauen. 4 Das durften sie jedoch erst nach dem Abendessen machen. 5 Nachdem die Kinder schlafengegangen waren, sahen sich die Eltern die Landkarte an und beschlossen, am Wochenende zu einem Campingplatz im Schwarzwald zu fahren, wo sie das Zelt richtig ausprobieren konnten. 6 Herr Ahrens bestand darauf, daß das Zelt wasserdicht sein müßte, da es neu war, aber trotzdem tropfte der Regen durch. 7 ,,Wir können unmöglich im Zelt bleiben," sagte Frau Ahrens. ,,Vielleicht kann der Bauer uns im Bauernhaus unterbringen." 8 ,,Sie hätten mir das Zelt nicht verkaufen dürfen. Es ist gar nicht wasserdicht!" schimpfte Herr Ahrens.

19 Ein Unfall mit dem Fahrrad

A cycling accident

1 Letzten Montagmorgen radelte Heike wie gewöhnlich die Straße entlang.

1 Last Monday morning Heike was cycling along the road to school as usual.

2 Ein Mann hatte eben ein blaues Auto neben einem kleinen Supermarkt kurz vor ihr geparkt.

2 A man had just parked a blue car next to a small supermarket a short distance in front of her.

3 Gerade als Heike an dem Auto vorbeifahren wollte, machte der Fahrer die Autotür auf.

3 Just as Heike was about to cycle past the car, the driver opened the car door.

4 Leider fuhr sie gegen die Tür und fiel zu Boden.

4 Unfortunately she drove into the door and fell to the ground.

5 Der Fahrer sprang aus dem Auto, um zu sehen, was geschehen war.

5 The driver leaped out of the car to see what had happened.

6 Zu seinem großen Entsetzen stellte er fest, daß das Mädchen das Bewußtsein verloren hatte.

6 To his great horror he realized that the girl was unconscious.

7 Zum Glück hatte eine Frau den Unfall gesehen und hatte sofort das Krankenhaus angerufen.

7 Fortunately a woman had seen the accident and had phoned the hospital immediately.

8 Kurz darauf kam der Krankenwagen an und fuhr Heike zum Krankenhaus, wo der Arzt feststellte, daß sie sich das linke Bein gebrochen hatte.

8 The ambulance arrived shortly afterwards and drove Heike to the hospital where the doctor diagnosed that she had broken her left leg.

9 Sobald sie das Krankenhaus erreicht hatte, kam Heike wieder zu Bewußtsein.

9 As soon as she reached the hospital, Heike regained consciousness.

10 Ihre Eltern besuchten sie im Krankenhaus und brachten ihr Weintrauben.

10 Her parents visited her in hospital and brought her some grapes.

A Comprehension

1 Von wem wurde die Autotür aufgemacht?
2 Was geschah mit dem Mädchen, nachdem es gegen die Tür gefahren war?
3 Unter welchen Umständen wäre der Krankenwagen nicht so schnell gekommen?
4 Von wem wurde Heike im Krankenhaus besucht?
5 Unter welchen Umständen wäre der Unfall nicht passiert?

B Translate into German

1 The blue car drove along the road and then the driver parked it next to the small supermarket. 2 The little girl was about a hundred meters from the supermarket when the man parked his car. 3 Without seeing the girl, the driver opened the car door.
4 Just as the driver was about to get out of his car, Heike drove into the door. 5 After the driver had leaped out of the car, he saw Heike lying on the ground. 6 As soon as the woman had seen the accident she phoned the hospital. 7 To their great horror the little girl's parents learned that their daughter was injured. 8 Fortunately she had regained consciousness when they arrived at the hospital. 9 She ate the grapes that her parents had brought her. 10 She had to stay in hospital a few days.

C Translate into English

1 „Ach du meine Güte, was habe ich getan?" dachte der Autofahrer, als er aus dem Wagen sprang. 2 Er beugte sich über das verletzte Mädchen, um festzustellen, ob sie noch atmete.
3 Er fürchtete, daß er sie getötet hatte. 4 Bald hörte man das Heulen des Krankenwagens in der Ferne. 5 Hätte die Frau das Krankenhaus nicht sofort angerufen, dann hätte das Mädchen sterben können. 6 Es tat dem Mann so leid um das Mädchen, daß er es deswegen täglich im Krankenhaus besuchte. 7 Obwohl sie Kopfschmerzen hatte und sehr blaß aussah, freute sich Heike sehr, als sie ihre Eltern in die Station kommen sah.

20 Der Totoschein

1 Letzten Sonntag-
nachmittag saß die Familie
Merkl in ihrem Wohn-
zimmer und sah fern.

2 Herr Merkl freute sich auf
die Fußballergebnisse, da
er feststellen wollte, ob er
im Toto gewonnen hatte.

3 Je mehr Ergebnisse er
hörte, desto aufgeregter
wurde er.

4 Schließlich sprang er auf
und schrie, ,,Wir haben
gewonnen!''

5 Sein Sohn, Achim, der
ihm gegenüber in einem
Sessel saß, errötete und
schwieg zunächst.

6 Dann stotterte er, ,,Nein,
Vati, wir haben nicht
gewonnen.''

7 Am vorigen Dienstag hatte
sein Vater ihm den Schein
gegeben, damit er ihn
einwerfen konnte.

8 Er hatte das Haus
rechtzeitig verlassen und
hatte den Schein auf dem
Wege zur Bushaltestelle
einwerfen wollen.

9 Leider hatte es zu regnen
begonnen, nachdem er ein
paar hundert Meter
gegangen war, und er
hatte beschlossen, nach
Hause zurückzukehren.

10 Er hatte seinen
Regenmantel geholt und
hatte den Schein in die
Tasche gesteckt.

The pools coupon

1 Last Sunday afternoon the
Merkl family was sitting in
their lounge watching
television.

2 Herr Merkl was looking
forward to the football
results as he wanted to see
if he had won the pools.

3 The more results he
heard, the more excited he
became.

4 Finally he jumped up and
shouted, 'We've won!'

5 His son, Achim, who was
sitting in an armchair
opposite, blushed and at
first said nothing.

6 Then he stuttered, 'No,
Dad, we haven't won.'

7 The previous Tuesday his
father had given him the
coupon to post.

8 He had left the house in
good time and had wanted
to post the coupon on his
way to the bus stop.

9 Unfortunately it had
begun to rain after he had
walked a few hundred
metres and he had decided
to return home.

10 He had fetched his
raincoat and had put the
coupon in his pocket.

11 Nachdem er das Haus zum zweiten Mal verlassen hatte, hatte er es eilig gehabt, und er hatte laufen müssen, um den Bus zu erreichen.	11 After he had left the house for the second time, he had been in a hurry and had had to run to catch the bus.
12 Er hatte völlig vergessen, den Schein einzuwefen!	12 He had completely forgotten to post the coupon!

A Comprehension

1 Was glaubte Herr Merkl zuerst, als er die Fußballergebnisse gehört hatte?
2 Woher wissen Sie das?
3 Was hätte Achim am vorigen Dienstag machen sollen?
4 Warum war Achim nach Hause gegangen, als es begonnen hatte, zu regnen?
5 Unter welchen Umständen hätte Herr Merkl im Toto gewonnen?

B Translate into German

1 Herr Merkl went into the lounge to watch television. 2 He wanted to listen to the football results. 3 He hoped that he had won the pools. 4 He became more and more excited. 5 Achim who was sitting opposite his father suddenly blushed. 6 He had remembered that he had forgotten to post the coupon. 7 He had returned home because of the rain. 8 After he had put on his raincoat, he put the coupon in his pocket. 9 If he hadn't run to the bus stop he would have missed the bus. 10 He shouldn't have forgotten to post the coupon!

C Translate into English

1 Herr Merkl, der ruhig in seinem Sessel saß und seine Pfeife stopfte, wandte sich seinem Sohn zu und sagte, „Achim, stell den Fernseher etwas lauter, bitte!" 2 Die Familie hatte sich an Sonntagnachmittage gewöhnt. 3 Jede Woche war es das Gleiche. Herr Merkl mußte unbedingt vor dem Apparat sitzen und die Fußballergebnisse hören. 4 Er träumte immer von dem Tag, an dem er im Toto gewinnen würde. 5 Er wußte genau, was er machen würde, wenn er reich wäre. 6 Er würde eine Kreuzfahrt um die Welt machen und exotische Länder besuchen, die bisher für ihn bloß Namen im Atlas gewesen waren. 7 Je aufgeregter sein Vater wurde, desto verlegener wurde Achim. 8 Nächste Woche würde sein Vater einen neuen Schein ausfüllen und sein Glück wieder versuchen müssen!

3 Getting ready for the examination: the written tests

In this chapter, the skills that are tested most frequently by the various examining boards are discussed. They include translation from German, translation into German, comprehension (reading and listening), essay writing, letter writing and dictation.

You should find out which syllabus you will be taking and for which board. Check carefully:

which type of questions you will be expected to answer;
how much time is allowed for each question;
how many marks each question carries.

Once you have this information you will be able to concentrate on the skills you will need for your particular examination. As these skills often overlap, however, you should try to spend some time on all the sections in this chapter if possible.

Have a look at some old question papers before you take the examination. Read the instructions carefully and familiarize yourself with the layout of the papers.

* Learn to time yourself.
* Read all the questions carefully.
* Answer all aspects of each question.
* Complete all questions to the specified length and with the specified detail.
* Leave enough time for a rough copy if necessary.
* Leave enough time to check your work carefully.

Translation from German

General advice

1 Read the passage through carefully two or three times.
2 There will usually be some words and phrases you don't know. Don't panic, you will often be able to make an intelligent guess.
3 Never leave gaps. You don't get marks for blank spaces!
4 You should practise working on timed passages as much as possible in class and at home. There should be time for you to make a rough copy first.
5 Remember that your final translation should read like a piece of natural English. If it doesn't (and you must be self-critical here), there is room for improvement.
6 Marks are often thrown away by missing out odd words, phrases or even whole lines. You should check your translation word for word, line by line against the original German version. Occasionally your translation will warrant you leaving out or even adding a word but there must be a good reason for this.
7 Each passage is usually divided up by the examiner into about five equal 'mark-carrying' areas; so even if you find one or two parts of the passage too difficult for you to translate well, don't worry, you can still score marks for the other sections. Don't waste too much time on these difficult parts; concentrate on getting a really good translation for those sections you can do. Even if you don't know vocabulary, try to get the syntax (i.e. the sentence construction) correct and guess all unknown words and phrases.
8 You must be decisive in your final choice of words. Don't leave alternatives. The examiner may mark both of your choices wrong even if one is technically correct. Very occasionally, however, you may wish to justify your particular choice of word with a footnote.

More points to watch

1 Always try to analyse each sentence clause by clause. First find the main clause(s).
   (a) Find the subject (nominative). It is singular or plural?
   (b) Find the verb. What tense is it?
   Watch the perfect and pluperfect tenses in particular.
   Always read to the end of the clause or sentence to see if there is an infinitive or past participle there. Mind you find the best English version for each tense (see 'Use of tenses', p. 38).
   (c) Is there a direct object (accusative)?
   (d) Is there an indirect object (dative)?

2 Is there a (are there) subordinate clauses(s)? If so, analyse each one as above.
3 Watch constructions with *seit*:
Er wohnt hier seit zwei Jahren. (*He has been living* here for two years.)
Er arbeitete seit fünf Jahren in der Fabrik. (*He had been working* in the factory for five years.)
4 Check all genders carefully. It is very easy to mistranslate plurals:
Er öffnete die Fenster. He opened the windows (*das* Fenster (-)).
5 Remember that the present participle is used far more in English than it is in German (see p. 49). Your English version will often sound more natural if you use present participles.
6 Translate as literally as possible if the English still makes sense. e.g. *nach einem Augenblick* should be translated by *after a moment* and not *a moment later*. Similarly, *Er kam im Dorf an* should be translated by *He arrived at the village* and not *He reached the village.*
7 You must, however, translate idiomatically where necessary. Some typical mistakes caused by not heeding this advice are:

die Frau des Mannes	the man's wife (*not* the wife of the man)
Er hatte Durst.	He was thirsty (*not* he had thirst).
nach dem Frühstück	after breakfast (*not* after the breakfast)
Er wartete auf seinen Freund.	He waited for his friend (*not* . . . on his friend).

8 Be careful with reflexive verbs. You rarely need to translate the reflexive word:

Er setzte sich.	He sat down.
Er wusch sich die Hände.	He washed his hands.

9 You should only translate *man* as *one* in English if there is no better alternative. *You, people* or the passive are usually preferable.

Man geht die Straße entlang.	You go along the street.
Man sagt, daß . . .	People say that . . .
Hier spricht man deutsch.	German is spoken here.

10 A wide vocabulary is the key to success in this section of the exam. Collect new words and expressions in a special notebook amd then learn them. Have a special section for the 'little' words (e.g. *vielleicht*, *etwa*, *sogar*). It is a good idea to write some of them down in sentences in context as their usage is sometimes wide and different.

Sample passage

A chance meeting in a bar

Eine Woche später, an einem Samstagabend, begegnete ich Mittermann und seiner jungen Frau in einem Lokal, wo ich manchmal am Wochenende zu essen pflegte. Sie saßen an der Theke auf hohen Barstühlen und hatten beide offenbar schon zuviel zu trinken gehabt. Mittermann schaute sich gerade um, als ich eintrat, und erblickte mich.

„Welch eine Überraschung!" rief er lauter als nötig war, glitt dabei vom Stuhl herab und reichte mir die Hand. „Darf ich dir Laura vorstellen?"

Diese hatte mich im Spiegel hinter der Bar gemustert, jetzt drehte sie sich ganz um, und ich konnte sehen, daß Wendler keineswegs übertrieben hatte: sie war wirklich hübsch, mit glattem, schwarzen Haar über die Ohren zurückgekämmt, braunen Augen, die für das schmale Gesicht fast zu groß waren und einem vollen weichen Mund. (WEL)

Commentary

First sentence This consists of two clauses: the main clause *Eine Woche . . . Lokal* and a subordinate clause introduced by *wo*.

(a) *Main clause*

Find the subject: *ich*.

Find the verb: *begegnen* (to meet by chance/bump into).

Identify the tense and person: 1st person singular, imperfect. (Translate: bumped into/met by chance.)

Is there a direct object? Yes there is, but as *begegnen* is always followed by the dative, what is technically the direct object will here be in the dative case, i.e. *Mittermann und seiner jungen Frau*. Are there any indirect objects? No.

Look for prepositional phrases and think what case follows the preposition and why:

an einem Samstagabend – on a Saturday evening (*an* + dat. with an expression of time).

in einem Lokal in a restaurant (*in* here + dat. as there is no movement).

eine Woche später is in the accusative case as it is an expression of definite time.

(b) *Subordinate clause*

wo is here used as a subordinating conjunction and we would expect to find the verb at the end of the clause.

Find the subject: *ich*.

Find the verb(s): *zu essen pflegte* (*pflegen* means *to be accustomed to* (used to) and is followed by *zu* + *infinitive*). *Manchmal*, (sometimes)/ *am Wochenende* (at the weekend).

> A week later, on a Saturday evening, I bumped into Mittermann and his young wife in a restaurant where I sometimes used to eat at the weekend.

Second sentence This consists of two main clauses linked by the coordinating conjunction *und*.

(a) *First main clause*

Sie (subject): They/*saßen* (verb – 3rd person pl. imperfect) – the continuous form 'were sitting' is better here./Where were they sitting? – *an der Theke* (*an* here + dat. – no movement) – *die Theke* (-n) bar (counter)/*auf hohen Barstühlen* (*auf* here + dat. – no movement). Note extra *n* in dat. pl.!/*hoch* (high) drops the *c* when it has an ending. *Barstuhl* is literally (bar chair). This, however, is not good English. Translate: 'bar stool'. (Note: *der Hocker* (-): stool.)

(b) *Second main clause*

The subject is still 'they' from the first clause.

Verb: *hatten . . . gehabt* (3rd person pl. pluperfect) – had had. What had they had? – *zuviel zu trinken* (too much to drink). Watch the three 'little' words: *beide* (both), *offenbar* (obviously) and *schon* (already).

> They were sitting on high bar stools at the bar and both had obviously already had too much to drink.

Third sentence Two main clauses: *Mittermann schaute . . . um*/*und erblickte mich* + the subordinate clause *als ich eintrat*.

(a) *First main clause*

Mittermann (subject)/*schaute sich um* (verb – 3rd person sg. imperfect + *gerade* (just) – continuous form better: 'was just looking round').

(b) *Subordinate clause*
   als (subordinating conjunction – verb at end of clause = 'when'/
   ich (subject)/*eintrat* (verb – 1st person sg. imperfect – *eintreten*
   (to come in/enter).

(c) *Second main clause*
   und (coordinating conjunction – no change in word order)/
   erblickte (verb – 3rd person sg. imperfect *erblicken*: to catch
   sight of)/*mich* (direct object): me.

> Mittermann was just looking round when I entered and caught
> sight of me.

Fourth sentence Three main pieces of information, the last two
linked by *und*. *Er* (subject)/*rief* (verb – 3rd person sg. imperfect –
called (cried). What did he call? – ,,*Welch eine Überraschung!*"
(direct object, acc. – 'What a surprise!'/How did he call it? – *lauter*
(comparative of *laut*) *als nötig war* (louder than was necessary)/*glitt*
herab (second verb from *herabgleiten* – to slide down) – could be
translated by the English present participle 'sliding down'/*vom* (=
von dem) – *von* (preposition + dat.)/*Stuhl* (the definite article *dem*
could be translated by 'his'. 'from his stool' (not chair)/*dabei* is
always difficult to translate. It means 'thereby' but may be translated
more freely: 'as he did so', etc./*reichte* (third verb (passed)) – offered
me his hand. The phrase *jemandem die Hand reichen* really means
'to shake someone's hand'.

Fifth sentence A question, therefore the verb is inverted.
Ich (subject)/*darf vorstellen* (verbs – 1st person sg. present of modal
verb *dürfen* + *infinitive* – *vorstellen* = to introduce/. *Laura* (direct
object acc./*dir* (indirect object, dat.) – to you.

> 'What a surprise!' he called louder than was necessary, sliding
> down from his stool as he did so, and shook hands with me. 'May
> I introduce Laura to you?'

Sixth sentence (as far as the colon) Three main pieces of information
+ a subordinate clause introduced by *daß*.

(a) *Diese* (subject) (*dieser* = the latter/*jener* = the former). *Diese* is
   the feminine form and refers to *Laura*/*hatte gemustert* (verb 3rd
   person sg. pluperfect). The continuous form sounds better: 'had
   been sizing up'/*mich* (direct object, acc.)/Where had she been
   sizing me up? – *im Spiegel* (dative here with *in* – no movement
   – in the mirror)/Where was the mirror? – *hinter der Bar* (dative

here with *hinter* – no movement)/*drehte sich um* (second verb –
'turned round'/Watch the two little words: *jetzt* (now) and *ganz*
(completely)/*ich* (subject)/*konnte sehen* (3rd person sg. imperfect
of modal verb *können* + *infinitive*).

(b) *Subordinate clause*

   daß (subordinating conjunction). Look for the verb at the end
   of the clause/*Wendler* (subject)/*hatte übertrieben* (verb – 3rd person sg. pluperfect of *übertreiben* – to exaggerate/*keineswegs* =
   'not at all'.

Sixth sentence (from the colon) One main clause with a relative
clause (introduced by *die*) in the middle.

(a) *Main clause*

   Sie (subject)/*war* (verb)/*wirklich* (really)/*hübsch* (pretty)/*mit* (preposition + dative)/*glatt* = smooth/*Haare* is not plural (the final
   e is an old dative ending sometimes found on masculine and
   neuter nouns)/*zurückgekämmt* is the past participle of *zurück-
   kämmen* (to comb back) used here as an adjective (combed-
   back) *über* (preposition used here with the accusative: over
   (across))/*die Ohren* – Remember to translate the definite article
   by the possessive adjective – her ears/*braunen Augen* (dative –
   still dependent on the *mit*/*und einem vollen weichen Mund* (dative
   – also dependent on the *mit*)/*voll* (full)/*weich* (soft).

(b) *Relative clause*

   die (subject) – Nominative plural of the relative pronoun: that
   (which). Look at the end of the clause for the verb/*waren* (verb)/
   fast (almost) *zu groß*/*für* (preposition + acc.)/*schmal* (narrow)/
   Remember to translate *das Gesicht* by 'her face'.

> She (the latter) had been sizing me up in the mirror behind the
> bar, now she turned round completely and I could see that
> Wendler hadn't exaggerated at all: she was really pretty, with
> smooth black hair combed back across (over) her ears, brown
> eyes that were almost too large for her narrow face, and a full,
> soft mouth.

Here are two passages for you to practise. You will find suggested
translations at the back of the book.

The master shot

**Ein paar Freunde gingen zusammen zum Jagen. Einer von ihnen
war Maler, ein anderer Lehrer, der dritte war Kaufmann. Sie gingen**

über Wiesen und Felder. Plötzlich blieb der Lehrer vor einer Scheune stehen und deutete auf das große Tor. Auf das Tor hatte jemand einen Hirsch gezeichnet, mit Kreide, und jemand hatte anscheinend auf den Hirsch geschossen. Er hatte genau ins Auge getroffen.

,,Ein toller Schuß'' sagte der Kaufmann. ,,Genau ins Auge.''

,,Wer kann das gewesen sein? Wer schießt so gut?'' überlegte der Lehrer.

,,Der Schuß ist von mir,'' sagte der Maler.

Die anderen lachten, weil sie wußten, daß er wirklich nicht so gut schoß.

,,Ihr braucht es ja nicht zu glauben,'' sagte er, ,,aber der Schuß ist wirklich von mir.''

Dann erklärte er ihnen, wie er es gemacht hatte: ,,Zuerst habe ich geschossen, dann habe ich den Hirsch gezeichnet.''

(SUJB)

Modern art

Das erste, was Herr Hallfeld sah, als er von der Arbeit nach Hause kam, war das Bild, denn es hing an der Wand gegenüber der Haustür. Dort, wo sonst immer die viel kleinere Alpenlandschaft gehangen hatte. Während er das Bild noch anstarrte, kam seine Frau lächelnd auf ihn zu.

,,Schön, nicht wahr? Gefällt es dir?''

An seinem Gesicht konnte man deutlich sehen, daß er es alles andere als schön fand.

,,Woher hast du es?'' fragte er.

,,Ein Geschenk von meinem Chef. Zu unserer Silberhochzeit. Wirklich nett von ihm, findest du nicht?''

,,Nur möchte ich gerne wissen, was das Bild eigentlich darstellt. Soll es ein Sonnenuntergang sein, oder eine Tomate auf Spinat . . .''

,,Es heißt, Nymphe im Bad,'' unterbrach ihn seine Frau.

,,Was du nicht sagst!'' rief er erstaunt. ,,Siehst du etwa die Nymphe?''

,,Leider auch nicht, aber mein Chef sagt, der Maler sei ein junger Künstler von großem Talent.''

,,Hm – weniger Talent und mehr Nymphe wäre mir lieber! Muß es denn gerade hier hängen?''

,,Ja, mein Lieber, wenigstens bis morgen früh.''

,,Wieso?'' Herr Hallfeld sah sie fragend an.

,,Ich habe den Chef und seine Frau zum Abendessen eingeladen. Da sollen sie sehen, wie schön ihr Geschenk zu unserer Wohnung paßt. Komm, zieh dich schenll um! Ich koche inzwischen Kaffee.`` Und da sie wußte, daß er ihren Chef nicht leiden konnte, eilte sie in die Küche, ehe er auf ihre Nachricht reagieren konnte. Er warf noch einen ärgerlichen Blick auf das Bild und schimpfte, ging aber dann nach oben ins Schlafzimmer.

(AEB)

Translation into German (prose composition)

The passages set for this test often look deceptively simple. Although the vocabulary is usually fair, you will have to have a good knowledge of German grammar if you are to translate into German with confidence. Work your way through Chapter 1 ('Revising grammar') and do the individual exercises on specific points as well as the translation sentences in Chapter 2 ('Revising vocabulary and useful constructions') before you tackle the passages for exam practice. These should be done as closely as possible under examination conditions. Check the time you should allow with your teacher. It is usually about forty minutes.

The following procedure may be helpful:

1 Read the passage right through making a mental note of any points that strike you immediately.
2 Leave enough time to make a rough version before attempting your fair copy.
3 Analyse each sentence separately.
   Which is the main clause (i.e. which is the clause that conveys the main piece of information)? There could, of course, be two or more main clauses. If there are, they will usually be linked by a coordinating conjunction (und; aber; oder; denn; sondern;).
4 Which is (are) the subordinate clause(s) (i.e. the clauses that provide additional information, telling you when, how, where, why, etc.)?
   They will be introduced by a subordinating conjunction:
   when? als; wenn; bevor; ehe; nachdem; während; bis; sobald; seitdem;
   how? wie
   where? wo; wohin; woher
   why? weil; damit; da
   Other common subordinating conjunctions you will need to know are:

obwohl; obgleich; daß; ob

Note also relative clauses introduced by relative pronouns (der; die; das, etc.) and *um . . . zu* clauses.

5 Analyse each clause carefully:
   (a) What is the subject (nominative)?
   (b) What is the verb? What tense is it? Is it singular or plural?
   (c) Is there a direct object – or several direct objects (accusative)? Are they nouns or pronouns?
   (d) Is there an indirect object (dative)? Are they nouns or pronouns?

6 Are there any instances of possession (e.g. 'of the man' (genitive): the man's car (das Auto des Mannes).

7 Identify the prepositions. What case should you use with each one?

8 Think about the word order:
   (a) Is the word order normal (i.e. subject/verb/rest of sentence)?
   (b) Do you have to invert the verb in the main clause? (Yes, if the sentence begins with an adverb (dann, sofort, lachend, etc.), a phrase (eine Woche später, nach dem Frühstück, etc.) or a subordinate clause (nachdem sie gefrühstückt hatten, etc.).
   (c) Does the verb go to the end of the clause? (It does if the clause is introduced by a subordinating conjunction or a relative pronoun.)
   (d) Check word order with direct and indirect objects in the same clause (see pp. 10, 126).
   (e) Remember: TIME/MANNER/PLACE!
   (f) Check the positions of infinitives and past participles. (They are usually at the end of a main clause.)
   Check that you have *not* used *zu* + *infinitive* with modal verbs (the infinitive is enough):
   Er wollte spielen. He wanted to play.
   Check the position of *zu* in the *um . . . zu* construction (see pp. 120, 127).

9 Are there any adjectives? (If they come before the noun, they must have endings.)
   (a) Which group of adjectival endings do you use? Check the case.
   (b) Are there any comparatives or superlatives? (see p. 28)?

10 If a verb is in the perfect or pluperfect tense, check whether it is conjugated with *haben* or *sein*.

11 Watch for particular verbs:
  (a) Are there any that are followed by the dative (helfen, folgen, etc.) (see p. 47)?
  (b) Are there verbs with separable prefixes? Watch the position of the prefix (see p. 42).
  (c) Is the verb used with a preposition (e.g. *warten auf* + *acc.* to wait for/*sich erinnern an* + *acc.* to remember/*riechen nach* + *dat.* to smell of)? Check the case carefully.
12 When you have sorted these problems out, you should concern yourself with the vocabulary:
  (a) What is the gender/plural of the individual nouns?
  (b) Check the principal parts of all the verbs in the passage.
  (c) Watch your spelling (including capital letters for nouns).

Before you make your fair copy, check your rough version five times (once each for each of the following):

W
O   (word order)
T   (tense)
A   (agreement: subject with verb/correct case after prepositions/ adjectival endings)
G   (gender)
S   (spelling)

Remember the word: W O T A G S !

Examination practice
Translate the following passages into German:

1 At half past seven that evening a young man got off the bus, went into the hotel, sat down at a table and asked for a cup of coffee. He was waiting for his girl-friend, who was to meet him there at eight o'clock.

After he had sat there for nearly an hour, the young man began to get anxious. He stood up, walked to the door and looked out into the street. Then he went back to his place.

At last he went over to a telephone-box (*Telefonzelle f.*) situated in the entrance hall, in order to ring up the girl's family. But at that moment the girl hurried into the hotel; she looked hot and excited. The young man ran to meet her.

'Why are you so late, my dear?' he cried. 'What has happened to you?'

'First I missed the bus, then I wanted to take a taxi, but they were all occupied. Finally I did get one, but there was so much traffic in the streets that we really couldn't go fast enough.'

'Anyway, here you are at last. Sorry you had such a bad journey,' said the young man. 'Shall we go into the restaurant? You must be terribly hungry and thirsty! Let's order something to eat and then we will decide what to do afterwards.' (SUJB)

2. Miss Renate Keller, who had just begun to type another letter, looked up as the door of the office slowly opened, and a tall young man entered.

'Excuse me,' he said politely, 'I would like to speak to Mr Hetherington, please.'

Renate shook her head. 'I'm afraid that is quite impossible,' she said. 'The boss went out a while ago to visit some customers and will not be back until about half past four.'

'Then I'll stay here until he comes if you don't mind. I've got nothing special to do this afternoon.' Without waiting for a reply the stranger sat down on a chair by the window and took a newspaper out of the pocket of his raincoat. Renate noticed, however, that he was not really reading but seemed to be watching the people on the street below. (WEL)

3 Mr Tate, accompanied by his wife, visited their doctor yesterday evening, before it got too dark; for he was an elderly man and there was a lot of traffic. The doctor was not surprised to see them, because the husband had for a long time been working too hard. He had not been taking enough walks, and had been eating too much of the good food his wife had cooked him. So it was easy for him to talk to both of them and give them good advice, and he also did not forget a bottle of medicine which Mr Tate was to take three times a day. 'Shut your eyes and imagine you are drinking wine,' he said with a smile, as they went out. 'The taste is nearly the same, and you will soon feel better, I hope. If you are still unwell after a week, come back again or telephone me before half past nine in the morning.' (OX)

Comprehension (including Use of German)

Most of the examinations set by the various boards include some sort of comprehension test. This may be a reading or listening comprehension. It could be a multiple choice test and the questions and answers could be in either English or German.

Reading and listening comprehension with questions and answers in German.

In this test you not only have to understand a passage (or passages) of German but you also have to show the examiner that you can use German accurately. In fact some boards will assess your answers purely on the accuracy of your language. You don't therefore, score any marks for conveying the correct information if your German is wrong!

General advice

1 Read carefully any instructions about answering in complete sentences. Some boards accept short answers. Check with your teacher before the exam about this and remember that the longer your answer is, the more likely you are to make mistakes.

2 Use pronouns wherever possible to shorten your answers.

3 Don't mis-spell any words given in the passages(s) or questions that you may reproduce in your answers. You can't afford to throw marks away!

4 Use the questions and text intelligently. You can, for example, frequently find out the genders of nouns by looking through the text and questions carefully.

5 Base your answers on the information in the passage. They should, however, be full in so far as they contain all the relevant information. (There could be several reasons, for example, why something was done. You would lose marks by only stating one reason.)

6 Remember that questions are usually designed so that you can't just copy answers from the text. Some form of manipulation has to take place. The basic vocabulary, however, will often be found in the passage albeit in a different form.

An analysis of question forms

If you are to do well in this section of the exam, you will need not only to understand the text or dialogue but also the questions that are asked and the implications that lie behind them.

Most texts will be about people (or things) who are doing something to other people or things at a particular time, in a particular way at a particular place and for a particular reason. This could be set out as follows:

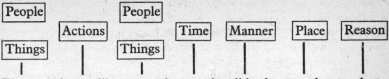

The examiner will want to know who did what to whom, when, how, where and why. To help him find out the answers, he will need a basic set of questions. Each question tests a specific linguistc point:

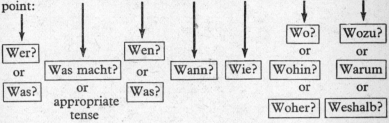

I People and things

You should revise the words for *who* and *what?* (interrogative pronouns) and the word for *which* (interrogative adjective) (see pp. 15, 16).

Learn to recognize the case used in the question. You will find that usually you need the same case in your answer.

Questions using the interrogative pronouns
(a) *People*

1 *Wer?* (nominative) Wer holte das Brot? or plural	*Answer with nominative* (subjects): Der Junge/die Frau/das Mädchen Sein Sohn/ihre Mutter/ihr Kind Die beiden Jungen Der Junge und sein Bruder Das kleine Mädchen und ihre Schwester, etc.
2 *Wen?* (accusative) Wen besuchten sie?	*Answer with accusative* (direct objects): (Sie besuchten) ihren Freund/den Mann/die Frau/ ihre Schwester/das Kind, etc.
3 *Wessen?* (genitive) Wessen Auto war es?	*Answer with genitive:* Es war das Auto des Mannes/der Frau/des Fräuleins. Es war das Auto seines Bruders/seiner Schwester/seiner Eltern (pl.)

Note:
no apostrophe: Es war Karls Auto
(Watch weak masculine nouns.
Es war Herr*n* Müllers Auto.

Remember to rephrase *the man's car* to *the car of the man*, etc.
Note: it is possible to answer this question with a possessive adjective, but this is less likely in a comprehension test: e.g. Es war sein/ihr Auto. (It was his/her car).

4 *Wem?* (dative)	*Answer with dative:*
(a) Wem gab er das Geschenk?	Er gab es seinem Vater/seiner Mutter/ dem Kind, etc.
	Note: watch weak masculine nouns:
	Er gab sie dem Junge*n*/dem Herr*n*/Herr*n* Müller
	Watch the dative plural. Don't forget to add an *n* where applicable:
	Er gab es seinen Brüder*n*/den Männer*n*
(b) Wem begegnete er auf der Hauptstraße?	Er begegnete seinem Freund. (NB *begegnen* + dat. (p. 47).

The interrogative pronouns above may also be used with prepositions. Repeat the preposition in your answer which should be in the same case as in the question:
Auf wen (acc.) wartete er? – (Er wartete) auf seinen Freund (acc.)
Mit wem (dat.) ging er ins Kino? (Er ging) mit seinem Freund (dat.)

(b) *Things*
More care is needed here as the nominative and accusative question forms are identical.

1 *Was?* (nominative) Was (subject) stand in der Garage?	*Answer with nominative:* Der Wagen/die Waschmaschine/das Fahrrad, etc. (stand dort)
2 *Was?* (accusative) Was (direct object) holte er aus der Garage?	*Answer with accusative:* (Er holte) seinen Wagen, das Fahrrad, etc.

Always look for the subject of the sentence first. Here *er* is the subject.

Note the special forms used with prepositions:

wo (*wor-* before a vowel)

You will of course need to know what case(s) follow the prepositions.

Womit (dat.) schrieb er den Brief? (Er schrieb ihn) mit einem Füller, mit einem Kuli, mit einem Bleistift (dat.) etc.

Worauf (acc.) wartete er? (Er wartete) auf einen (acc.) Bus, einen Zug, eine Straßenbahn, etc.

Questions using the interrogative adjectives

In a more complicated situation, the examiner may wish to know *which* person or *which* thing is involved.

You will find that the most frequent answers to a question with *welcher* will contain:

(a) *The definite article and an adjective* (Group 1, p. 23).

Note: the adjective could be in the positive, comparative or superlative form (p. 28).

Welcher Mann (nom.) las die Zeitung? – Der alte Mann (The old man)/Der ältere Mann (The older man)/Der älteste Mann (The oldest man) (las sie (read it)).

(b) *A possessive adjective (and an adjective)* (Group 2 p. 24);

Again the adjective could be in the positive, comparative or superlative form.

Welchen Sohn (acc.) schickte sie in die Stadt? (Sie schickte) ihren jungen Sohn (her young son)/ihren jüngeren Sohn (her younger son)/ihren jüngsten Sohn (her youngest son).

Welchem Bruder (dat.) half er? (Er half) seinem jungen Bruder/seinem jüngeren Bruder/seinem jüngsten Bruder. (*helfen* + dat.)

Note that in the examples above (a) and (b), the answers are again in the same case as the question.

(c) *A relative clause*

You must be very careful with answers involving a relative clause. Remember that although the noun in the answer will be in the same case as the one in the question, the relative pronoun functions independently and need not necessarily be in the same case.

Welcher Mann (nom.) telefonierte mit der Polizei? (Which man phoned the police?) Der Mann (nom.), der (nom., subject) die Leiche gefunden hatte. (The man who had found the corpse.)

Welchen Mann (acc., direct object) verhafteten die Polizisten? (Which man did the policemen arrest?) (Sie verhafteten) den Mann (acc.), der (nom., subject) die Leiche gefunden hatte. (They arrested) the man who had found the corpse.)

Welchem Mann (dat.) folgten die Polizisten? (Which man did the policemen follow?) (Sie folgten) dem Mann (dat.) den (acc., direct object) sie verhaften wollten. ((They followed) the man whom they wanted to arrest.)

Was für ein . . .? (What sort of a . . .?)
The examiner may want to know what sort of a person or thing is involved.

There are two main answers to the question: *Was für ein . . .?* Once again you should look carefully at the question and identify the case used. Your answer will be in the same case:

(a) *An answer containing a compound noun, the make or brand of a product or a particular type of thing or person* (bungalow, detached house/butcher, baker, etc.)

Was für ein Wagen (nom., subject) stand vor dem Haus? Ein Sportwagen (compound noun)/ein Ford (type of car) (stand da) (nom.).

Was für einen Wagen (acc., subject) fuhr er? – (Er fuhr) einen Sportwagen/einen Ford (acc., direct object).

Mit was für einem Wagen (dat.) fuhr er? (Er fuhr) mit einem Sportwagen/mit einem Ford (dat.)
In was für einem Haus (dat.) wohnte er? (Er wohnte) in einem Bungalow/in einem Einfamilienhaus (dat.).

(b) *An answer including the indefinite article and an adjective* (Group 2, p. 24)

Was für ein Mann (nom., complement) war der Einbrecher? – Er war ein alter Mann (nom., complement).

Was für einen Lehrer (acc. direct object) hatten sie? Sie hatten einen jungen Lehrer (acc.)

Neben was für einer Frau (dat.) saß er? – Er saß neben einer hübschen Frau (dat.).

II Actions

1 You should look carefully at each question and identify the tense. In a lot of questions you will be asked what the various people in the passages were/will be/had been doing, etc.

Most narrative passages will be written in the imperfect tense. The following observations may also be useful for the oral examination.

You should revise the formation of each tense as you work through this section.

There are two verbs that are used for *to do*. They are: *tun* (tut, tat, getan) and *machen* (wk.).

They are often linked to an expression of time or place and the preposition *mit*.

Was machte er *an seinem Geburtstag (am Samstag)?* Er hatte eine Party.
Was machten sie *im Garten?* Sie spielten Fußball.
Was machten die Löwen *mit dem Fleisch?* (What did the lions do with the meat?) Sie fraßen es. (They ate it.)

In most situations you should use the same tense that was used in the question.

Examples
Present

Was macht (tut) er?	Er raucht/er spielt/er sitzt, etc.
Was machen (tun) sie?	Sie rauchen/sie spielen/sie sitzen, etc.

Future

Was wird er machen (tun)?	Er wird seinen Freund besuchen.
Was werden sie machen (tun)?	Sie werden in die Stadt gehen.

Note: a lot of questions are asked about what people are/were about to do. Again you should reflect the form of the question in your answer.

Was will er eben (gerade) machen (tun)?	Er will eben (gerade) in den Bus einsteigen. (He is about to get on to the bus.)
Was wollten sie eben (gerade) machen (tun)?	Sie wollten eben das Haus verlassen. (They were about to leave the house.)

Imperfect

Was machte (tat) er?   Er mähte den Rasen.
                                     Er ging in die Stadt.
Was machten (taten) sie?   Sie badeten.
                                     Sie tranken den Wein.

Perfect

You must be very careful indeed with this tense. Although the
question will always be formed with *haben* and the past participle,
the answer will sometimes be with *haben + the past participle* and
sometimes with *sein + the past participle*. (Remember that the past
participle of strong verbs ends in *en* (getrunk*en*) and that of weak
verbts in *t* (gespiel*t*.)

Was hat er gemacht (getan)?   Er hat den Wein getrunken.
                                     Er ist in die Stadt gegangen.
Was haben sie gemacht (getan)? Sie haben gebadet.
                                     Sie sind ins Wasser gesprungen.

Pluperfect

As with the perfect tense be careful with the auxiliaries (*hatte* and
war) and the past participles:

Was hatte er gemacht (getan)?   Er hatte seinen Freund
                                     besucht.
                                     Er war in die Stadt gegangen.

Watch particularly for the pluperfect (and word order) in questions
beginning with *Wann*?

Wann ging er in die Stadt?   Nachdem er gefrühstückt
                                     hatte.
Wann badeten sie?   Nachdem sie ins Wasser
                                     gesprungen *waren*.

Conditional

This is an unlikely tense to be tested on the comprehension paper.
You should watch for it, however, in the oral or in a letter.

Was würden Sie machen (tun),   Ich würde nach Amerika
wenn Sie reich wären?   fahren.
   (What would you do if you   Ich würde einen Rolls-Royce
   were rich?)   kaufen.
Note also:
Was würdest Du gern machen   Ich würde gern viele Ausflüge
(tun)?   machen.
   (What would you like to do?)   (I'd like to go on a lot of
                                        trips.)

Future perfect

This tense is very rarely used in exam questions. You should, however, be able to recognize it. Again watch the auxiliary verb in your answer.

Was wird er gemacht (getan) haben?
(What will he have done?)

Er wird Fußball gespielt *haben*.
(He will have played football.)
Er wird in die Stadt gefahren *sein*.
(He will have gone into the town.)

Conditional perfect

You should be prepared to use this tense. The longer form is less frequent. Use the forms with the *past participle* + *hätte* or *wäre*:

Was hätte er gemacht (getan), wenn er das früher gewußt hätte (hätte er das früher gewußt)?
(What would he have done if he had known that earlier?)

Er hätte das Auto nicht genommen.
(He wouldn't have taken the car.)
Er wäre länger geblieben.
(He would have stayed longer.)

Watch for questions beginning with: *Unter welchen Umständen . . .?* (Under/in what circumstances . . .?)

Unter welchen Umständen hätte er das nicht gemacht (getan)?
(In what circumstances would he not have done that?)

Wenn er mehr Geld gehabt hätte.
(If he had had more money).
Wenn er in die Stadt gegangen wäre.
(If he had gone into the town.)

2 Many questions will contain a *modal verb*. The tense will usually be the imperfect. Usually you can answer with the same *modal verb* + *infinitive*:

Was sollte Hans machen?
(What was Hans to do?)
Was sollte später geschehen?
(What was to happen later?)

Er sollte seinem Vater helfen.
(He was to help his father.)
Sie sollten baden gehen.
(They were to go for a swim.)

Was wollte die Frau kaufen?
(What did the woman want
to buy?)

Sie wollte ein neues Kleid
kaufen.
(She wanted to buy a new
dress.)

Was mußte er machen?
(What did he have to do?)

Er mußte seine Hausaufgaben
machen.
(He had to do his
homework).

Was durfte sie nicht machen?
(What wasn't she allowed to
do?)

Sie durfte nicht allein
hingehen.
(She wasn't allowed to go
there by herself.)

Occasionally you will have to change the modal verb:

Konnte er den Fernseher allein
tragen?
(Could he carry the television
set by himself?)

Nein, sein Freund mußte ihm
helfen.
(No, his friend had to help
him.)

3 Other possible questions with verbs:

Was beschloß er zu machen (tun)? (What did he decide to do?) Er
beschloß, zu Hause zu bleiben. (He decided to stay at home.)
Nennen Sie einige Tiere, die im Zoo zu sehen sind! (Name some
animals that are to be found at the zoo). Löwen, Tiger, Affen,
Elefanten.
Wie sah der Mann aus? (What did the man look like?) Er *war*
groß und dick.
Was wollte er wissen, als er das Abteil betrat? (What did he want
to know when he entered the compartment?) Er wollte wissen,
ob der Platz besetzt sei (war). (He wanted to know if the seat was
taken.)
Wo fand die Geschichte statt? (Where did the story take place?) Sie
fand in Hamburg statt. (It took place in Hamburg.)
Was verstehen Sie unter 'Besteck'? (What do you understand by
'cutlery'?) Ich verstehe Messer, Gabeln und Löffel darunter. (I
understand knives, forks and spoons.)

III Time

1 Many questions to do with time are specific and are used with prepositions. Remember to repeat the preposition in your answer.

Um wieviel Uhr . . .?	*Um* sechs Uhr, etc.
An welchem Tag . . .?	*Am* Dienstag, etc.
An was für einem Tag . . .?	*An* einem regnerischen (rainy)/nebligen (foggy)/ sonnigen (sunny) Tag, etc.
In welchem Monat . . .?	*Im* August, etc.
Zu welcher Jahreszeit . . .?	Im Sommer, etc. (Note different preposition!)
Zu welcher Zeit des Jahres . . .? (At what time of the year . . .?)	*Zu* Weihnachten (At Christmas)/zu Ostern (At Easter)
In welchem Jahr . . .?	*Im* Jahre 1967
Bis wann spielten sie?	*Bis* acht Uhr (Until eight o'clock)
Von wann bis wann?	*Von* acht Uhr bis neun Uhr
Seit wann war er verheiratet? (How long had he been married?)	*Seit* einem Jahr (For a year)
Vor wievielen Tagen war er da gewesen? (How many days ago had he been there?)	*Vor* vier Tagen (Four days ago)

Other questions might be more general but could still have a preposition in the answer:

Wann fuhren sie aufs Land?	Letzten Sonntag
(When did they go into the country?)	An einem heißen Sommertag Vor zwei Wochen Während der Sommerferien

2 Revise the subordinating conjunctions that introduce temporal (time) clauses: *wenn* (when, whenever); *als* (when); *während* (while); *bevor/ehe* (before); *nachdem* (after); *seitdem* (since); *bis* (until).

Wann holte er sein Auto?	Nachdem (als) er gefrühstückt hatte. Bevor er frühstückte.
Wann hörte sie Radio?	Während sie einen Pullover strickte. (While she was knitting a sweater.)
Bis wann spielten sie?	Bis sie zu müde wurden, weiterzuspielen. (Until they became too tired to go on playing.)
Wie lange spielten sie?	(Sie spielten) eine Viertelstunde/eine halbe Stunde/eine Stunde/ anderthalb Stunden (lang)
Wie oft gehst du ins Kino?	Einmal (once)/zweimal/ dreimal in der Woche (im Monat/im Jahr)

IV Manner

The most frequent question is: *Wie?* (how/in what way?) There are, however, other questions that may be used: *auf welche Weise/Art?* (in what way?); *womit* (with what?/how?); *mit wem?* (with whom?)

    (a) *Wie?/Auf welche Weise?*
        Typical answers to this question would be adverbs or adverbial phrases:

Wie ging er die Straße entlang?	schnell (quickly); langsam (slowly); so schnell wie möglich (as quickly as possible); schneller als gewöhnlich (quicker than usual)

    (b) *Wie?/Womit?/Mit wem?*

Wie (Womit) fuhr er in die Stadt?	mit dem Wagen/mit dem Zug/ mit der Straßenbahn, etc.
Wie sprach er?	mit lauter Stimme (in a quiet voice); leise (quietly), etc.
Mit wem ging er wandern?	mit seinem Freund; mit seiner Freundin; mit seinen Freunden, etc.

Note also the question:

Woher wissen Sie, daß sie unglücklich war? (How do you know that she was unhappy?)	Ich weiß das, weil sie weinte. (I know that because she was crying.)

V Place

There are three main question words that indicate position. They are: *Wo?* – where? (no movement); *Wohin* – where to? (movement into, on to, under, towards, etc.); *Woher?* – from where? (usually only movement from and out of).

Sometimes the last two questions are split into two parts, the *hin* and *her* usually being at the end of the sentence:

Wo gehen Sie heute abend *hin*? Where are you going (to) tonight?
Wo kommst du denn *her*? Where do you come from then?

Be certain, therefore, that you understand the full implications of the question before answering.

1 You must be very careful indeed with questions to do with place.

  (a) You will often have to change a phrase from the dative to the accusative and vice versa if the phrase contains a preposition that may be used with either of those cases. Consider the following two examples that could be sentences in your exam passage:

    (i) Sie bereitete das Mittagessen in *der* Küche (dative). (She was preparing the lunch in the kitchen.)
The question you have to answer could be:
Wohin ging sie, un das Mittagessen zu bereiten? (Where did she go, to prepare the lunch?)
Wohin + *gehen* suggest movement and therefore in + *accusative* must be used in your answer:
(Sie ging) in *die* Küche.

    (ii) Sie ging in *die* Küche (accusative) um das Mittagessen zu bereiten. (She went into the kitchen to prepare the lunch.)
The question you have to answer here could be:
Wo bereitete sie das Mittagessen? (Where did she prepare the lunch)?
Wo + *bereiten* does NOT suggest movement and therefore *in* + *dative* must be used in your answer: (Sie bereitete es) in *der* Küche.

(b) Revise the nine prepositions that may be used with both the accusative and dative cases:

---

in, an; auf; vor; hinter; neben; zwischen; unter; über

Compare and contrast (and if possible learn by heart) the following pairs of sentences used with these positions. Note that the verb in the right-hand column suggests movement.

Wo? (no movement – dative)	Wohin? (movement – accusative)
Er war *im* Garten.	Er ging *in den* Garten.
Das Bild hing *an der* Wand.	Er hängte das Bild *an die* Wand.
Er saß *auf dem* Stuhl	Er setzte sich *auf den* Stuhl.
Das Auto war *vor/hinter dem* Haus.	Er fuhr das Auto *vor/hinter das* Haus.
Sie saß *neben ihrem* Freund.	Sie setzte sich *neben ihren* Freund.
Sie saß *zwischen ihrem* Vater und *ihrer* Mutter.	Sie setzte sich *zwischen ihren* Vater und *ihre* Mutter.
Die Katze war *unter dem* Tisch.	Die Katze ging *unter den* Tisch.
Der Hubschrauber schwebte *über dem* Dorf. (The helicopter hovered over the village.)	Der Hubschrauber flog *über das* Dorf. (The helicopter flew over the village.)

(c) Note that *zu* and *nach* also often suggest movement towards and that phrases containing them could be in answers to the question *Wohin?* They are, however, both always followed by the *dative* case. (*nach* is used with names of places and most countries, *zu* is used with buildings, shopkeepers, etc.)
As above compare the following pairs of sentences:

Wo? (no movement – dative)	Wohin? (movement – dative!)
Er wohnte *in* München/*in* Deutschland, etc.	Er fuhr *nach* München/*nach* Deutschland, etc.
(Er wohnte *in der* Schweiz)	(Er fuhr *in die* Schweiz)
Er wartet *am* Bahnhof/*am Flughafen*/*in meinem* Haus	Er fuhr *zum* Bahnhof/*zum* Flughafen/*zu meinem* Haus
Er kaufte sie *beim* Bäcker (at the baker's)	Er ging *zum* Bäcker (to the baker's)
Er wohnte *zu* Hause (at home)	Er fuhr *nach* Hause (home)

Note:

Er ging *zum* Kino. He went to the cinema (but he didn't go in).
Er ging *ins* Kino. He went to the cinema (to the pictures, i.e. he went in and saw the film).

2 Revise the other prepositions that indicate position.
  (a) *Dative only*
      bei (at someone's house/shop)
      Er wohnte bei seiner Schwester (with his sister/at his sister's house)
      gegenüber (opposite)
      Note: *gegenüber* usually comes after a pronoun and before a noun.
      Er wohnte gegenüber der Schule. (He lived opposite the school.)
      Er saß ihm gegenüber. (He was sitting opposite him).
  (b) *Accusative only*
      entlang (along) (er ging die Straße entlang) *bis* (up to) is often used with another preposition and then means *right up to* (bis ans Fenster) *um* (around): Er trug einen Schal um den Hals; *gegen* (towards, against): Er pochte gegen die Tür. (He hammered against the door.)
  (c) *Genitive only*
      innerhalb (within); *außerhalb* (outside); *diesseits* (on this side); *jenseits* (on that side); *links* (to the left of); *rechts* (to the right of); *links* (to the left of); *nördlich/südlich/westlich/östlich* (to the north/south/west/east of)

3 Look carefully at questions using *welch*. Identify the case used in the question. Usually you will use the same case in your answer even if there is a different case in the passage:
  Er ging *ins* Wohnzimmer (acc.), um fernzusehen. (He went into the lounge to watch television);
  In *welchem* Zimmer (dat.) sah er fern? – er sah *im* Wohnzimmer (dat.) fern.

4 You may have to use an adjective in your answer:
  In was für einem Haus wohnte er? Er wohnte in einem *großen* (Haus).

VI Reason

1 There are three main question words that mean *why?* They are: *Warum?/Wozu?* (for what purpose) and *Weshalb?* They are often interchangeable.

2 You may find it helpful to think of three standard answers to the question *why* in English. German has three corresponding structures when some sort of *purpose* is required in the answer.

Why did he go into the garden?	*Warum ging er in den Garten?*
(a) (in order) to cut the grass.	(a) um das Gras zu mähen (*um . . . zu* + *infinitive*)
(b) because he wanted (had to) cut the grass.	(b) weil er das Gras mähen wollte (mußte) (imperfect tense of *wollen* (*müssen*) + *infinitive*)
(c) so that he could cut the grass.	(c) damit er das Gras mähen konnte (imperfect tense of *können* + *infinitive*.

If you are answering questions on a single picture, you may be required to answer in the present tense:
Weil er das Gras mähen *will* (*muß*)
Damit er das Gras mähen *kann*.
Note: The *um . . . zu* construction does not vary.

3 *Weil* is, however, used in a variety of other ways in answering questions beginning with *warum*. Again most structures correspond to their English equivalents:

(a) *With the ordinary tense of the verb* (usually the imperfect in a comprehension passage)

Warum aß sie das Brot?	Weil sie hungrig *war*.
Warum konnte sie nicht zahlen? (Why couldn't she pay?)	Weil sie kein Geld *hatte* (Because she *had*n't any money.)

(b) *With a pluperfect*

Warum weinte das Mädchen? (Why was the girl crying?)	(Sie weinte), weil sie ihre Puppe *verloren hatte*. (because she *had lost* her doll.)
Warum war er glücklich?	Weil er im Toto *gewonnen hatte*. (Because he *had won* the pools.)
Warum kam sie spät zur Arbeit?	Weil sie spät *aufgestanden war*. (Because she *had got up* late.)

Examination practice
Suggested answers will be found at the back of the book.

News of examination success

Am Freitagmorgen ging Frau Lampe wie gewöhnlich in den Supermarkt. Als sie zurückkam, half ihr ihre Tochter, die Lebensmittel auszupacken.

„Mutti", sagte diese plötzlich, „Post ist da. Ich habe das Staatsexamen bestanden." Frau Lampe ließ die Tüte mit den Tomaten fallen. Sie rollten in alle Richtungen, während Mutter und Tochter sich freudig umarmten.

Endlich dachten sie wieder an die Tomaten, die überall herumlagen. Einige waren unter dem Küchenschrank, und die beiden mußten sogar den Gasherd von der Wand wegziehen, weil einige dahinter waren.

1 Woher war die Mutter gekommen?
2 Warum war sie dorthin gegangen?
3 In welchem Zimmer spielte sich diese Szene ab?
4 Was machten Mutter und Tochter zuerst, d.h. bevor die Tochter vom Staatsexamen sprach?
5 Was hatte die Tochter eben erfahren?
6 Wie hatte sie es erfahren?
7 Was wollte die Mutter tun, als sie die Tomaten fallen ließ?
8 Wohin, zum Beispiel, rollten die Tomaten?

The watch thieves

„Sie kommen", flüsterte der Polizeikommissar. Endlich! Das hohe Gras, wo sie lagen, war unangenehm naß, und sie hatten mehr als eine Stunde gewartet.

Ein Auto kam den Weg entlang und hielt nicht weit von den Polizisten. Drei Männer stiegen aus und gingen zu Fuß weiter. Nach zehn Minuten erreichten sie eine Turmruine und verschwanden darin.

Drinnen war ein großer Raum. Einer der Männer nahm aus einem Loch in der Steinmauer einen Koffer, den er vor zwei Tagen dort versteckt hatte. Er machte den Koffer auf. Hunderte von Armbanduhren lagen im Schein seiner Taschenlampe da.

„Jetzt gehen wir feiern," sagte einer der Diebe.

„Im Gefängnis gibt's kein Feiern", sagte eine Stimme. Die Diebe drehten sich um, völlig perplex.

„Also, Sie kommen mit," sagte der Kommissar. „Den Koffer mit den Uhren nehme ich."

9 Wo lagen die Polizisten versteckt?
10 Was machten sie da?
11 Wohin gingen die Diebe?
12 Wozu waren sie hierher gekommen?
13 Wie hatten sie so viele Armbanduhren bekommen?
14 Warum waren die Diebe so erstaunt, als der Kommissar sprach?
15 Was geschah mit dem Koffer, als man die Ruine verließ?

(AEB)

Reading and listening comprehension with questions/answers in English

This is really a disguised translation test. Your answers will be a précis in English of the original passage. Be careful not to make your answers too long but be sure to include all the relevant points.

Reading and listening comprehension with multiple choice answers.

1 In these tests you will have to choose an answer from four or five possible options and you will have to make your choice on a specially prepared grid. You don't have to write any German or English. If possible try to see one of these grids before your exam and familiarize yourself with the layout.
2 To do well in this test you need a *wide vocabulary* and you need to *think logically*.
3 Never leave a blank and never mark in two answers.
4 Pace yourself to allow time for tackling the longer passages or dialogues that usually follow the shorter items that start the test.

Types of question

1 There is often an overlap with the role-playing test. Familiarize yourself with the situations given in this book and try to anticipate others. Many of the situations you might read or listen to could be to do with *where* people are, *who* they are and *what they are doing* – are they in a theatre, at a station, an airport, in a restaurant, etc.? Is it a producer talking to an actress, a butcher to a customer, a customs official talking to a motorist, etc.?

You could keep a separate section in your notebook where you can collect relevant vocabulary. Make a list of as many professions as possible and link them together where you can, e.g. der Regisseur (director), der Schauspieler/die Schauspielerin (actor/actress). Similarly – der Polizist (policeman), der Verbrecher (criminal), der Dieb (thief), Taschendieb (pickpocket).

Do the same for buildings, places, etc. and think of the verbs that could occur in these situations. If you don't understand the vocabulary on the question paper, you won't be able to answer the questions.

Examiners often use synonyms (words of similar meaning). You might hear the word *Polizist* on tape, for example, and find the word *Schutzmann* on your question paper. Both words mean *policeman* (cf. also – Fleischer/Metzger/Schlachter (butcher)). The same applies to adjectives – *glücklich, heiter, munter, froh* all have similar meanings.

2 You might have some visual questions. You could have:
   (a) A plan of a building and you might have to work out from the information you are given *where* in that building people are.
   (b) A series of menus. *Which one* does a person choose?
   (c) A series of pictures. *Which one* fits the description given? You need to be logical and to eliminate the irrelevant facts.

3 There are often questions to do with time and prices. Make certain that you can deal with numbers easily.
   (a) Trains, buses, planes leave and arrive at certain times. How long does the journey last? Alternatively you could be given the time of departure and told how long the journey lasts. You could be asked the time of arrival.
   (b) You might hear a short dialogue where somebody is buying two or three items in a shop. The prices will be given and you will be expected to know the total amount spent.

   There are many variations on these themes so don't be surprised by what you may find on your question paper.

4 Watch out for the tense used in the question. If you are asked what someone *is going to do*, don't choose an answer in the *past* tense!

   Multiple-choice tests are very relentless as you usually have twenty-five to thirty questions to answer. Above all keep calm and think clearly.

In order to practise samples of these tests, write to your examination board (see addresses, p. 7) or ask your teacher for past papers.

Essay writing

Most of the boards set an essay or essays of some sort. There may be a story based on a series of pictures, a story based on an outline or continuation of an outline, an essay based on a single title, a *Nacherzählung* (reproduction essay) or a letter.

The principles for all these types of essay are similar except for the letter, but remember the following points:

1 If it is an essay based on a series of pictures, make certain that you deal with *each* of the pictures as fully as possible.
2 If it is a story based on an outline, bring in all the points mentioned in the outline. (Make certain you don't mis-spell any of the words given to you!)
3 In a reproduction essay you normally hear a short story two or three times and then have to write down what happened in your own words with the help of a printed summary which is provided. The original story usually has about 250 words and your version will have to be written in about 150 words.

   This test is very demanding as it is partly a memory test. Try to remember the main points of the action and concentrate on getting these down as accurately as possible. Don't waste time (and space) adding your own inventions as you might in a picture essay. (Again don't mis-spell any words given in the printed summary!)

You might find it useful to familiarize yourself with the twenty stories in Chapter 2 ('Revising vocabulary and useful constructions'). These may be treated as model essays. Study the constructions used and try to produce similar ones in the essays you write yourself. Adjust the length to suit the requirements of the exam your particular board sets.

General advice
1 Read carefully all instructions about the number of words you have to use. Try to keep to this number. You will certainly lose marks if you write less and you could lose marks if you write more.
2 Some boards ask you to write your essay from a special viewpoint. (For example, you may have to be one of the characters in the story. If this is the case, you will have to be able to use the *ich* and *wir* forms of the verbs.)
3 Plan your essay before you start. It should have at least three paragraphs – a beginning, a middle and an end.

4 Remember that you are much more in control of what you write in this test than you are in a translation or comprehension. Only use words, phrases and constructions that you can deal with. If you find the construction of a sentence is becoming too complicated for you to handle, forget it and begin a simpler one. Above all aim for accuracy rather than complicated sentences if you think you can't manage them.

5 Try to think your essay out in German. Always start from a basic outline and then expand it into a rough copy.

6 Check your rough copy very carefully (see WOTAGS, (p. 104) before you copy out your neat version.

Additional advice

1 It is a good idea to start your essay with an expression of time (see p. 34).

2 If you do start with an expression of time, remember to invert the verb.

3 The main tense of your essay will be the IMPERFECT.

4 Always check for AGREEMENT between the subject and the verb (singular subject – singular verb/plural subject – plural verb).

5 Watch out for direct objects (accusative) and be very careful indeed with masculine nouns: Er fuhr seinen Wagen.

6 Always ask yourself what case follows a preposition (see p. 31). Watch out particularly for prepositions that are followed by either the accusative or the dative.

7 Have you got an indirect object in your sentence? Remember to put it in the dative case. Watch the word order (see p. 10).

8 You can impress the examiner by using adjectival endings correctly (see p. 23). If you don't know your endings, don't use adjectives before nouns!

9 *Word order*. Check for:
   (a) Inversion
   If you start your sentence with something other than the subject, you must invert the verb. This 'something' could be:
   A single word: zuerst/dort/dann/plötzlich.
   A phrase: nach dem Frühstück/am nächsten Morgen, etc.
   A subordinate clause (i.e. if your clause begins with a subordinating conjunction: als, nachdem, während, etc., (see p. 35). Remember to put the verb at the end of the subordinate clause before you invert the verb in the main clause! You will in fact have these two verbs next to each other (separated by a comma) in the middle of your sentence:

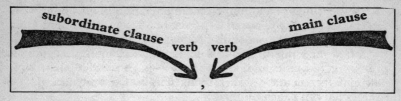

e.g. Nachdem er sein Fahrrad geholt *hatte*, *machte* er sich auf den Weg in die Stadt.

(b) Verb to the end
Have you put the verb at the end of
all your subordinate clauses? (see above)
all your relative clauses? (e.g. Der Junge, der auf dem Ufer *spielte*.)

(c) Remember that there is no change in word order when a clause is introduced by a coordinating conjunction (i.e. und/aber/oder/denn/sondern).

(d) Remember that expressions of time precede those of manner and those of manner precede those of place:
T – When? (Wann?)
M – How? (Wie/Womit? etc.)
P – Where? (Wo?); Where to? (Wohin?); Where from? (Woher?)

(e) Another reminder about the word order if you have a direct and indirect object in the same sentence.
Two nouns: Indirect object (dat.) precedes direct object (acc.)
  Er gab seinem Freund (indirect object) *einen Apfel* (direct object).   (He gave his friend an apple.)
Two pronouns: Direct object (acc.) precedes indirect object (dat.)
  Er gab ihn (direct object) *ihm* (indirect object). (He gave it to him.)
Noun + pronoun: Pronoun precedes noun (regardless of case)
  Er gab ihm den Apfel. (He gave him the apple.)
  Er gab ihn seinem Freund. (He gave it to his friend.)

10 Bring in as many *good points* as you can to earn your bonus ('grace') marks. Here are some suggestions:

- *beginnen* (i, a, o) + zu + infinitive (to begin):
  Sie begannen, Fußball zu spielen.

- *beschließen* (beschließt, beschloß, beschlossen) + zu + infinitive (to decide):
  Sie beschlossen, einen Spaziergang zu machen.
- *to have just* . . . (in essays usually the pluperfect + eben (gerade)):
  Er hatte eben (gerade) seine Hausaufgaben gemacht. (He had just done his homework.)
- *to be about to* . . . (in essays usually the imperfect of wollen + eben (gerade) + infinitive):
  Er wollte eben (gerade) ins Schwimmbecken springen. (He was about to jump into the swimming pool.)
- *to be on the point of* (im Begriff sein + zu + infinitive):
  Er war im Begriff, auszugehen. (He was on the point of going out.)
- *a direct object* (acc.) and *indirect object* (dat.):
  Sie gaben ihrem Sohn ein Fahrrad. (They gave their son a bike.)
- *inversion*:
  Eine Viertelstunde später *kamen* die ersten Gäste.
- *a relative clause*:
  Er telefonierte mit seinem Freund, der im nächsten Dorf wohnte. (He phoned his friend who lived in the next village.)
- *a subordinate clause* (verb inverted in a following main clause):
  Während sein Vater das Auto wusch, schälte seine Mutter Kartoffeln. (While his father was washing the car, his mother was peeling potatoes.)
- *modal verbs* + infinitive (usually the imperfect in essays):
  Sie wollte ins Kino gehen. (She wanted to go to the pictures.)
  Er mußte zu Hause bleiben. (He had to stay at home.)
  Sie konnte ihre Handtasche nicht finden. (She couldn't find her handbag.)
- *TMP* (expressions of time, manner and place in the same sentence):
  Gestern abend (time) ging sie mit einem Freund (manner) ins Kino (place). (Last night she went to the pictures with a friend.)
- *um* . . . *zu* + infinitive (in order to . . .); remember the four variations for this construction:
  Sie ging in ihr Schlafzimmer, um Platten zu hören.

Sie ging ins Badezimmer, um sich zu waschen.
Sie ging ins Wohnzimmer, um fernzusehen.
Sie ging ins Schlafzimmer, um sich anzuziehen.

Remember that you are in control of what you write in an essay. If you don't know a construction or word, don't attempt to use them!
Always check your work carefully. (WOTAGS!)

Your basic outline and how to improve it

1 In most essays your basic tense is the imperfect. Jot down the main story line in simple sentences:

Peter und sein Freund Karl wollten zu einem See fahren.
Sie trafen sich an der Straßenecke.
Die Fahrt zum See dauerte eine halbe Stunde.
Sie lehnten ihre Fahrräder an einen Baum.
Sie zogen sich aus.
Sie zogen ihre Badehosen an.
Sie liefen ins Wasser.
Sie badeten, etc.

2 Think about how you could vary the constructions:

(a) You could start with an expression of time and use *beschließen* + *infinitive*. Invert verb!
Letzten Sonntag beschlossen Peter und sein Freund Karl, zu einem See zu fahren.

(b) You could add an adjective and a relative clause.
Letzten Sonntag beschlossen Peter und sein Freund Karl, zu einem kleinen See zu fahren, der in der Nähe war.

(c) More inversion!
Nach dem Frühstück trafen sie sich an der Straßenecke.

(d) Use a subordinate clause. Change tense of verb to pluperfect:

Nachdem sie ihre Fahrräder an einen Baum gelehnt hatten, zogen sie sich aus.

(e) Add the word *dann* (inversion).
. . . und dann zogen sie ihre Badehosen an.

(f) You could add another subordinate clause + an *um . . . zu* clause.
Da es ein sehr heißer Tag war, liefen sie gleich (immediately) ins Wasser, um zu baden. (Change the imperfect to the infinitive.)

3 Final version:
Letzten Sonntag beschlossen Peter und sein Freund Karl, zu einem kleinen See zu fahren, der in der Nähe war. Nach dem Frühstück trafen sie sich an der Straßenecke. Die Fahrt zum See dauerte eine halbe Stunde. Nachdem sie ihre Fahrräder an einen Baum gelehnt hatten, zogen sie sich aus, und dann zogen sie ihre Badehosen an. Da es ein sehr heißer Tag war, liefen sie gleich ins Wasser, um zu baden.

Sample titles

1 You were out with friends in the countryside when a fog came down and you found yourself alone. Explain how you managed to find your way back to the youth hostel where you were staying. (100 words)   (LOND)

2 Sie sind mit dem Flugzeug nach Hannover gefahren, um dort Ihre Ferien bei einer deutschen Familie zu verbringen. Am Flughafen aber wartete niemand auf Sie. Erzählen Sie, was Sie dann getan haben. (about 150 words)   (SUJB)

3 Do not write out the following paragraph, but continue the story in German, using about 150 words.
    Als ich spät abends auf dem Weg nach Hause war, sah ich in einem Bauernhof Rauch und Flammen.   (OX)

4 Tell the story outlined below, keeping to three paragraphs of at least sixty words. You may use as you wish the suggestions given and may add any relevant detail.
    You have been asked by an uncle to help him in his shop during the holidays. Describe your experiences there.
    Lebensmittel- oder Schreibwarengeschäft? – in den Ferien – Taschengeld verdienen – bedienen – im Laden aufräumen – freundliche und schlechtgelaunte Kunden – was die Leute Ihnen erzählen – interessante aber ermüdende Arbeit. (180–200 words)
                                                                                        (WEL)

Series of pictures

There are sample answers to the following three essays based on a series of pictures. The instructions for each could be:
    Tell, using past tenses, the story of the events that have occurred in the following series of pictures.

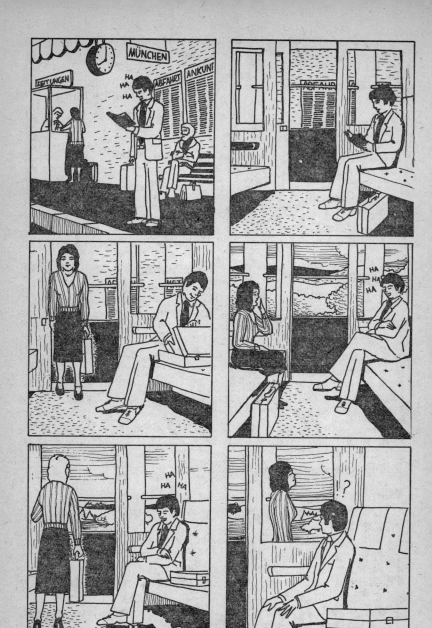

Letter writing

General advice

1 You should be prepared to write about the following subjects:
 (a) Yourself and your family.
 (b) Your house and garden.
 (c) Your town or village.
 (d) Your school (types of school, subjects, times, meals, exams, sixth form, university, etc.).
 (e) Hobbies (spare-time activities, part-time jobs, sport, playing instruments, music you like, etc.).
 (f) Meeting your pen friend (from the station/airport); visiting your pen friend.
 (g) Holidays – Christmas, New Year's Eve, Easter, Whitsun, summer holidays.
 (h) Thank-you letters for birthday/Christmas presents/a party/a holiday.
 (i) Complaining about a bad hotel.
 (j) Saying you are sorry you can't come to Germany; cancellation of a holiday because of illness.
 (k) Writing to someone who is ill/had an accident.
 (l) Formal letters: hotel/camp site/caravan site/youth hostel/au pair or holiday job.

2 A letter is a sort of one-sided conversation. You will often be expected to ask and answer questions as well as make factual statements.
　　You should familiarize yourself with the subject matter in the general conversation section (p. 142) and the section on role-playing (p. 159). You could find a lot of the material useful.

3 Some boards give you a theme for your letter, others print a letter to which you must reply.

4 If there is a letter for you to read, study it very closely.
 (a) Look carefully at the questions which are asked in different tenses.
 Was machst Du? (What do you do?) present
 Was wirst Du machen? (What will you do?) future
 Was hast Du gemacht? (What did you do?) perfect
 Was würdest Du gern machen? (What would you like to do?) conditional, etc.
 As you will be expected to use the same tenses in your answers, be sure that you can handle them.

(b) Make certain that you deal with each point or reply you are supposed to make in your letter. Tick them off (in pencil) on the question paper one by one.

5 Before you start your letter, think whether you are going to use the *du*, *ihr* or *Sie* form of the verb. (*Du* and *ihr* are used for friends and relatives, etc., while *Sie* is more formal.) Be sure that you use the corresponding form for *your* (dein, euer, Ihr).

6 All words for *you* and *your* are written with an initial capital in German letters:
*D*u/*D*ich/*D*ir/*D*ein, etc. (singular familiar)
*I*hr/*E*uch/*E*uch/*E*uer, etc. (plural familiar)
*S*ie/*S*ie/*I*hnen/*I*hr, etc. (singular and plural formal)

7 Germans don't usually put their full address at the top of the page. They put it on the back of the envelope.
Just put the town (or village) and the date at the top of your letter: Bristol, den 16. Juni

8 Follow the opening greeting with an exclamation mark, although increasingly a comma is being used: Lieber Klaus!

How to start your letter
Lieber Achim! (Dear Achim,)
Liebe Jutta! (Dear Jutta,)
Lieber Achim, liebe Jutta! (Dear Achim and Jutta,)
Sehr geehrter Herr! (Dear Sir,)
Sehr geehrte Herren! (Dear Sirs,)

How to close your letter
Jetzt muß ich Schluß machen. (Now I must close.)
Alles Gute. (All the best.)
Schreib (Schreibt/Schreiben Sie) bald wieder! (Write soon.)
Einen schönen Gruß an Deine (Eure/Ihre) Eltern. (Best wishes to your parents.)
Nochmals vielen Dank. (Once more many thanks.)
Ich wünsche Euch (Ihnen) allen frohe Weihnachten und ein glückliches Neues Jahr! (I wish you all a merry Christmas and a happy New Year.)
Auf ein baldiges Wiedersehen! (I hope we see each other again soon.)
Hochachtungsvoll! (Yours faithfully)

A few useful phrases

Entschuldige/Entschuldigt/Entschuldigen Sie bitte, daß ich so lange nicht geschrieben habe. (Please excuse me for not having written for such a long time.)

Vielen Dank für Deinen/Euren/Ihren netten Brief. (Many thanks for your nice letter.)

Hoffentlich geht es Dir/Euch/Ihnen gut. (I hope you are well.)

Hoffentlich hast Du/habt Ihr/haben Sie meinen letzten Brief bekommen. (I hope you have received my last letter.)

Zuerst ein paar Zeilen über + acc. . .(First a few lines about. . .)

Ich lege Dir/Euch/Ihnen ein paar Fotos/Ansichtskarten/ein kleines Geschenk/eine Kassette bei. (I am enclosing a few photos/postcards/a small present/a cassette for you.)

Sample titles

1 Write a letter to your German pen friend explaining why you will not be able to visit his (her) family in Germany. (100 words) (LOND)

2 Schreiben Sie einen Dankbrief an Ihre Großeltern, die Ihnen £10 zum Geburtstag eben geschenkt haben. Erzählen Sie ihnen, was Sie damit tun werden. (150–160 words)   (SUJB)

3 You have just returned very dissatisfied from a holiday which you have booked through a travel firm. Write a letter of complaint to the firm with details of what went wrong.   (WEL)

4 Sie haben an eine deutsche Jugendherberge geschrieben, die Sie schon früher einmal besucht haben, um zu fragen, ob man im August noch Platz frei hat. Sie haben jetzt den folgenden Brief bekommen. Schreiben Sie eine passende Antwort darauf! (100 words)

> Lieber Herr David!
>
> Ihren Brief vom 1.6.77 habe ich dankend erhalten. Ich glaube, Sie waren schon einmal bei uns? Ich freue mich auf ein Wiedersehen. Im August haben wir noch Platz; würden Sie mir bitte schreiben, wann Sie kommen wollen, und wie viele Sie sind. Wir haben jetzt eine neue Herberge. Im August aber haben wir auch die alte Herberge in der Burg offen; Sie können dort wohnen, wenn Sie wollen.
>
> Anfang September hat die Stadt eine „englische Woche" und möchte junge Besucher aus England einladen, kostenlos in der Herberge oder bei Familien zu wohnen. Ich lege eine Broschüre bei, falls Sie sich dafür interessieren.
>
> Noch eins möchte ich erwähnen, falls Sie mir helfen

können. Hier in der Herberge haben wir jede Woche einen Briefmarkenklub und wir möchten mit Briefmarkensammlern aus anderen Ländern Kontakt aufnehmen.

Mit freundlichen Grüßen,

Johann Kordaß

(AEB)

Dictation

In this test you have to write down as accurately as possible a passage of German that will be read to you three times – twice right through and once in sections. Don't worry if you find this exercise difficult. Most other candidates will feel the same way!

Suggested procedure

1 It is a good idea to write dictations on alternate lines as you will have more space to make alterations later. Try to practise this in advance.

2 Take a pencil and rubber into the exam with you as well as your pen.

3 You are not allowed to write anything down during the first reading. Usually you will be given a title and this should give you some idea as to what the passage will be about. Listen carefully and try to get the gist of the text. Try to sort out how many people are involved, who they are and what they are doing.

4 When the passage is read slowly in sections, write each phrase down as carefully and neatly as you can. You won't really have time to copy out your version again as you should use the five minutes at the end to check what you have written.

5 There will always be some words and phrases you have never heard before. Don't panic, you will have to guess how to spell them. Concentrate on getting the words you think you know right.

6 Try to make sense of what you are writing. It could help you with the spelling.

7 During the final reading use your pencil to mark those parts of your dictation that will need to be looked at and given thought to during the final five minutes.

8 Make certain that every word you have written is clear. It is better to cross a word out and rewrite it rather than leave it unclear.

9 Don't leave alternative spellings. You must be decisive! Examiners are not generous here and will tend to cross out both your versions even if one is correct.

10 Punctuation will be given to you in German. Familiarize yourself with the German punctuation given in this section.

Points to watch

1 *wurde/würde?*
   (a) Er wurde naß. (imperfect of *werden*) He got (became) wet.
   (b) Er wurde durch den Regen durchnäßt. (*wurde* + past participle = imperfect passive) He was soaked by the rain.
   (c) Er würde naß werden. (*würde* + infinitive = conditional) He would get wet (e.g. if he went outside).

2 *das/daß?*
   it is important to identify the part of speech.
   (a) Was ist *das*? (demonstrative pronoun) What's that?
   (b) *Das* ist mein Bruder. (demonstrative) That's my brother.
   (c) *Das* Haus ist groß. (definite article) The house is large.
   (d) Das Haus, *das* meinem Bruder gehört, ist neu. (relative pronoun) The house that belongs to my brother is new.
   (e) Er sah, *daß* das Haus groß war. (subordinating conjunction) He saw that the house was large.
   Note the position of the verb in the last two examples. The subordinating conjunction *daß* is frequently found in the combination: Er sah/erfuhr/fand/sah, daß. . . etc.

3 *Mann/man?*
   Think about the difference between the noun *der Mann* (man, husband) and the prounoun *man* (one, you, people, they).

4 Watch *Sie/sie* and *Ihr/ihr*
   Think of the meaning! (You/they/she? – your/their/her?)

5 Remember *capital letters for nouns!*
   Watch particularly adjectives that are used as nouns: der dicke *A*lte.

6 Watch expressions like: alles *G*ute (all the best), etwas *I*nteressantes (something interesting), nichts *N*eues (nothing new).

7 Watch compound nouns like *N*acht*t*isch and *S*treichholz and compound adjectives like *hellrot*.

8 Note the difference in pronunciation between the noun *der W*eg (prounounced like the English word 'vague') and the prefix *weg* (pronounced 'veck' to rhyme with the English word 'peck')

9 Think of what happens with the plurals of nouns when deciding on similar sounds, e.g. *äu* or *eu* (*oi* is very rare in German): Haus/Häuser (compare sound with *Leute*).
Watch the *e* sound of plurals: Gegenstand/Gegenstände and Schrank/Schränke, etc. Also compare *gebe* and *gäbe*.

10 Compare *nur/für* and *Bruder/Brüder*, etc.

11 Watch adjectival endings – particularly -*e* and -*er*. Also nouns used like adjectives: der Alt*e* but ein Alt*er*.

12 Watch verbs with *er*- as a prefix.
These can be tricky particularly as words are repeated during the second reading:
erfahren (to learn, find out), erfinden (to invent), erblicken (to catch sight of), etc.
Er erfuhr, daß sein Bruder nicht da war. (He found out that his brother wasn't there.)

15 Watch similar sounds: *der Tod* (death) and *tot* (dead)
   gütig (kind) and *glücklich* (happy)
   nackt (naked) and *Nacht* (night)
   Arz*t* (doctor) and *letzt* (last)
   Ziel (destination) and *Seil* (rope)
Be very careful with *ei/ie* and *sch* sounds.

14 Watch out for the prefixes *ver*- and *vor*-. (You will never find them spelled *fer*- and *for*- except on a bad candidate's script;)
Also learn to distinguish between *v* and *w*.

15 Remember that separable prefixes are joined to the verb in infinitives, and present and past participles: *ausgehen*, *auffallend*, *angezogen* and in the present and imperfect tenses at the end of a clause or sentence: *ausgeht/ausging*.

Punctuation

, (das) Komma
. (der) Punkt
„ (die) Anführungszeichen (unten) (pl.)
" (die) Anführungszeichen (oben) (pl.)
: (der) Doppelpunkt
; (das) Semikolon
! (das) Ausrufezeichen
? (das) Fragezeichen
– (der) Gedankenstrich = dash
- (der) Bindestrich = hyphen
() (die) Klammern (pl.)

Exam practice

Here are three sample dictations. If you can't find anyone to give
them to you, read through them carefully and analyse where you
think you would have gone wrong in an exam and why.

Interesting presents

Fritz saß | in der kleinen Küche, | und da *Anke* gerade | zwei
Wochen schulfrei hatte, | war sie auch | zu Besuch gekommen. |
Jedesmal wenn sie kam, | pflegte sie | ein hübsches Geschenk |
mitzubringen. | Einmal war es | eine Glaskugel, | in der | eine
winzige Landschaft | zu sehen war, | und wenn man | die Kugel
schüttelte, | dann schneite es darin. | Ein anderes Mal | schenkte
sie *Fritz* | einen bunten Sonnenschirm | aus Papier | oder einen
Bleistiftspitzer | in der Form | einer kleinen Lokomotive. |

   Diesmal aber | hatte sie ihm | einen wunderschönen Malkasten
| mitgebracht. | So saßen die beiden Kinder | nun an dem kleinen
Küchentisch | einander gegenüber | und malten. | Zwischen ihnen
| saß Frau *Waas*. | Sie hatte sich | eine Brille aufgesetzt | und las |
aus einem dicken Buch vor, | während sie an einem Schal | für
den Jungen strickte. |

                                                              (JMB)

A cat narrowly misses its prey

Ich stand am Küchenfenster | und sah einer Katze zu, | die in einer
Ecke des Hofes saß. | Sie rührte sich nicht. | Auf einmal aber |
wurde die Katze lebendig. | Ganz gespannt | schaute sie nach der
Seite, | streckte den Kopf vor | und spitzte die Ohren. | Sie mußte
wohl | etwas gemerkt haben. | Leise und vorsichtig, | dicht am
Boden | und mit zuckendem Schwanz | schlich sie | an der niedrigen
Wand entlang. | Ein junger Buchfink | saß piepend | auf der Mauer.
| Ich wollte das Fenster aufreißen | und den frechen Räuber ver-
jagen, | aber der Fensterflügel klemmte. | Immer näher kam die
schleichende Katze | an den Vogel heran, | nur noch drei Schritte
| war sie davon entfernt. | Jetzt duckte sie sich | ganz an den Boden,
| und dann setzte sie zum Sprung an. | Aber umsonst! Der kleine
Buchfink | konnte sich im letzten Augenblick | noch retten.

                                                              (O & C)

A coffee-cup reminisces

Niemand weiß, | daß ich | vor fünfundzwanzig Jahren | unter einem
Weihnachtsbaum | geboren wurde, | und daß einfache Kaffeetassen
| selten | dieses hohe Alter erreichen. | Meine Eltern, | meine
Geschwister, | sogar meine Kinder | sind längst gestorben, | wäh-

rend ich | die letzten Lebensjahre | auf einem Fensterbrett in *Köln* | verbringen muß. | Mein Vater war ein Kuchenteller, | und meine Mutter eine Obstschale. | Ich hatte drei Geschwister: | zwei Untertassen und eine Butterdose, | doch blieb unsere Familie | nur wenige Monate vereint. | Die meisten Tassen | sterben jung und plötzlich, | und so wurden | die Brüder und die liebe Schwester | am folgenden Osterfest | vom Tisch gestoßen. | Bald danach | mußte ich in die Stadt fahren, | um einem Verwandten unseres Besitzers zu dienen.

(LOND)

4 Getting ready for the examination: the oral tests

You should check carefully well in advance of your exam which skills will be tested by your particular examining board. Some boards give as much as twenty-five per cent of the total marks for the oral examination, while others give considerably less.

A book can only give you limited help with oral work but you should try to answer the questions in this section aloud. If you have a cassette recorder you should record and rerecord as many aspects of the exam as possible to help improve your accent, intonation and fluency.

Reading aloud a prepared passage

Use your preparation time carefully to work out the general meaning of the passage. You have to convince the examiner that you understand what you are reading (even if you don't!) and he will be assessing your pronunciation and intonation (i.e. the way your voice goes up and down). Remember that many words belong together (e.g. in einem kleinen Dorf) and that there are natural breaks often indicated by a comma. Don't rush the passage, don't mumble, and be sure to pronounce vowels (particularly those with umlauts) and consonants clearly.

Here is a passage for you to practise:

Wollo

Eines Abends, während wir friedlich beisammen saßen, wurde unser Haus wie von einem Erdbeben erschüttert. Die Bilder wackelten, der Tisch bebte, und die Würstchen rollten von meinem Teller. Ich wollte aufspringen, mich nach der Ursache umsehen, als ich unterdrücktes Lachen auf den Gesichtern meiner Kinder bemerkte.

„Was ist hier los?" schrie ich. Zum ersten Mal in meinem Leben war ich wirklich außer Fassung.

„Walter," sagte meine Frau leise und legte die Gabel hin, „es ist ja nur Wollo."

„Wer ist Wollo?" fragte ich müde, und in diesem Augenblick wurde das Haus wieder durch ein Beben erschüttert.

„Wollo," sagte meine jüngste Tochter, „ist der Elefant, den wir jetzt im Keller haben."

(CAM)

General Conversation

You should be prepared to answer everyday questions that a German may ask you about yourself, your own background, your family, their ages and occupations, your home and how you help, your daily routine at home and at school, what you intend to do when you leave school or go into the sixth form, your town or village, travel and holidays, your hobbies and sports. You must also be able to show the examiner that you can answer questions in different tenses and that you can move easily from one tense to another. Some boards have a prescribed list of questions that you have to prepare in advance. Here are some general questions (some easy, some more difficult). You should adapt the answers to suit your own circumstances.

I

1 *Wie heißen Sie?*
   Ich heiße Lynn Jackson.
2 *Wie alt sind Sie?*
   Ich bin sechzehn Jahre alt.
3 *Wann sind Sie geboren?*
   Ich bin am siebten November neunzehnhundertfünfundsechzig geboren.
4 *Was tun Sie, wenn Sie Geburtstag haben?*
   Normalerweise gebe ich eine Party, wo wir tanzen und plaudern und essen und trinken.

5 *Was für Geschwister haben Sie?*
Ich habe zwei Geschwister – einen Bruder und eine Schwester.

6 *Wie alt sind Ihre Geschwister, und was tun sie?*
Mein Bruder ist jünger als ich; er ist vierzehn Jahre alt. Er geht noch in die Schule. Meine Schwester ist älter als ich. Sie ist neunzehn Jahre alt, und sie arbeitet in einer Bank.

7 *Was für Verwandte haben Sie noch?*
Ich habe einen Vater, eine Mutter, einen Großvater, zwei Groß-mütter, Onkel, Tanten, Kusinen und Vettern.

8 *Beschreiben Sie Ihre Eltern!*
Mein Vater ist fünfundvierzig Jahre alt. Er ist groß und ziemlich dick. Er hat dunkles Haar und braune Augen. Meine Mutter ist jünger als mein Vater. Sie ist ziemlich groß und schlank. Sie hat blondes Haar und blaue Augen.

9 Wo arbeitet Ihr Vater?
Er arbeitet in einem Büro in Bristol.

10 *Arbeitet Ihre Mutter?*
Ja, sie arbeitet in einem Laden in der Stadt.

II

1 *Was sind Zwillinge?*
Es sind zwei Geschwister, die kurz nacheinander geboren sind.

2 *Haben Sie Tiere zu Hause? Wenn ja, welche?*
Ja, wir haben einen kleinen grauen Hund, der Dougal heißt, eine schwarze Katze namens Jilly, zwei Goldfische und einen Wellensittich.

3 *Wann sind Sie heute morgen aufgestanden?*
Heute morgen bin ich um etwa halb acht aufgestanden.

4 *Was haben Sie heute morgen gemacht, bevor Sie zur Schule gekom-men sind?*
Zuerst bin ich ins Badezimmer gegangen, wo ich mich ge-waschen und mir die Zähne geputzt habe. Danach habe ich mich im Schlafzimmer angezogen. Anschließend habe ich mit der Familie in der Küche gefrühstückt, und schließlich habe ich das Haus um etwa zwanzig Minuten nach acht verlassen.

5 *Was werden Sie heute abend machen, wenn Sie die Schulaufgaben fertig haben?*
Wenn ich die Schulaufgaben fertig habe, werde ich wahrschein-lich ein bißchen fernsehen und danach ein Buch lesen. Vielleicht werde ich eine Freundin besuchen und Schallplatten hören.

6 *Wie helfen Sie im Haushalt?*
Ich mache mein Bett. Manchmal gehe ich für meine Mutter im Supermarkt einkaufen. Ich koche auch, und ich wasche ab.

7 *Wie nennt man die Mahlzeiten in Deutschland?*
  Sie heißen das Frühstück, das Mittagessen und das Abendessen
  oder das Abendbrot.

8 *Was ißt man in Deutschland normalerweise zum Frühstück?*
  Zum Frühstück ißt man in Deutschland normalerweise
  Brötchen mit Butter und Marmelade oder Honig. Viele Leute
  essen auch Käse, Wurst und Schinken oder ein gekochtes Ei.

9 *Beschreiben Sie ein typisches deutsches Mittagessen!*
  Ein deutsches Mittagessen beginnt vielleicht mit einer Suppe.
  Dann ißt man Fleisch mit Kartoffeln und Gemüse wie z.B.
  Erbsen, Karotten oder grünen Bohnen. Danach ißt man Obst
  oder ein Eis.

10 *Was sagen die Deutschen, bevor sie mit dem Essen beginnen?*
  Viele sagen ,,Guten Appetit!'' Andere sagen ,,Gesegnete Mahl-
  zeit!'' oder ,,Mahlzeit!''

III

1 *Was muß man vor und nach dem Essen machen?*
  Vor dem Essen muß man den Tisch decken und nach dem Essen
  muß man abräumen.

2 *Beschreiben Sie ein typisches deutsches Abendessen!*
  Zum Abendessen ißt man in Deutschland normalerweise kalten
  Aufschnitt. Das heißt Schinken, Bierwurst, Teewurst usw. . .
  Dazu ißt man Brot und Butter, Fleischsalat, Tomatensalat, Gur-
  kensalat und Käse. Die Deutschen essen sehr gern Roggenbrot
  und Pumpernickel.

3 *Was fragt eine deutsche Mutter ihre Familie nach dem Essen?*
  Vielleicht fragt sie, ,,Habt ihr genug gegessen?'' oder ,,Hat das
  Essen geschmeckt?''

4 *Beschreiben Sie, wie man schnell Kaffee machen kann!*
  Am besten nimmt man einen Kaffeelöffel voll Nescafé und tut
  ihn in eine Tasse. Dann gießt man kochendes Wasser darüber.

5 *Was haben Sie letzten Samstag gemacht?*
  Während des Tages, von neun bis sechs, habe ich in einem
  Laden in der Stadtmitte gearbeitet. Dort habe ich Schuhe ver-
  kauft. Am Abend bin ich mit einem Freund ins Kino gegangen.

6 *Nennen Sie einen großen Unterschied zwischen einem typischen
  deutschen und einem typischen englischen Haus!*
  Die meisten deutschen Häuser haben einen Keller.

7 *Wohnen Sie in einer Wohnung?*
  Nein, ich wohne in einem ziemlich großen Doppelhaus.

8 *Ist Ihr Haus in der Stadt oder auf dem Lande?*
Es ist am Stadtrand.

9 *Wie viele Einwohner hat die Stadt, in der Sie wohnen?*
Sie hat ungefähr fünfundfünfzigtausend Einwohner.

10 *Seit wann wohnen Sie in Ihrem Haus?*
Wir wohnen seit zehn Jahren dort.

IV

1 *Wie viele Zimmer hat Ihr Haus?*
Es hat acht Zimmer – fünf oben und drei unten.

2 *Wie heißen die Zimmer?*
Oben sind die drei Schlafzimmer, das Badezimmer und die Toilette, und unten sind das Wohnzimmer, das Eßzimmer und die Küche.

3 *Haben Sie ein eigenes Zimmer?*
Nein, ich teile ein Zimmer mit meiner Schwester.

4 *Beschreiben Sie Ihr Schlafzimmer!*
Mein Schlafzimmer ist ziemlich groß. Es hat weiße Wände und blaue Vorhänge. Es hat zwei Betten, einen großen weißen Kleiderschrank, einen Toilettentisch, einen Schreibtisch, zwei Stühle und einen Sessel. Ein Bett ist neben dem Fenster. Ich habe auch einen Plattenspieler und ein kleines Radio in meinem Schlafzimmer.

5 *Was für Möbel gibt es in einem Wohnzimmer?*
In einem Wohnzimmer gibt es Sessel und ein Sofa. Manchmal sieht man auch einen Couchtisch, eine Stehlampe, einen Bücherschrank und Bilder. Gewöhnlich ist dort auch ein Fernseher und manchmal auch eine Stereoanlage.

6 *In welches Zimmer gehen Sie, um fernzusehen?*
Ich gehe ins Wohnzimmer.

7 *In welchem Zimmer essen Sie?*
Ich esse im Eßzimmer.

8 *Wo schlafen Sie?*
Ich schlafe in meinem Bett im Schlafzimmer.

9 *Wann gehen Sie ins Badezimmer?*
Ich gehe dorthin, wenn ich mich waschen oder ein Bad nehmen will.

10 *Wie ist Ihr Haus geheizt?*
Es hat Zentralheizung.

V

1 *Was gibt es in einer modernen Küche?*
In einer modernen Küche gibt es vielleicht einen Spültisch,
einen Gasherd bzw. einen Elektroherd, einen Kühlschrank,
eine Geschirrspülmaschine, eine Waschmaschine, einen Ge-
frierschrank, Wandschränke, einen Tisch und Stühle oder
Hocker.

2 *Können Sie kochen?*
Ja, ich kann kochen aber nicht besonders gut.

3 *Was kochen Sie?*
Ich koche allerlei Sachen – Fleischgerichte, Omelettes, Fisch-
stäbchen usw..

4 *Haben Sie eine Garage? Wenn ja, wo ist sie?*
Ja, wir haben eine. Sie ist neben dem Haus.

5 *Was findet man in einer Garage?*
Es kommt darauf an, aber normalerweise findet man einen
Wagen und Fahrräder.

6 *Beschreiben Sie Ihren Garten!*
Wir haben zwei Gärten – einen kleinen vor dem Haus und einen
größeren hinter dem Haus. In diesem Garten haben wir einen
ziemlich großen Rasen und Blumenbeete mit schönen Blumen
und Sträuchern. Wir haben auch einige Apfelbäume und eine
schöne Weide.

7 *Was machen Sie dort?*
Manchmal mähe ich den Rasen, aber im Sommer sitze ich lieber
in einem Liegestuhl oder liege auf dem Rasen, um mich zu
sonnen.

8 *Was findet man in einem Gartenschuppen?*
In einem Gartenschuppen findet man normalerweise Gartenge-
räte, einen Rasenmäher und vielleicht Liegestühle.

9 *Womit mäht man den Rasen?*
Man mäht ihn mit einem Rasenmäher.

10 *Beschreiben Sie Ihr ideales Haus!*
Mein ideales Haus würde sehr modern, aber nicht zu groß sein.
Jedes Mitglied der Familie würde sein eigenes Zimmer haben.
Wir würden einen großen Abstellraum haben, wo wir Tischten-
nis spielen könnten, und natürlich würde es auch einen Swim-
mingpool geben.

VI

1 *Was für eine Schule besuchen Sie?*
Ich besuche eine Gesamtschule.

2 *Wie viele Schüler(innen) hat Ihre Schule?*
Sie hat ungefähr elfhundert.

3 *Wie weit ist Ihre Schule von Ihrem Haus entfernt?*
Sie liegt ungefähr fünf Kilometer davon entfernt.

4 *Wie kommen Sie zur Schule?*
Ich fahre mit dem Bus.

5 *Wie lange dauert Ihre Fahrt zur Schule?*
Sie dauert ungefähr zehn Minuten.

6 *Was sehen Sie auf dem Schulweg?*
Nichts Besonderes – Häuser, eine Kirche, einige Läden und eine Schule.

7 *Wann beginnt die erste Unterrichtsstunde?*
Sie beginnt um fünf Minuten vor halb zehn.

8 *Wie viele Unterrichtsstunden haben Sie am Tag?*
Wir haben acht Stunden

9 *Wie lange dauert eine Unterrichtsstunde?*
Sie dauert fünfunddreißig Minuten.

10 *Welche Fächer haben Sie in der Schule?*
Ich habe Deutsch, Französisch, Englisch, Mathematik, Geschichte, Erdkunde, Chemie, Physik und Kunst.

VII

1 *Was sind Ihre Lieblingsfächer?*
Ich habe Sprachen besonders gern, also Deutsch und Französisch. Ich mag auch Geschichte.

2 *Seit wann lernen Sie schon Deutsch?*
Ich lerne es seit drei Jahren.

3 *Wann endet die letzte Stunde am Vormittag?*
Sie endet um fünf Minuten nach zwölf.

4 *Von wann bis wann dauert die Mittagspause?*
Sie dauert von fünf Minuten nach zwölf bis ein Uhr.

5 *Essen Sie in der Schule zu Mittag? Warum?/Warum nicht?*
Nur selten. Ich ziehe es vor, meine eigenen belegten Brötchen mitzubringen.

6 *Beschreiben Sie Ihre Schuluniform!*
Ich trage einen blauen Pullover, eine weiße Bluse, einen blauen Rock, einen roten Schlips, eine Strumpfhose und schwarze Schuhe.

7 *Welcher Schultag ist für Sie der schönste in der Woche und warum?*
Dienstag ist für mich der schönste Tag, weil ich vormittags eine Doppelstunde Deutsch habe. Am Nachmittag haben wir Sport; das ist mein Lieblingsfach.

8 *Was sieht man in einem Klassenzimmer?*
In einem Klassenzimmer sieht man Tische, Stühle, eine Tafel, Bilder, Kreide, Hefte und Bücher.

9 *Beschreiben Sie Ihren Mathematiklehrer bzw. Ihre Mathematiklehrerin!*
Er ist mittelgroß und ziemlich dick. Er hat eine Glatze und einen Bart und er trägt einen Brille.

10 *Ein deutsches Mädchen sagt, sie sei letztes Jahr sitzengeblieben. Was meint sie damit?*
Sie meint, daß sie wegen ihrer schlechten Noten nicht in die nächste Klasse versetzt wurde.

VIII

1 *Verlassen Sie die Schule am Ende des Schuljahres?*
Nein, ich hoffe, in die 11. Klasse zu gehen.

2 *Was ist ein Abiturient?*
Er ist ein Schüler, der das Abitur machen will.

3 *Was wollen Sie machen, wenn Sie die Schule verlassen haben?*
Ich hoffe, auf die Universität zu gehen.

4 *Haben Sie Hobbys? Welche?*
Ja, ich lese gern und höre gern Schallplatten. Ich tanze viel und gehe gern in Diskos. Ich reise auch gern ins Ausland.

5 *Was lesen Sie gern?*
Am liebsten lese ich Romane, besonders Krimis. Ich lese auch gern Zeitungen und Illustrierte.

6 *Wo bekommt man Bücher, die man nicht kaufen will?*
Man bekommt sie in der Leihbibliothek.

7 *Was braucht man, um Schallplatten zu spielen?*
Man braucht einen Plattenspieler.

8 *Wie viele Stunden verbringen Sie jeden Abend vor dem Fernseher? Welche Programme haben Sie am liebsten?*
Ach, vielleicht eine oder zwei. Am liebsten sehe ich Filme, besonders Kriminalfilme, Fernsehspiele, Programme über Tiere und Popsendungen.

9 *Spielen Sie ein Instrument? Welches?*
Ja, ich spiele seit Jahren Klavier. Als ich jünger war, spielte ich auch Blockflöte und Klarinette.

10 *Haben Sie je etwas gesammelt? Was?*
Ja, als ich kleiner war, habe ich Briefmarken und Trachtenpuppen gesammelt.

IX

1 *Haben Sie einen Brieffreund oder eine Brieffreundin?*
Ja, ich habe zwei Brieffreundinnen – eine deutsche, die in München wohnt und eine französische, die in Paris wohnt.

2 *Welchen Sport treiben Sie im Sommer? Und im Winter?*
Im Sommer spiele ich gern Tennis und im Winter Hockey und Federball. Ich schwimme auch gern.

3 *Was tragen Sie, wenn Sie Hockey spielen?*
Wenn ich Hockey spiele, trage ich ein rotes Hemd, einen grauen Rock, rote Socken und Hockeyschuhe.

4 *Wo kann man schwimmen?*
Man kann in einem Freibad oder in einem Hallenbad, im Meer, in einem See oder in einem Fluß schwimmen.

5 *Was tragen Sie, wenn Sie schwimmen?*
Wenn ich schwimme, trage ich einen Badeanzug normalerweise einen Bikini. (Mein Bruder trägt eine Badehose.)

6 *Was ist Ihre Lieblingsfußballmannschaft?*
Fußball interessiert mich gar nicht, aber mein Bruder ist ein Arsenalfan.

7 *Wo hat die Schule ihre Sportplätze?*
Ganz hinten, hinter der Turnhalle.

8 *Ihre Uhr ist stehengeblieben. Wie fragen Sie nach der Zeit?*
Ich würde fragen: „Wie spät ist es, bitte?" oder „Wieviel Uhr ist es?"

9 *Den wievielten haben wir heute?*
Heute haben wir den siebten Mai, neunzehnhundertzweiundachtzig.

10 *Wozu dient eine Wettervorhersage?*
Sie dient dazu, einem Auskunft über das Wetter zu geben, wie z.B., ob es regnen oder schneien wird, ob die Sonne scheinen wird, oder ob es neblig oder stürmisch sein wird.

X

1 *Wann gehen Sie gewöhnlich einkaufen?*
Normalerweise gehe ich/gehen wir am Wochenende einkaufen,
entweder am Freitagabend oder am Samstagmorgen.

2 *Wohin gehen Sie, um einzukaufen?*
Normalerweise gehe ich/gehen wir zum Supermarkt.

3 *Was ist der Unterschied zwischen einem Supermarkt und einem
gewöhnlichen Laden?*
Man kann Lebensmittel usw. entweder in einem Supermarkt
oder in einem kleinen Laden kaufen. In einem Supermarkt
jedoch bedient man sich selber, und die Waren sind öfters
billiger zu bekommen.

4 *Wer verkauft Fleisch?*
Der Metzger (Der Fleischer) (Der Schlachter).

5 *Sie wollen verschiedene Fleischsorten für drei Mahlzeiten kaufen.
Was sagen Sie zum Metzger?*
Ich würde sagen: „Ich möchte ein Kilo Rindfleisch, ein Kilo
Schweinefleisch und sechs Koteletts, bitte."

6 *Wohin geht man, um Obst und Gemüse zu kaufen?*
Man geht zum Gemüsehändler.

7 *Wo kauft man Brot und Brötchen?*
Man kauft sie beim Bäcker.

8 *Und wo kauft man Kleider?*
Man kauft sie in einer Boutique, in einem Kaufhaus oder in
einem Damenmodengeschäft.

9 *Und Briefmarken?*
Man kauft sie auf der Post.

10 *Was ist der Unterschied zwischen einer Drogerie und einer Apotheke?*
In einer Drogerie kauft man Seife, Parfüm, Filme, Sonnen-
creme, Sonnenbrillen usw., und in einer Apotheke kauft man
Tabletten und Medikamente.

XI

1 *In was für einem Geschäft kauft man Tonbandgeräte, Platten-
spieler und Fernseher?*
Man kauft sie in einem Radiogeschäft (in einem
Elektrogeschäft)

2 *Was kauft man in einem Tabakgeschäft?*
Dort kauft man Zigaretten, Zigarren, Tabak, Pfeifen, Streichhölzer, Feuerzeuge usw.

3 *Was ist ein Warenhaus/Kaufhaus?*
Es ist ein großes Geschäft, wo man fast alles kaufen kann.

4 *Was ist ein Ladentisch?*
Er ist eine Theke in einem Laden, hinter der der Verkäufer
steht und die Kunden bedient.

5 *Wie kommt man zu den oberen Stockwerken in einem großen
Warenhaus?*
Man fährt entweder mit dem Fahrstuhl oder mit der Rolltreppe,
oder man geht die Treppe hinauf.

6 *Warum gehen viele Leute auf dem Markt einkaufen?*
Sie gehen da einkaufen, weil Lebensmittel, Obst und Gemüse
meistens billiger und frischer, und die meisten anderen Waren
auch preiswerter als in den Läden zu bekommen sind.

7 *Nennen Sie fünf Obstsorten!*
Äpfel, Apfelsinen, Birnen, Pflaumen und Weintrauben.

8 *Nennen Sie fünf Gemüsesorten!*
Kartoffeln, Erbsen, Karotten, Zwiebeln und Kohl.

9 *Nennen Sie fünf Lebensmittel!*
Butter, Käse, Milch, Mehl und Zucker.

10 *Am Schaufenster steht das Wort, ,,Schlußverkauf". Was bedeutet
das?*
Ein Schlußverkauf ist ein Verkauf, wo Waren billiger als gewöhnlich verkauft werden, damit man im Laden Platz für neue
Waren bekommt.

XII

1 *Wohin gehen Sie, um sich die Haare schneiden zu lassen?*
Ich gehe zum Friseur.

2 *Was tut ein Schneider?*
Er macht Kleider – Hosen, Jacken, Anzüge, Röcke, Kostüme
usw. . .

3 *Was benutzen Sie für die Einkäufe in einem Supermarkt?*
Ich benutze entweder einen Einkaufskorb oder einen
Einkaufswagen.

4 *Wo zahlen Sie in einem Supermarkt?*
Ich zahle an der Kasse.

5 *An welchem Tag sind die meisten Geschäfte in Ihrer Stadt
geschlossen?*
In meiner Stadt sind sie am Mittwoch geschlossen.

6 *Wo sind die besten Läden in Ihrer Stadt?*
Sie sind in der Hauptstraße. (In vielen Städten sind sie in der
Fußgängerzone.)

7 *Stellen Sie sich vor, Sie sind im Postamt. Wenn das Porto für eine Postkarte sechzig Pfennig kostet, wie verlangen Sie Briefmarken für fünf Postkarten?*
Ich würde sagen: ‚Ich möchte fünf Briefmarken zu sechzig Pfennig, bitte.'

8 *Was sind ein Bäcker, ein Metzger und ein Lebensmittelhändler?*
Ein Bäcker ist ein Mann, der in einer Bäckerei arbeitet, und der Brot und Brötchen bäckt, ein Metzger ist ein Mann, der in einer Metzgerei arbeitet, und der Fleisch und Würste verkauft, und ein Lebensmittelhändler ist ein Mann, der in einem Lebensmittelgeschäft arbeitet, und der Lebensmittel verkauft.

9 *Was sagt die Verkäuferin, wenn Sie in einen Laden kommen?*
Vielleicht sagt sie: ,,Guten Tag, was darf es sein?"

10 *Wenn die Verkäuferin sagt: ,,Sonst noch etwas?" was will sie wissen?*
Sie will wissen, ob der Kunde noch etwas kaufen will.

Prepared topics

Some boards publish (before the exam) a list of about ten or twelve topics from which you will have to prepare two or three. You will have to give a lecturette on one of these in the exam and then answer questions on it. Prepare your topics well in advance and keep on practising and improving them. Keep your account of each topic simple and only use language that you can handle. The examiner will spot any 'chunks' you may have learned by heart from books that are really too difficult for you at this stage and you won't get many marks for them. You should certainly try to record your efforts on cassette.

Narrative on a series of pictures

Here you will be given a picture-series just before your exam and you will be required to relate (in the third person) the story depicted. Your story will have to be told in the past tense.

You could use the three picture-series on pp. 130–2 to practise this part of the exam. The skills required are discussed in the essay writing section on pp. 124–29. Sample versions of these picture series are given at the end of the book.

The single picture

This test usually takes one of two forms:

1 You may be given the picture in advance, in which case you will have to talk about it without the examiner asking you set questions. Use the same techniques as in writing an essay. Remember that most of your verbs will be in the present tense but you should be prepared to say what has just happened (perfect tense + *eben/ gerade*), e.g. *Sie ist eben (gerade) gefallen*; or what is about to happen (wollen + *eben/gerade* + infinitive), e.g. *Er will eben (gerade) ins Auto einsteigen.*

2 You may be handed the picture in the exam room with no preparation time. The examiner will have a printed set of questions in front of him that he is not allowed to alter or rephrase. You will be assessed on the fluency, accuracy and intelligibility of your answers rather than on your accent. Think before you answer but don't delay your answer too long! Revise the section on comprehension (p. 125) and remember that the questions are often designed to test your ability to manipulate the language by changing a verb, case or adjectival ending. Some questions may be of a general nature about travel, camping or whatever the theme of the picture may be.

Before you try to answer the questions on the four pictures that follow, use each picture to revise vocabulary.

1. Write down all the noun vocabulary with gender and plural.
2 Write down all the verbs with their principal parts if they are irregular.
3 What adjectives or adverbs could you use?

Sample answers to the questions are given at the end of the book.

Bild A

1 Wo findet diese Szene statt?

2 Was, glauben Sie, machen die zwei Männer, die arbeiten, beruflich?

3 Was hat der Kellner eben gemacht?

4 Womit fegt der Straßenfeger die Straße (die Fußgängerzone)?

5 Wo sitzen die Leute links?

6 Wie sind die Tische?

7 Was macht die Frau rechts?

8 Was wird sie wohl da machen?

9 Was für Tiere sehen Sie auf dem Bild?

10 Was macht der Hund?

11 Wann findet diese Szene statt, und woher wissen Sie das?

12 Was macht der junge Mann, der am Brunnen kniet?

13 Was für Fahrzeuge sehen Sie auf dem Bild?

14 Wo kommt man hin, wenn man nach rechts geht?

15 Was sehen Sie im Hintergrund?

Bild B

1 Wo findet diese Szene statt?

2 Wie spät ist es?

3 Was macht der Vater am Tisch?

4 Essen die anderen Mitglieder der Familie auch?

5 Warum, glauben Sie, ißt der Vater erst jetzt?

6 Was macht die Tochter, die am Tisch sitzt?

7 Was macht die Mutter?

8 Was macht die jüngste Tochter (die Tochter mit Zöpfen)?

9 Der wievielte ist es?

10 Was hört die Familie im Radio?

11 Wo ist die Katze, und was macht sie?

12 Was macht die älteste Tochter?

13 Wo sitzt der kleine Junge?

14 Wo sitzt der Großvater, und was macht er?

15 Was macht man mit einem Bügeleisen?

(A)

(B)

Bild C

1 Wo findet diese Szene statt?
2 Was verkauft die Marktfrau links?
3 Was macht sie in diesem Augenblick?
4 Nennen Sie vier Obstsorten und vier Gemüsesorten!
5 Was will die Katze eben machen?
6 Was hat die Frau, die Obst kauft, schon in der Stadt gemacht?
7 Wieviel Uhr ist es?
8 Was trägt der Markthändler rechts?
9 Was verkauft er?
10 Was für Spielzeug verkauft er zum Beispiel?
11 Was macht das kleine Mädchen in diesem Augenblick?
12 Warum macht sie das?
13 Was kann man in einer Tabakhandlung kaufen?
14 Steigt ein Mann gerade aus dem Bus?
15 Warum, glauben Sie, schiebt der Mann das Fahrrad?

Bild D

1 Wo findet diese Szene statt?
2 Was machen die Leute auf dem See?
3 Was hat der Hund eben gemacht?
4 Was macht die Frau, die auf dem Gras kniet?
5 Warum macht sie das?
6 Was will der Junge, der auf dem Sprungbrett steht, eben machen?
7 Was hat die Frau vorne am Tisch schon gemacht?
8 Was macht sie im Augenblick?
9 Was macht ihr Mann?
10 Warum trägt er eine Brille?
11 Wo übernachten die Leute auf dem Campingplatz?
12 Wie spät ist es?
13 Was verkauft der Mann in Geschäft wohl außer Coca-Cola?
14 Was machen die zwei jungen Leute, die rechts vor dem Geschäft sitzen?
15 Wie ist das Wetter, und woher wissen Sie das?

(C)

(D)

Role-playing situations

Although this section of the exam does not usually carry many marks, it is very demanding as the range of possible situations is considerable. You will be given a card or piece of paper just before your exam with instructions in English about the things you will have to say in German. Use your preparation time not only to think out answers to the instructions given but also try to imagine how the conversation could develop. Listen carefully to what the examiner says to you in the exam room and react accordingly. Don't forget that the examiner will also be playing a role (e.g. he may be the customs official while you are the traveller).

Here are some sample situations that you should be able to deal with. When you have worked through them, cover the German version and use the English to test yourself.

There are two test role-playing situations at the end of this section. Answers in the form of sample dialogues are given at the end of the book. Remember that you must always think who you are supposed to be talking to. Do you use *du*, *ihr* or *Sie*? (Watch the corresponding forms of *dein*, *euer* and *Ihr*!)

Finding your way around

Entschuldigen Sie bitte. Ich bin hier fremd.

Excuse me please. I'm a stranger here.

Wie komme ich am besten zum Bahnhof/zum Rathaus/zum Marktplatz/zum Dom/zur Post/ zur Stadtmitte?

What's the best way of getting to the station/ to the town hall/to the market place/to the cathedral/to the post office/to the town centre?

Gehen Sie zu Fuß oder fahren Sie? Am besten nehmen Sie den Bus/ die Straßenbahn (Linie 12).

Are you walking or driving? The best thing for you to do is to catch the (No. 12) bus/tram.

Sie könnten mit der U-Bahn/mit der S-Bahn fahren.

You could go by tube/by suburban railway.

Gehen Sie diese Straße hinunter (hinauf/entlang)!

Go down (up/along) this street.

Gehen Sie immer geradeaus, bis Sie zu den Verkehrsampeln kommen!

Keep straight on until you come to the traffic lights.

Dort müssen Sie nach links (nach rechts) abbiegen.

There you have to turn left (right).

Nehmen Sie die erste Straße links und dann die dritte rechts!

Take the first road on the left and then the third on the right.

At the customs

Guten Morgen. Darf ich bitte Ihren Paß sehen?

Good morning. Can I see your passport please?

Haben Sie etwas zu verzollen?

Have you anything to declare?

Nein, ich habe nur 200 Zigaretten, eine Flasche Whisky und ein paar kleine Geschenke und Andenken für meine Familie.

No, I've only got 200 cigarettes, a bottle of whisky and a few small presents and souvenirs for my family.

Machen Sie bitte den Koffer/die Mappe (Aktentasche)/die Handtasche/die Tasche auf!

Open your suitcase/your briefcase/your handbag/bag, please.

In Ordnung. Machen Sie den Koffer zu!

Fine. You can shut your suitcase.

Wie lange bleiben Sie in der BRD?

How long are you staying in West Germany?

Zwei Wochen ungefähr.

About two weeks.

Na schön. Sie können weitergehen.

Fine, you can go through.

Schöne Ferien. Auf Wiedersehen.

Have a pleasant holiday. Good-bye.

At the post office

Was kostet ein Brief nach England?

How much does a letter to England cost?

Ich möchte auch einen Brief in die Schweiz schicken.

I'd also like to send a letter to Switzerland.

Geben Sie mir bitte fünf Briefmarken zu 80 Pfennig!

Give me five 80 pfennig stamps please.

Zu welchem Schalter muß ich gehen, um ein Telegramm/ein Päckchen/ein Paket aufzugeben?

Which counter must I go to, to send a telegram/a packet/a parcel?

Leider wiegt das mehr als 1000 Gramm.

Unfortunately it weighs more than 1000 grammes.

Sie müssen es als Paket schicken.

You'll have to send it as a parcel.

Wenn Sie es ins Ausland schicken, müssen Sie einen grünen Zettel für den Zoll ausfüllen.

If you are sending it abroad, you'll have to fill in a green form for the customs.

Das geht schneller per Luftpost, aber es wird teuer, wenn es schwer ist.

It will go quicker by airmail but it will be expensive if it's heavy.

Entertainments

Hast du Lust am Samstag ins Kino/ ins Theater/ins Konzert/in die Oper zu gehen?

Would you like to go to the pictures/the theatre/a concert/the opera on Saturday?

Ich gehe lieber ins Theater.

I prefer to go to the theatre.

Was gibt es im Theater/im Kino/im Fernsehen/im Radio?

What's on at the theatre/ the cinema/on television/the radio?

Es gibt ein Stück von Brecht im Theater, einen guten amerikanischen Film im Kino, Nachrichten und Sport im Fernsehen und Popmusik im Radio.

There's a Brecht play on at the theatre, a good American film on at the cinema, news and sport on TV and pop music on the radio.

Du sollst anrufen und Karten bestellen.

You should phone and book some tickets.

Wo möchten Sie sitzen? – im Parkett/im ersten Rang/im zweiten Rang/im Balkon/in einer Loge?

Where would you like to sit? – in the stalls/in the dress circle/in the upper circle/in the balcony/in a box?

Wir haben noch ein paar Plätze vorne/in der Mitte/hinten.

We still have a few seats at the front/in the middle/at the back.

Einmal (zweimal/dreimal) zweiter Rang, bitte.

One (two/three) seats in the upper circle, please.

Also, Sie haben zwei Plätze in der fünften Reihe im Parkett für morgen abend.

Right then, you have two seats in the fifth row in the stalls for tomorrow evening.

Wann beginnt die Vorstellung?

When does the performance begin?

162 German

Shopping

Was darf es sein, bitte?

Sonst noch etwas?/Sonst noch einen Wunsch?

Werden Sie schon bedient?

Was kostet das, bitte?

Alles zusammen macht das zehn Mark fünfundzwanzig, bitte.

Ich möchte/Ich hätte gern + acc.

Ich hätte gern einen Pullover/eine Flasche Wein/ein neues Kleid.

Ich möchte ein halbes Pfund/ein Pfund/zwei Pfund Kirschen, bitte.

Ich möchte ein Kilo Käse und zwei Kilo Kartoffeln, bitte.

Ich hätte gern 250 g Schinken, bitte.

Ich möchte einen Liter Milch, bitte.

Ich möchte eine Schachtel Zigaretten/Streichhölzer/Pralinen und eine Tafel Schokolade, bitte.

Ich möchte eine Dose Cola, ein Paket Waschpulver und eine Tube Senf, bitte.

Was kostet das die Flasche/das Pfund?

Die kosten zwei Mark das Stück.

Welche Größe/Welche Farbe?

Haben Sie etwas Billigeres/ Größeres/Kleineres, bitte?

Nimm den Wagen/den Korb und stelle dich an!

Leider habe ich gar kein Kleingeld bei mir.

Can I help you?

Would you like anything else?

Are you being served?

How much is it please?

That makes 10 marks 25 (pfennigs) altogether, please.

I'd like. . .

I'd like a sweater/a bottle of wine/a new dress.

I'd like half a pound/a pound/two pounds of cherries, please.

I'd like a kilo of cheese and two kilos of potatoes, please.

I'd like 250 grammes of ham, please.

I'd like a litre of milk, please.

I'd like a packet of cigarettes/(a box of) matches/chocolates and a bar of chocolate, please.

I'd like a can of coke, a packet of washing powder and a tube of mustard, please.

How much does it cost a bottle/a pound?

They cost two marks each.

What size/What colour?

Have you anything cheaper/larger/smaller, please?

Take the trolley/basket and join the queue.

Unfortunately I have no change at all on me.

At the lost property office

Guten Tag, kann ich Ihnen helfen?	Good day, can I help you?
Ja, hoffentlich.	Yes, I hope so.
Ich habe meinen Fotoapparat/meine Handtasche/meine Mappe/meine Brieftasche/mein Portemonnaie/ meinen Paß/meine Reiseschecks/ meinen Regenschirm/meinen Mantel/meine Uhr/meinen Ring/ mein Armband/meine Halskette verloren.	I've lost my camera/my handbag/my briefcase/ my wallet/my purse/ my passport/my traveller's cheques/my umbrella/my coat/my watch/my ring/my bracelet/my necklace.
Wo haben Sie ihn/sie/es verloren?	Where did you lose it?
Irgendwo in der Fußgängerzone/ auf der Hauptstraße.	Somewhere or other in the pedestrian precinct/in the high street.
Ich habe ihn/sie/es im Bus/im Zug/ in der Straßenbahn/im Café/in einer Gaststätte liegengelassen.	I left it on the bus/train/ tram/in the café/in a restaurant.
Können Sie ihn/sie/es beschreiben?	Can you describe it?
Wie sieht er/sie/es aus?	What does it look like?
Er/sie/es ist aus Leder/aus Plastik/ aus Gold/aus Silber.	It's made of leather/ plastic/gold/silver.
Er hat einen großen Kragen/drei Knöpfe vorne/einen Reißverschluß.	It's got a large collar/ three buttons at the front/a zip fastener.
Welche Marke?/Welche Farbe?/ Welche Größe?	What make?/What colour?/What size?
Was war drin?	What was in it?
Wann haben sie ihn/sie/es verloren?	When did you lose it?
Gestern abend/heute morgen/heute nachmittag.	Last night/this morning/ this afternoon.
Es tut mir leid. Er/sie/es ist nicht hier.	I'm sorry. It's not here.
Soll ich wiederkommen?	Shall I come back?

At the railway station

Entschuldigen Sie bitte, wo ist der Schalter/Gleis vier/die Gepäckaufbewahrung/der Wartesaal/die Auskunft?

Excuse me please, where is the ticket office/platform four/the left luggage office/the waiting room/the information desk?

Wie fährt man am besten nach München?

What is the best way to get to Munich?

Muß man umsteigen?

Do you have to change?

Nein, der Zug fährt direkt nach München.

No the train goes straight to Munich.

Sie müssen eine Zuschlagkarte haben, wenn Sie mit dem Intercity fahren wollen.

You must have a supplementary ticket, if you want to go by Intercity.

Einmal/zweimal/nach München, bitte.

One (ticket)/two/ to Munich, please.

Einfach oder hin und zurück?

Single or return?

Erster Klasse oder zweiter Klasse?

First class or second class?

Wann fährt der Zug nach München ab?

When does the train to Munich leave?

Wann kommt der Zug in München an?

When does the train arrive in Munich?

Von welchem Gleis fährt der Zug nach München ab?

From which platform does the train to Munich leave?

In a restaurant

Wir möchten gern einen Tisch für vier.	We'd like a table for four.
Möchten Sie am Fenster sitzen oder dort drüben in der Ecke?	Would you like to sit by the window or over there in the corner?
Ich bringe Ihnen gleich die Speisekarte.	I'll bring you the menu straightaway.
Herr Ober, die Weinkarte, bitte!	Waiter, the wine list, please.
Haben Sie schon gewählt?	Have you decided what you would like yet?
Wir möchten jetzt bestellen.	We'd like to order now.
Was möchten Sie trinken?	What would you like to drink?
Möchten Sie eine Vorspeise/eine Nachspeise (Nachtisch)?	Would you like a hors d'oeuvre (starter)/a dessert (pudding)?
Ich möchte einen Krabbencocktail/ eine Tagessuppe/eine Spargelcremesuppe.	I'd like one prawn cocktail/one soup of the day/one cream of asparagus soup.
Ich möchte Schweinebraten/ Rinderbraten/Steak/Wiener Schnitzel/Huhn/Forelle.	I'd like roast pork/roast beef/steak/Viennese schnitzel (veal cutlet)/ chicken/trout.
Ich möchte Bratkartoffeln/ Salzkartoffeln/Pommes Frites/ Reis.	I'd like fried potatoes/ boiled potatoes/chips/ rice.
Ich möchte Erbsen/Karotten/ Blumenkohl/Rosenkohl/ Champignons/Zwiebeln/ gemischten Salat.	I'd like peas/carrots/ cauliflower/brussel sprouts/mushrooms/ onions/mixed salad
Ich möchte ein Eis/Obstsalat/ Apfelstrudel/frisches Obst/Käse.	I'd like an ice-cream/ fruit salad/apple strudel/fresh fruit/ cheese.
Fräulein, zahlen, bitte (die Rechnung bitte)!	Miss, the bill, please.

Staying at a hotel

Können Sie mir ein gutes/billiges Hotel in der Nähe empfehlen?

Can you recommend a good/cheap hotel nearby?

Haben Sie noch Zimmer frei?

Have you still got some rooms free?

Ich möchte ein Einzelzimmer für meinen Sohn und ein Doppelzimmer für meine Frau und mich.

I'd like a single room for my son and a double room for my wife and me.

Möchten Sie ein Zimmer mit Bad/ Dusche/WC/fließendem Wasser?

Would you like a room with a bath/a shower/a lavatory/running water?

Wie lange wollen Sie bleiben?

How long would you like to stay?

Wir wollen nur eine Nacht/zwei Nächte/bis zum Wochenende bleiben.

We would like to stay only one night/two nights/until the weekend.

Wo liegt das Zimmer?

Where is the room?

Im Erdgeschoß/im ersten (dritten/ siebten) Stock/vorne/hinten.

On the ground floor/on the first (third/ seventh) floor/at the front/back.

Was kostet das Zimmer pro Nacht mit Frühstück?

What does the room cost per night including breakfast?

Ich finde das etwas teuer. Haben Sie etwas Billigeres?

I find that a little expensive. Have you got something cheaper?

Gut, ich nehme es.

Fine, I'll take it.

Ich habe Ihnen geschrieben und ein Doppelzimmer mit Balkon reserviert.

I wrote to you and reserved a double room with a balcony.

Mit Vollpension/mit Halbpension.

With full board/with half board.

Einen Augenblick, bitte. Sie müssen einen Meldeschein ausfüllen.

Just a moment, please. You have to fill in a registration form.

Test card 1

> **At the dry-cleaner's**
> The examiner is the person behind the counter.
> 1 List 2/3 items you have brought to be cleaned.
> 2 Point out an oil stain on one of the items.
> 3 Say that your mother collected an item that had been cleaned but it is still dirty.
> 4 Ask when the items will be ready.
> 5 Ask when the shop closes.
>
> *Additional points*
> What type of oil – where the stains are – have you got your mother's ticket still? – cost – does the shop close for lunch?

Test card 2

> **At a taxi-rank**
> The examiner is the taxi driver.
> 1 Ask the taxi driver if he is free.
> 2 Ask him if he can take you to the airport.
> 3 Tell him that you have to be at the airport by 4.30.
> 4 Ask him if he can get you there in time.
> 5 Tell him that you will give him a large tip if he gets you there in time.
>
> *Additional points* (during the taxi ride)
> Where are you flying to? – are you going on business or on holiday? – how long are you staying? – ask the driver if he often goes to the airport – ask if the traffic is always so heavy.

5 Answers to tests

Revising grammar

Use of cases with articles and limiting adjectives (p. 15)

1 Welcher Mann wohnt in *dem* (in jenem) Haus? 2 Ihr Mann hat ein Motorrad, aber er hat kein Auto (keinen Wagen). 3 Sie kaufte ihrem Sohn einen Regenmantel. 4 Sein Bruder hat keine Freunde. 5 Das Haus ihrer Schwester hat kein Badezimmer. 6 Er las die Zeitung seines Bruders. 7 Die Lehrerin der Kinder trug einen Rock und eine Bluse. 8 Sein Onkel schickte dem Freund seines Sohnes einen Brief.

Personal pronouns (p. 16)

1 Sie sahen mich. 2 Ich sah sie. 3 Sie sah ihn. 4 Sie sah ihn. 4 Er sah uns. 5 Hat sie sie gesehen? 6 Sie ging mit uns. 7 Ich ging mit ihm. 8 Wir gingen mit ihr. 9 Sind Sie (Bist du/Seid ihr) mit mir gegangen? 10 Sie gingen mit Ihnen (mit dir/mit euch).

Relative clauses (p. 17)

1 Der Mann, der eine Pfeife raucht, trägt eine Sonnenbrille. 2 Die Frau, deren Mann die Zeitung liest, schreibt einen Brief. 3 Hast du (Haben Sie/Habt ihr) deinen (Ihren/euren) Bruder besucht, der in Köln wohnt? 4 Die Kinder, deren Vater den Wagen (das Auto) wäscht, spielen im Garten. 5 Der Freund, dem er eine Postkarte schickte, wohnte in Wien. 6 Die Freundin, mit der sie ins Kino ging, hieß Sally. 7 Der Freund, mit dem sie ins Theater ging, hieß John. 8 Die Mädchen, mit denen sie nach Frankreich fuhr, arbeiteten in ihrem Büro.

The complement and the use of articles (p. 18)

1 Er ist mein Bruder. 2 Sie wurde Ärztin. 3 Er ist Lehrer. 4 Er ist ein guter Lehrer. 5 Das schöne Frankreich. 6 Der kleine Rainer ist älter als die kleine Anna. 7 Er sprach mit lauter Stimme. 8 Er steckte die Pfeife in den Mund. 9 Fährst du vor oder nach dem Mittagessen nach Garmisch? 10 Er liest die Zeitung immer beim Frühstück. 11 Ich habe Fieber. 12 Hast du (Haben Sie) Kopfschmerzen?

Adjectival endings (p. 24)

1 Dieser junge Mann hat eine hübsche Frau. 2 Seine kleine Tochter hat einen braunen Hund, eine schwarze Katze und zwei weiße Mäuse. 3 Welchen neuen Film haben Sie (hast du/habt ihr) gesehen? 4 Ihr junger Bruder lief aus seiner neuen Schule und stieg in ihr kleines Auto ein. 5 Unser junger Arzt wohnt in einem kleinen Haus. 6 Arbeitet der Freund seines jungen Bruders in dieser großen Fabrik? 7 Sein neuer Nachbar trinkt gern kaltes Bier, kalte Milch und heißen Kaffee. 8 Diese jungen Kinder wohnen in *den* (jenen) alten Häusern.

The comparison of adjectives and adverbs (p. 29)

1 Dieser junge Mann ist mein älterer Bruder. 2 Er kam mit einem schnelleren Zug. 3 Mein Vater ist älter als meine Mutter. 4 Sie ist größer als ihre Schwester aber nicht so groß wie ihr Bruder. 5 Bist du (Sind Sie/Seid ihr) jünger als ich? 6 Er stieg immer höher. 7 Er ist der kleinste Junge in seiner Klasse. 8 Je mehr er spielte, desto besser wurde er. 9 Er war sein bester Freund. 10 Karl läuft schnell, Achim läuft schneller, aber Rainer läuft am schnellsten. 11 Singst du so gut wie deine Schwester? 12 Er spricht spanisch gut, deutsch besser und französisch am besten. 13 Er ißt mehr als ich, aber nicht so viel wie sein Bruder. 14 Er raucht gern Zigaretten, er raucht lieber Zigarren, aber am liebsten raucht er Pfeife.

Prepositions (p. 33)

(a) 1 trotz des Regens 2 (an)statt seines Bruders 3 gegenüber dem Rathaus 4 bei seinem Bruder 5 mit seinem Vater 6 um den Garten (herum) 7 nach dem Frühstück 8 am Morgen 9 während des Frühlings 10 um seiner Mutter willen 11 aus dem Garten 12 von der Stadt 13 außer ihrem Hund 14 die Straße entlang 15 zum Flughafen 16 wegen des Schnees 17 ohne seinen Mantel 18 durch die Küche 19 für seinen Onkel 20 diesseits des Berges 21 innerhalb einer Stunde 22 unweit des Dorfes

(b) 1 Er saß in einem Sessel. 2 Er setzte sich in einen Sessel. 3 Sie hängte den Spiegel an die Wand. 4 Der Spiegel hing an der Wand 5 Sie legte sich auf das Bett. 6 Sie lag auf dem Bett. 7 Er steckte das Geld in die Tasche. 8 Das Geld war in der Tasche. 9 Das Postamt war zwischen dem Kino und dem Supermarkt. 10 Er setzte sich neben den Mann.

Measurements and quantity (p. 33)

1 Ich möchte 250 Gramm Schinken, ein halbes Pfund Kirschen und fünf Kilo Kartoffeln, bitte. 2 Das kostet dreiunddreißig Mark. 3 Ich möchte drei Tassen Tee und zwei Flaschen Cola, bitte. 4 Er wollte zwei Pfund Apfelsinen. 5 Sie wohnen einen Kilometer von der Stadtmitte entfernt.

Expressions of time (p. 35)

(a) 1 um 3.30 2 am Dienstag 3 im Herbst 4 zu Weihnachten 5 im Januar 6 gestern abend 7 früh am Morgen 8 an einem Tage in der letzten Woche 9 an einem nebligen Novembermorgen 10 abends 11 am Wochenende 12 während des Nachmittags 13 heute nachmittag 14 am sechzehnten Februar 15 vor zwei Tagen 16 vor einem Monat 17 nächsten Donnerstag 18 eines Samstags 19 einmal in der Woche 20 jeden Monat

(b) 1 eine Viertelstunde später 2 eine halbe Stunde später 3 eine Stunde später 4 anderthalb Stunden später 5 zwei Stunden später

(c) 1 plötzlich 2 zuerst 3 kurz darauf 4 bald darauf 5 dann/anschließend 6 kurz vorher 7 schließlich 8 endlich 9 einige Minuten später 10 nach ein paar Minuten

The present tense (p. 39)

1 Sie ißt einen Apfel. 2 Was trinkst du (trinken Sie/trinkt ihr) abends? 3 Sie sehen fern. 4 Steht er, oder sitzt er? 5 Er steigt in den Wagen (ins Auto) ein. 6 Er zieht sich in seinem Schlafzimmer an. 7 Singt sie gut? 8 Sie gehen einmal in der Woche ins Kino.

The imperfect tense (p. 40)

1 Sie deckte den Tisch. 2 Sie wohnten (früher) in Köln. 3 Sie ging in den Supermarkt und kaufte ein Pfund Äpfel. 4 Er las ein Buch, als das Telefon klingelte. 5 Sie besuchte ihren Großvater sonntags. 6 Sie arbeitete (früher) in einem Reisebüro. 7 Sie liefen die Straße entlang. 8 Er lag im Bett.

The future tense (p. 41)

1 Ich werde meine Hausaufgaben heute abend machen. 2 Er wird bald aufstehen. 3 Kommen sie heute nachmittag? (Werden sie heute nachmittag kommen?) 4 Am Samstag werden wir ins Kino gehen. 5 Wirst du (Werden Sie/werdet ihr) mich im Krankenhaus besuchen?

The conditional tense (p. 41)
1 Wir würden nach München fahren. 2 Sie würden ein größeres Haus kaufen. 3 Ich würde fliegen. (Ich würde mit dem Flugzeug reisen.) 4 Was würdest du (würden Sie/würdet ihr) machen (tun)? 5 Sie würde bis elf Uhr im Bett bleiben.

The perfect tense (p. 43)
1 Wir sind früh aufgestanden. 2 Wann haben Sie (hast du/habt ihr) gefrühstückt? 3 Er hat eben das Haus verlassen. 4 Warum sind Sie (bist du/seid ihr) nach Deutschland gefahren? 5 Haben Sie (hast du/habt ihr) den Brief geschrieben? 6 Er ist Arzt geworden. 7 Hat sie den Mantel gekauft? 8 Sein Vater ist vor zwei Tagen gestorben. 9 Sie sind verreist. 10 Ist das Ruderboot gekentert?

The pluperfect tense (p. 43)
1 Er war im Sessel eingeschlafen. 2 Warum waren sie zu Hause geblieben? 3 Wir hatten eben den Film gesehen. 4 Was war dort geschehen (passiert)? 5 Er hatte Fußball gespielt. 6 Nachdem das Segelboot gekentert war. 7 Als sie die Betten gemacht hatte. 8 Weil sie den Zug verpaßt hatte. 9 Sie hatte sich gerade angezogen. 10 Warum hatten sie ferngesehen?

The future perfect and conditional perfect tenses (p. 44)
1 We would have played tennis if it hadn't rained. 2 Will you already have eaten? 3 He would have bought himself a car if he had been richer. 4 What would you have done if you hadn't stayed at home? 5 He will already have seen him. 6 That wouldn't have happened if the police had come earlier.

Modal verbs (p. 46)
1 We shall have to hurry otherwise we shall have to go on foot. 2 He couldn't come last night. 3 He could (i.e. would be able to) come tomorrow evening. 4 He had to write a letter. 5 He had a letter to write. 6 He had written a letter. 7 She will have to go to work tomorrow. 8 The beer is said to be very good. 9 He shouldn't have done that. 10 May I have another cup of tea, please?

Reflexive verbs (p. 46)
1 Wir fühlten uns müde. (Wir waren müde) 2 Hast du dich (Haben Sie sich/Habt ihr euch) an die Fotos erinnert? 3 Nachdem sie sich gewaschen hatte, zog sie sich an. 4 Ich ging nach oben, um mich auszuruhen. 5 Hast du dir (Haben Sie sich/Habt ihr euch) die Hände und das Gesicht gewaschen?

The imperative (p. 47)
1 Mach (Machen Sie/Macht) die (jene) Tür zu! 2 Wollen wir ins Kino gehen? 3 Schick (Schicken Sie/Schickt) ihm eine Postkarte! 4 Sei (Seien Sie/Seid) pünktlich! 5 Lies (Lesen Sie/Lest) diesen Roman!

Verbs with the dative (p. 48)
1 Der Wagen (Das Auto) gehörte seinem Bruder. 2 Er dankte seinen Söhnen. 3 Hat sie dir (Ihnen/euch) verziehen? 4 Nachdem sie ihrem Vater geholfen hatten, folgten sie ihm ins Haus. 5 Sie erlaubte ihrer Tochter zur Party zu gehen. 6 Der Zug näherte sich dem Bahnhof.

Verbs with prepositions (p. 48)
1 Hast du dich an seinen Geburtstag erinnert? 2 Er freute sich auf seine Ferien. 3 Er wartete auf den Zug. 4 Er mußte sich auf seinen Freund verlassen. 5 Er bat um noch eine Flasche Wein. 6 Er hatte Angst vor dem Hund.

Translation of the English present participle (p. 49)
1 She heard him singing. 2 They saw us coming. 3 without hesitating a moment. 4 instead of going to the theatre. 5 Before getting dressed I get washed. 6 She was lying in the garden sunbathing. 7 The man reading the newspaper has a moustache. 8 He left the house without me noticing him. 9 He came running along the street. 10 I heard him mowing the lawn. 11 I like drinking beer. What do you like drinking most of all? 12 It's marvellous hiking through the forest.

The passive (p. 50)
1 The cathedral was built in the thirteenth century. 2 After the boys had been rescued, they were taken to the hospital. 3 The thieves have been arrested by the police. 4 You will easily be seen. 5 The plates have been broken by the woman. 6 He was murdered with a pair of scissors.

The subjunctive (p. 51)
1 He said (that) he *was* poor. 2 He asked if I *had* been in Germany. 3 She said that she *had* already eaten. 4 He asked if she *had* already seen the film. 5 It seemed as if it had been raining. 6 It seemed as if he had stolen the valuable picture.

Revising vocabulary and useful constructions

1 Ende gut, alles gut (p. 55)
A 1 (Er spielte) mit zwei Freunden (Fußball). **2** (Er wohnte) im
Nachbarhaus (im Haus nebenan). **3** (Er war böse auf sie), weil sie
sein (eines seiner) Fenster zerbrochen hatten (weil sie den Fußball
durch eines seiner Fenster geschossen hatten). **4** Sie kauften eine
neue Fensterscheibe. **5** Sie setzten sie ein. **6** Sie brachte sie den
Jungen.
B 1 Letzten Dienstagnachmittag gingen die Jungen in den Garten,
um Fußball zu spielen. **2** Einer der Jungen zerbrach ein Fenster. **3**
Sie hörten ihn den Rasen mähen. (Sie hörten, wie er den Rasen
mähte.) **4** Er war böse auf sie, weil sie das Fenster zerbrochen
hatten. **5** Nachdem sie das Glas zusammengefegt hatten, holten sie
Geld. **6** Sie gingen zum Glaser, wo sie eine neue Scheibe kauften.
7 Es gelang dem Jungen, die neue Scheibe einzusetzen, weil er
praktisch veranlagt war. **8** Die Jungen waren überrascht, als Herr
Schulze sie in sein Haus einlud (. . .sie einlud, in sein Haus zu
kommen). **9** Die Jungen dankten Herrn und Frau Schulze für die
Limonade und den Kuchen, die sie ihnen angeboten hatten. **10** Am
folgenden Tag mußte Uwe den Rasen in seinem eigenen Garten
mähen.
C 1 Instead of continuing their game (instead of going on playing),
the three boys decided to go to the glazier's straight away. **2** They
saw their neighbour talking to his wife. **3** 'Don't be angry with
him,' said Frau Schulze. **4** 'Let's try to buy a new pane,' suggested
Uwe. **5** 'Do you think we'll manage to put the pane in?' **6** 'Watch
out (Take care), otherwise (or) you'll break the new pane, too,' said
Uwe. **7** 'Well boys, are you thirsty? Come in, won't you?' said Herr
Schulze. **8** As they were very hot, they were pleased when the
neighbour invited them to have a drink but they were a little
embarrassed.

2 Ein Banküberfall (p. 57)
A 1 Sie wollten die Bank in der Hauptstraße überfallen. **2** (Es war)
in Säcken im Kofferraum des Fluchtautos. **3** (Er folgte) den Bank-
räubern. **4** Sie wußte es, weil der Autofahrer sie angerufen hatte
(und ihr erzählt hatte, wo sie sich aufhielten). **5** Er zahlte es auf
der Bank in der Hauptstraße ein.
B 1 Die drei maskierten Männer hatten vor (beabsichtigten/hatten
die Absicht), die Bank in der Hauptstraße zu überfallen. **2** Der
Überfall war sorgfältig von den drei maskierten Männern geplant

worden. **3** Einer der Männer blieb im Auto (im Wagen), und die anderen zwei gingen in die Bank. **4** Sie steckten das Geld in Säcke und trugen sie aus der Bank. **5** Nachdem sie wieder ins Auto (in den Wagen) eingestiegen waren, fuhren sie so schnell wie möglich ab. **6** Sie wollten sich auf einem einsamen Bauernhof aufhalten. **7** Nachdem der Autofahrer den Männern gefolgt war, telefonierte er mit der Polizei (rief er die Polizei an). **8** Nachdem die Polizei den Bauernhof umstellt hatte, gelang es ihr, die Räuber zu überreden, herauszukommen. **9** Sie wurden verhaftet und zur Polizeiwache gefahren. **10** Das Geld wurde von dem Autofahrer auf der Bank eingezahlt.

C 1 The poor female bank clerk was afraid of the two masked men who had suddenly rushed into the bank. **2** She had neither (the) time nor (the) opportunity to defend herself against the robbers. **3** 'Come on, get a move on (hurry up) won't you? Hand over the money!' said one of the men brusquely (rudely) (growled one of the men). **4** The woman behind the counter looked at them in wide-eyed astonishment. **5** The robbers hadn't noticed at all, however, that someone had followed them (had been following them). **6** When they had reached the farm, the laughed themselves silly (they laughed their heads off). **7** 'We've done it,' said the tall man with the grey beard. **8** 'You were unlucky,' said the policeman. 'Now you won't be able to rob any more banks!'

3 Vollbad (p. 59)

A 1 Er war der dreijährige (kleine) Sohn von Herrn und Frau Braun. (Er war Herrn und Frau Brauns dreijähriger (kleiner) Sohn.) **2** Sie war ihre Schwester. **3** Sie wäre nicht nach unten gegangen, wenn das Telefon nicht geklingelt hätte (. . .hätte das Telefon nicht geklingelt). **4** (Es tropfte (dort) da durch), weil die Badewanne übergelaufen war (. . . weil Hansi den Hahn aufgedreht hatte). **5** Sie fanden, daß Hansi in der Badewanne stand und weinte, daß die Badewanne übergelaufen war, und daß der Boden im Wasser schwamm.

B 1 Es war Samstagmorgen. **2** Die zwei (beiden) Töchter frühstückten mit ihrem Vater. **3** Seine Frau ging nach oben ins Badezimmer, um ihren kleinen Sohn zu baden. **4** Plötzlich hörte sie das Telefon im Flur klingeln (läuten). **5** Während der kleine Junge den Hahn aufdrehte, sprach (unterhielt sich) seine Mutter mit ihrer Schwester. **6** Nachdem sie bemerkt hatten, daß Wasser durch die Decke tropfte, stürzten sie nach oben. **7** Sie sahen, daß die Badewanne übergelaufen war, und daß Hansi weinend in der Badewanne stand. **8** Herr Braun war böse auf seine Frau und seinen kleinen Sohn. **9** Er hätte den Hahn nicht aufgedreht, wenn seine Mutter ihn nicht allein gelassen hätte (...hätte seine Mutter ihn nicht allein gelassen). **10** Frau Braun hätte ihren Sohn nicht allein lassen sollen!

C 1 'Inge,' Herr Braun called upstairs. 'Your sister is on the phone.' **2** 'Now be good,' said Frau Braun to her little son. 'I'll be back straightaway (immediately).' **3** She shouldn't (ought not to) have talked (spoken) to her sister for so long. **4** Without hesitating a moment, the two girls rushed upstairs. **5** They realized what had happened. **6** If they hadn't rushed upstairs immediately, the accident would have been even worse. **7** I wonder if the boy will turn the tap on again, if (when) his mother isn't there? **8** 'You shouldn't have done that,' he said angrily.

4 Episode am Strand (p. 61)

A 1 Es war heiß und sonnig. **2** (Sie saßen) in Liegestühlen. **3** Jutta baute Sandburgen, und Hans spielte mit einem Schiff in einer Pfütze. **4** (Sie waren besorgt), weil sie bemerkt hatten, daß ihr Sohn verschwunden war (daß ihr Sohn nicht mehr da (dort) war). **5** Er spielte mit einem kleinen Hund.

B 1 Während des Sommers fuhr die Familie Meyer ans Meer, um zwei Wochen in einem kleinen Hotel zu verbringen, das am Strand war. **2** Sie setzten sich auf die Liegestühle, die sie mitgebracht hatten. **3** Ihr kleiner Sohn half seiner jüngeren Schwester, Sandburgen zu bauen. **4** Nachdem sie sich eine halbe Stunde lang gesonnt hatten, liefen sie ins Meer, um zu baden. **5** ,,Reich mir die Sonnencreme!'' sagte sie. ,,Ich will (möchte) keinen Sonnenbrand bekommen.'' **6** Während ihre Mutter die Zeitung las, spielten die zwei (beiden) Kinder mit ihren kleinen Schiffen (Booten). **7** Da es ein sehr heißer sonniger Tag war, amüsierten sie sich alle am Strand. **8** Sie war sehr besorgt, als sie bemerkte, daß ihr kleiner Sohn verschwunden war. **9** Wohin war er gegangen? (Wo war er hingegangen?) **10** Sie war so erleichtert, als sie ihn und einen kleinen schwarzen Hund in der Ferne sah.

C 1 'Shall we go for a swim now or would you prefer to go on reading your novel?' she asked in a quiet voice. **2** 'Actually I'm not hungry at all (I'm not really hungry at all) but I would like an ice (cream). Will you fetch (get) me one?' **3** 'Shall we go for a little (short) walk to the old lighthouse?' he asked suddenly. **4** At that moment she didn't want to (she wasn't keen) as she was busy putting on (rubbing in) some suntan cream. **5** 'What shall we do this afternoon? I'd like to go on a motorboat trip round the bay. What about it?' 6 'Take care,' she said to Hans. 'The water can suddenly get (become) very deep.' 7 'Where is Hansi? I can't see him anywhere. I shouldn't have let him go off by himself (alone), should I?' 8 'Don't worry! I can see him over there in the distance.'

5 Ein kleiner Junge wird vor dem Ertrinken gerettet (p. 65)
A 1 Ein kleiner Junge und seine kleine Schwester (spielten dort). **2** Er fiel in den Fluß (ins Wasser). **3** (Sie wußten das), weil er im Wasser herumzappelte. **4** (Sie standen) auf der Brücke. **5** (Sie brachten sie nach Hause), nachdem sie den Jungen aus dem Wasser gezogen hatten.
B 1 Nach dem Mittagessen beschlossen sie, einen Spaziergang am Fluß zu machen, da die Sonne hell schien. **2** Ein kleines Mädchen spielte mit ihrem älteren Bruder am gegenüberliegenden Ufer (am Ufer gegenüber). **3** Plötzlich fiel er ins Wasser und begann im Wasser herumzuzappeln, da er nicht schwimmen konnte. **4** Zum Glück (Glücklicherweise) sahen sie, was geschehen (passiert) war. **5** Es gelang ihm, einen großen Ast aufzuheben, den er ins Wasser warf. **6** Nachdem der Mann den Ast aufgehoben hatte, trug er ihn zum Fluß, um ihn ins Wasser zu werfen. **7** Sie standen auf der niedrigen, hölzernen Brücke (auf der niedrigen Holzbrücke) und zogen den Jungen, der sich an dem Ast festhielt, aus dem Fluß. **8** Das kleine Mädchen hörte auf zu weinen (hörte zu weinen auf), als sie sah, daß ihr Bruder in Sicherheit war. **9** Sie brachten den Jungen, den sie gerettet hatten und das Mädchen, das geweint hatte, nach Hause. **10** Die Eltern der Kinder waren erleichtert, ihren Sohn und ihre Tochter zu sehen und dankten dem jungen Paar (bedankten sich bei dem jungen Paar).
C 1 The boy could have drowned if the young couple hadn't seen him **2** 'Hurry up, won't you (Come on, hurry up), or (otherwise) the little boy will drown!' she shouted. **3** They ran up to the little girl to comfort (console) her. **4** Although it was a marvellous day, it was still slippery on the river bank and the boy slipped and fell into the water. **5** If he hadn't been able to swim, the accident would have been even worse. **6** If the branch hadn't been there, then the young man would probably (I suppose) have had to jump into the water himself. **7** The father ought to (should) have been angry with his son but he could not help smiling when he looked at the sad, wet boy. **8** 'Go upstairs straightaway (immediately), have a shower and get changed (change) or (otherwise) you will catch cold!' said his mother.

6 Ein ‚Terrorist' wird beinahe verhaftet (p. 65)

A 1 (Er kaufte es ihm) in einem Spielwarengeschäft. **2** Er wollte ein Glas Bier trinken. **3** (Er rief sie an), nachdem er bemerkt hatte, daß im Paket des Mannes ein Gewehr war. **4** (Er fuhr) mit seinem Auto (dahin). **5** (Sie klopften), nachdem Herr Becker schon ins Haus gegangen war (als er schon im Haus war). **6** Der kleine Junge (Sohn) von Herrn Becker (Herrn Beckers kleiner Sohn) hatte es.

B 1 Letzte Woche kaufte Herr Becker seinem Sohn ein herrliches Geschenk in einem Spielwarengeschäft. **2** Kurz darauf verließ er das Geschäft (den Laden) und beschloß in eine Gaststätte zu gehen, weil er durstig war (weil er Durst hatte). **3** Der Kellner kam auf ihn zu, und er (dieser) bestellte ein Glas Bier. **4** Sobald er dem Mann sein Bier gebracht hatte, beschloß der Kellner die Polizei anzurufen (mit der Polizei zu telefonieren). **5** Nachdem er die Gaststätte verlassen hatte, stieg er in sein Auto (in seinen Wagen) (ein). **6** Einige Minuten später kam die Polizei an und folgte seinem Auto (seinem Wagen). **7** Der kleine Junge dankte seinem Vater (bedankte sich bei seinem Vater), als er ihm das Gewehr gab. **8** Nachdem die zwei (beiden) Polizisten aus ihrem Auto (Wagen) ausgestiegen waren, klopften sie an die Haustür des Mannes. **9** Er war überrascht, die Polizisten an der Haustür zu sehen. **10** Die Polizisten lächelten, als sie den Sohn von Herrn Becker (Herrn Beckers Sohn) mit dem Gewehr spielen sahen.

C 1 He wanted to buy (his son) something unusual for his birthday (for his son's birthday). **2** The brand new rifle was to be (was supposed to be) a big (great) surprise for him. **3** 'Is that right (correct/the right change)?' said the salesman, after the man had paid for the present. 'Yes, that's fine (perfectly correct),' he replied. **4** The waiter became highly suspicious and thought that the man was a dangerous terrorist. **5** He thought (considered) for a moment what he should (ought to) do. **6** There was (existed) only one possibility – he had to inform the police immediately. **7** He knew that he could always rely on the police and was relieved when he caught sight of them opposite the restaurant. **8** 'Well I never,' said one of the policemen when he saw the boy, who was dressed up as a cowboy, playing with the rifle.

7 Pilze zum Mittagessen (p. 67)

A 1 (Sie wohnten) in einer schönen Hütte am Rande eines Waldes. **2** Sie hatten eben (gerade) gefrühstückt. **3** Sie sammelten sie. **4** Er öffnete eine Flasche Wein (Er machte den Wein auf). **5** Er brachte sie) zum Krankenhaus. **6** (Sie mußten die Nacht dort verbringen), weil sie zu krank waren, nach Hause zu fahren (weil sie krank waren).

B 1 Letzten August verbrachte Rainer eine Woche mit seiner Verlobten und zwei Freunden auf dem Lande. **2** Die gemütliche Hütte war in der Nähe eines großen Waldes. **3** ,Wollen wir einen Spaziergang im Wald machen (Wollen wir im Wald spazierengehen?' schlug Rainer nach dem Frühstück vor. **4** Sie sammelten die Pilze, die unter der großen Eiche wuchsen. **5** Gisela ging in die Küche, um die Kartoffeln zu schälen. **6** Nachdem Rainer die Pilze gewaschen hatte, deckte Peter den Tisch im Eßzimmer. **7** Sie saßen am Tisch, genossen gerade das Essen und tranken den Wein, den Rainer geöffnet hatte. **8** Nach dem Mittagessen begannen (sie) alle, sich krank zu fühlen. **9** Es gelang ihm, das Krankenhaus anzurufen (mit dem Krankenhaus zu telefonieren). **10** Der Krankenwagen fuhr sie zum Krankenhaus, wo sie die Nacht verbringen mußten (. . .wo sie über Nacht bleiben mußten).

C 1 'I like it here,' said Gisela. 'The cottage is in such a marvellous position, isn't it, so close to the forest.' **2** 'Shall we go for a walk after breakfast or do you prefer to do some shopping?' asked Helga. **3** 'Just look at those lovely mushrooms growing over there.' **4** 'I wonder if they are poisonous,' Gisela asked her fiancé. **5** 'Not at all. You don't need to worry,' answered Rainer. **6** It was bad luck that he had been wrong. **7** The doctor insisted that they couldn't go home straight away and that they had to spend the night in hospital. **8** They ought not to have eaten (shouldn't have eaten) the mushrooms.

8 Die Geburtstagsparty (p. 69)

A 1 (Er wurde) am dritten Mai (sieben Jahre alt). **2** Der Briefträger (brachte sie ihm). **3** Er putzte sich die Zähne. **4** Er zog ihn sofort. **5** (Er dankte ihnen), als (nachdem) sie ihm ihre Karten und Geschenke gegeben hatten.

B 1 Karl war aufgeregt, weil es sein Geburtstag war (weil er Geburtstag hatte). **2** Er hoffte, daß der Briefträger ihm einige Karten und Päckchen bringen würde. **3** Er wollte das neue Fahrrad ausprobieren, das seine Eltern ihm zum Geburtstag geschenkt (gegeben) hatten. **4** Nach dem Frühstück ging er nach oben, damit er sich die Zähne putzen konnte. **5** Leider mußte er zum Zahnarzt gehen, weil er Zahnschmerzen hatte. **6** Er fühlte sich krank, als der Zahnarzt seinen schlechten Zahn gezogen hatte. **7** Anstatt sich auf seine Party zu freuen, fühlte er sich elend. **8** Er dankte seinen Freunden (Er bedankte sich bei seinen Freunden) für die Ge-

schenke, die sie ihm gegeben (geschenkt) hatten. 9 Er wollte nichts
essen. 10 Anstatt mit seinen Freunden zu spielen, mußte der arme
Karl ruhig (still) in einem Sessel sitzen.
C 1 Karl didn't know at all in advance what he was to get (receive)
for his birthday. 2 He had been looking forward to his party for
days. 3 'Just look, Mum, what the postman has brought me,' he
said excitedly. 4 'Does your tooth really hurt?' his mother asked. 5
'We really must go to the dentist's,' she said. 'Do we have to?'
replied little Karl sadly. 6 'We are really sorry that you are not very
well,' they said. 7 He should have tried (ought to have tried) to
drink a glass of orange juice. 8 It was a pity, that he could neither
drink nor eat (that he wasn't allowed to either drink or eat).

9 Das Horoskop (p. 71)

A 1 (Sie wollte sie darein stellen), nachdem sie sie abgewaschen
hatte. 2 (Sie ließ sie fallen), weil sie ausrutschte. 3 Sie war (draußen)
im Garten. 4 (Sie mußte sie ins Haus zurücktragen), weil es zu
regnen begann (weil es regnete). 5 (Sie hätte es wohl nicht ver-
brannt), wenn ihre Freundin nicht angerufen hätte (wenn sie nicht
so lange mit ihrer Freundin geplaudert hätte).
B 1 Frau Mainzer nahm die Zeitung, um ihr Horoskop zu lesen.
2 Nachdem sie gelesen hatte, daß ihr Tag erfolgreich sein sollte,
begann sie ihre Hausarbeit. 3 Sie ließ die Teller fallen, die sie gerade
in den Schrank stellen wollte, weil sie ausrutschte. 4 Sie mußte die
Teller auffegen, die sie gerade zerbrochen hatte. 5 Sie nahm die
saubere Wäsche aus der Waschmaschine und hängte sie auf die
Leine. 6 Sie ärgerte sich, als es zu regnen anfing, da sie die
Wäsche, die auf der Leine hing, wieder ins Haus bringen mußte.
7 Gerade als sie den Tisch decken wollte, läutete (klingelte) das
Telefon im Flur. 8 Sie plauderte eine dreiviertel Stunde lang mit
der Freundin, die sie angerufen hatte. 9 Sobald sie roch, daß etwas
angebrannt war, stürzte sie aus dem Flur, um zu sehen, was los
war. 10 Sie hoffte, daß der nächste Tag besser für sie sein würde.
C 1 She thumbed through the newspaper and when she found the
(her) horoscope, she started to read it eagerly. 2 She had believed
in the stars for years. 3 'I can't sit around all day long, can I?' she
thought to herself. 4 She had just set to work (She had just started
work) when she suddenly slipped and dropped the crockery that
she had just washed up. 5 'Oh, good heavens,' she said to herself,
'Now it's starting to rain.' 6 'But now I really must go,' she said to
her friend. 'I think there's something burning in the kitchen.' 7 'I'll
call (phone) you next week. Cheerio.' 8 In the evening she told her
husband everything that had happened during the day.

10 Die verpaßte Fähre (p. 73)

A 1 Die deutschen Freunde (Deutsche Freunde) der Familie Robinson wohnten dort. **2** Sie konnten sich rechtzeitig (früh) auf den
Weg (nach Dover) machen. **3** (Sie wollten dann da sein), weil sie
die Fähre (die um 12.00 Uhr abfahren sollte) nicht verpassen wollten. **4** Sie mußten anhalten und anderthalb Stunden an der Unglücksstelle warten. **5** (Sie wären rechtzeitig angekommen), wenn
es keinen Unfall gegeben hätte.

B 1 Letzten Sommer fuhr die Familie Robinson nach Bonn, um
ihre deutschen Freunde zu besuchen. **2** Da sie sich früh am Morgen
auf den Weg machen mußten, beluden sie das Auto (den Wagen)
am Vorabend (am Abend vorher). **3** Sie wollten bis ein Uhr (bis
eins) in Dover sein. **4** Sie wollten die Fähre nicht verpassen, die
um zwei Uhr (um 14.00 Uhr) abfahren sollte. **5** Plötzlich mußte
Mr (Herr) Robinson anhalten, weil es einen schweren Unfall gegeben hatte (weil ein schwerer Unfall passiert war). **6** Sie konnten
einen Krankenwagen und einen Abschleppwagen in der Ferne sehen. **7** Sie mußten etwa anderthalb (eineinhalb) Stunden warten,
bevor sie ihre Fahrt fortsetzen konnten (bevor sie weiterfahren
konnten). **8** Der Unfall war etwa dreißig Kilometer (30 km) von
Dover entfernt passiert (geschehen); **9** Als sie in Dover ankamen,
war die Fähre schon abgefahren. **10** Sie sprachen (unterhielten
sich) über den Unfall, während sie auf die nächste Fähre
warteten.

C 1 'You ought to go to bed straight away,' said Mr Robinson to
his children. 'We've got (We have) a long day ahead of us tomorrow.' **2** 'For God's sake (For Heaven's sake) what's happened there?'
said Mrs (Frau) Robinson to her husband. **3** 'There must have been
a serious accident,' he replied. **4** 'I hope nobody is badly hurt
(injured).' **5** 'We shall certainly have to wait (for) a long time,' he
added. **6** 'We should have (ought to have) set off earlier, shouldn't
we?' he said sadly. **7** 'We won't manage it now (We can't do it
now). The ferry will certainly already have gone (left/departed)
when we arrive in Dover.' **8** Mrs Robinson thought (was of the
opinion) that they should (ought to) ring (phone) to let their friends
know that they would be arriving (would arrive) later.

11 Ein Unfall beim Schlittschuhlaufen (p. 75)

A 1 Er brachte seinen Schlitten und seine Schlittschuhe mit. **2** (Sie
gingen dorthin), um einen Schneemann zu bauen (weil sie einen
Schneemann bauen wollten/damit sie einen Schneemann bauen
konnten). **3** (Sie wollten) auf einem kleinen (zugefrorenen) See

(Schlittschuh laufen). **4** (Er wäre nicht ins Wasser gefallen), wenn das Eis nicht gebrochen wäre (. . .wäre das Eis nicht gebrochen). **5** (Er lief dorthin), nachdem er gesehen hatte, was passiert (geschehen) war (nachdem er gesehen hatte, daß Achim ins Wasser gefallen war). **6** (Er zog ihn) mit einem Seil (daraus) (mit dem Seil, das er aus dem Kofferraum seines Wagens geholt hatte).

B 1 Dieter freute sich, als er sah, daß es die ganze Nacht hindurch geschneit hatte. **2** Achim holte seine Schlittschuhe aus seinem Schlafzimmer und seinen Schlitten aus dem Schuppen. **3** Sie gingen in den Garten, um einen großen Schneemann zu bauen. **4** Sie setzten sich auf den Schlitten, damit sie den Hügel hinunterrodeln konnten. **5** Sie zogen ihre Schlittschuhe an und gingen auf das Eis. **6** Es machte Spaß, auf dem zugefrorenen See Schlittschuh zu laufen. **7** Plötzlich sah Dieter den armen Achim ins eisige Wasser fallen. **8** Zum Glück (Glücklicherweise) sah ein Mann, was geschehen (passiert) war. **9** Er zog ihn mit dem Seil, das im Kofferraum seines Autos (Wagens) gewesen war, aus dem Wasser. **10** Achim war sehr erleichtert und dankte dem Mann (bedankte sich bei dem Mann).

C 1 'Just look at the snow, Mum! Can Achim come round to our house?' **2** 'Let's build a snowman,' he suggested. **3** Dieter disappeared into the house and after a moment returned with a carrot for the (his) nose and two buttons for the (his) eyes. **4** They put a hat on his head and tied a scarf around his neck. **5** 'Be careful and don't get up to any nonsense (don't do anything stupid),' said the mother before the boys set off. **6** 'Keep calm,' the man called (shouted) to poor Achim. 'I'll throw you the rope.' **7** 'Oh, thank God (thank Heavens),' sighed Achim. 'I would (certainly) have drowned for sure (certain) without your help.' **8** The man looked at the shivering boy and his friend. 'Come (on). 'I'll take you home otherwise (or) you'll catch cold!'

12 Der neue Couchtisch (p. 77)

A 1 Er wollte ihn nach Hause bringen und ihn seinen Eltern als Geschenk geben (Er wollte ihn seinen Eltern schenken). **2** Er wartete auf den Bus. **3** (Ich weiß das), weil er (der Fahrer) Uwe (ihm) nicht erlaubte, mit dem Tisch in den Bus einzusteigen. **4** Er mußte ihn nach Hause tragen. **5** (Er setzte sich darauf), nachdem er oben angekommen war, weil er sich sehr müde fühlte.

B 1 Uwe wollte seinen Eltern den Couchtisch schenken (geben), den er in der Schule gebastelt (gemacht) hatte. **2** Er war sehr stolz auf seinen Couchtisch. **3** Letzten Montag holte er ihn aus dem Werkraum. **4** Da er seine Eltern überraschen wollte, beschloß er den Tisch nach Hause zu tragen. **5** Er durfte nicht mit dem Tisch in den Bus einsteigen. **6** Er war böse auf den Fahrer. **7** Nachdem er den steilen Hügel hinaufgegangen war, setzte er sich auf den Couchtisch, weil er erschöpft war (weil er sich müde fühlte). **8** Wenn er sich nicht auf den Tisch gesetzt hätte (Hätte er sich nicht auf den Tisch gesetzt), (dann) wäre er nicht zusammengebrochen. **9** Er hätte weinen können. **10** Er hoffte, daß er den Tisch reparieren könnte (reparieren können würde).

C 1 'The table looks really good,' said the teacher. 'Your parents will certainly be pleased with it.' **2** I'm sorry,' said the driver, 'You can't get on with that thing there.' **3** 'He could have been more friendly,' though Uwe. **4** The further he walked (went), the heavier the table seemed to get (become). **5** Perhaps Uwe ought to have (should have) asked his teacher to drive (take) him home with the (his) table. **6** He had already covered a good distance (He already had a good distance behind him) when he decided to rest a moment (a while). **7** 'Oh, blast,' he cursed. 'I shouldn't have done that.' **8** 'It doesn't matter,' said his parents, when they saw the collapsed table. 'You'll be able to repair it for sure (We are sure, you'll be able to repair it).'

13 Ein Zufall (p. 79)

A 1 Sie waren die zwei (beiden) Kinder von Herrn und Frau Gauglitz. **2** Sie hatten Geld aus ihren Spardosen (heraus)genommen. **3** Es war in den (ihren) Spardosen (gewesen) (die in ihren Schlafzimmern waren). **4** (Sie gingen dorthin), nachdem sie den Pullover (für ihre Mutter) gekauft hatten. **5** Er mußte zum Geschäft zurückgehen und den Pullover gegen eine Handtasche umtauschen.

B 1 Herr Gauglitz wohnte mit seiner Frau und seinen zwei (beiden) Kindern in einem kleinen Einfamilienhaus. **2** Die Kinder wollten ihrer Mutter Geschenke kaufen, weil am Freitag ihr Geburtstag war (weil sie am Freitag Geburtstag hatte). **3** Anna nahm Geld aus der Spardose, die auf dem Toilettentisch in ihrem Schlafzimmer stand. **4** Ihr Bruder ging in sein Schlafzimmer, um Geld zu holen. **5** Nachdem sie ihrer Mutter einen neuen Pullover in einem Warenhaus gekauft hatten, gingen sie zur Blumenhandlung (zum Blumenhändler), um ihr ein paar Blumen zu kaufen. **6** Herr Gauglitz wußte nicht, was seine Kinder gekauft hatten. **7** Am nächsten Tag mußte Herr Gauglitz mit dem Pullover zum Geschäft zurückgehen, wo er ihn gegen eine Handtasche umtauschte. **8** Als er wieder zu Hause war, gab er sie seiner Frau. **9** Zum Glück (Glücklicherweise) gefiel sie ihr. **10** Jetzt (Nun) hatte sie eine schöne neue

Handtasche, einen neuen roten Pullover und ein paar schöne Blumen.
C 1 'Do you know what mum would like (wants) for her birthday?' Bernd asked his sister suddenly. 2 'Not really,' she replied. 'Let's go into town after breakfast and buy her something.' 3 They were able to (could) do that because they had the day off school. 4 They fetched their money and hurried to the bus stop as they lived a fairly long way away (a fair distance) from the town centre. 5 When they were in a large department store, Anna suddenly remembered the nice pullover that her mother had seen recently and which she had liked. 6 'Shall we buy it?' asked Bernd. 'I think so. It's really good value,' answered Anna. 7 Their father was completely perplexed when he saw what the (his) children had given their mother. 8 Frau Gauglitz smiled at her husband. 'It doesn't matter, dear. You can change it tomorrow. Besides, I would like (love) (to have) a new handbag.'

14 Der Kinobesuch (p. 81)
A 1 (Es klingelte) am Nachmittag, während Rita oben in ihrem (Schlaf-) Zimmer saß, Schallplatten hörte und eine Illustrierte las. 2 Sie wollten ins Kino gehen. 3 Sie hatte eben (gerade) Abendbrot gegessen (Sie hatte eben (gerade) (zu) Abend gegessen). 4 (Sie fuhr) mit dem Bus (dorthin). 5 (Sie fühlte sich) unruhig und verlegen), weil Robert nicht kam. 6 (Sie wäre nicht gleich nach Hause gefahren), wenn Robert gekommen wäre.
B 1 Nach dem Mittagessen ging Rita nach oben in ihr (Schlaf) Zimmer. 2 Sie wollte die Platte hören, die sie am Vormittag gekauft hatte. 3 Sie hatte sich gerade hingesetzt, um ihre Illustrierte zu lesen, als das Telefon im Flur läutete (klingelte). 4 Sie freute sich (Sie war froh/glücklich), als Robert sie einlud, ins Kino zu gehen, da sie ihn sehr gern hatte (mochte). 5 Sie zog das neue Kleid an, das sie zu ihrem Geburtstag bekommen hatte. 6 Als sie am Kino ankam, war Robert nicht da. 7 Je länger sie wartete, desto (umso) verlegener fühlte sie sich (wurde sie). 8 Nach einer halben Stunde beschloß sie, nach Hause zu fahren. 9 Sie war sehr böse auf ihren Freund. 10 Sie erzählte (sagte) ihrer Mutter, was geschehen war.
C 1 'Rita,' her mother called, 'Turn the (your) record player down, please! Do you always have to play your records so loud(ly)?' 2 'Would you like to go to the cinema (the pictures) tonight?' he asked. 'I would love to,' she replied. 3 'Will Robert see (take) you home straight after the film?' her mother asked. 'Yes, of course, Mum.' 4 'The dress suits you well. You look really nice,' she said.

5 'Bye, Mum. I must hurry,' she called, when (as) she shut the front door. **6** She had the feeling that the other people were looking at her in a funny (strange) way, but that wasn't (really) true (the case). **7** Although she would have liked to have seen the film, she had no wish (desire) at all to go there alone. **8** Robert phoned later to apologize to her.

15 Ein Brand (p. 83)

A 1 (Sie fand) im Winter (statt). **2** Er sollte seine Frau von dem Haus ihrer Freundin abholen. **3** (Es wäre nicht geschehen), wenn Herr Krause die Lampe auf seinem Schreibtisch ausgemacht hätte (wenn die Katze die Lampe nicht umgestoßen hätte). **4** (Er rief sie an), als (sobald) er den Rauch sah/als (sobald) er sah, daß es bei Krauses brannte. **5** Einer der Feuerwehrleute (rettete sie). **6** (Sie waren entsetzt), weil ihr Haus gebrannt hatte (wegen des Brandes) (über den Brand).

B 1 Herr Krause war Geschäftsmann. **2** Letzten Dienstagabend hatte er sich gerade an seinen Schreibtisch gesetzt, als das Telefon klingelte (läutete). **3** Seine Frau bat ihn, sie abzuholen. **4** Sie war bei einer Freundin. **5** Leider (unglücklicherweise) machte er die Lampe nicht aus. **6** Nachdem die Katze auf den Schreibtisch gesprungen war und die Lampe umgestoßen hatte, begannen die Papiere zu brennen. **7** Der Nachbar rief die Feuerwehr an (telefonierte mit der Feuerwehr), sofort als (sobald) er den Rauch sah (erblickte). **8** Der Brand war bald unter Kontrolle. **9** Herr Krause sah einen der Feuerwehrleute (Feuerwehrmänner) mit der Katze. **10** Herr Krause hätte die Lampe ausmachen sollen.

C 1 Last Tuesday evening Herr Krause had to work especially (particularly) hard, for (as) he had to fly to Hamburg the following morning on business. **2** He had already been working for two and a half hours when his wife phoned (rang). **3** She said (that) she was at her friend's house and she wanted to know if he could fetch her. **4** 'Yes, I'll come straight away (immediately),' he said. **5** He was, however, a little (slightly) annoyed, because he was busy writing an important letter. **6** As he was still thinking about the letter, he left his study without turning the lamp off. **7** 'Quickly. Just look over there, Ilse!' the neighbour said to his wife. 'Is the Krause's house on fire?' **8** 'You're right. Phone the fire-brigade quickly!'

16 Von der Flut eingeholt (p. 85)

A 1 Es ist ein angenehmer Badeort. **2** Sie hätten in die Schule
gehen sollen. **3** (Sie wären argwöhnisch gewesen), wenn die zwei
Jungen (Brüder) das Haus nicht zur gewöhnlichen Zeit verlassen
hätten (hätten die Jungen. . .verlassen). **4** (Sie standen) oben auf
einigen Felsen. **5** Sie mußten ein Seil herablassen.

B 1 Letzten Mittwoch schwänzten Karl und Uwe die Schule. **2** Es
war ein herrlicher Tag, und sie beschlossen zum Strand zu gehen
(fahren). **3** Ihre Eltern waren gar nicht argwöhnisch (mißtrauisch),
da die Jungen das Haus zur gewöhnlichen Zeit verließen. **4** Es war
viel schöner am Strand als in der Schule; Karl schwamm (badete)
im warmen Meer (in der warmen See), während Uwe sich neben
einigen Felsen sonnte. **5** Danach spielten sie mit dem Volleyball,
den sie mitgebracht hatten. **6** Dann (Anschließend) schlug Karl vor,
daß sie auf die Felsen klettern sollten. **7** Sie hatten nicht bemerkt,
daß die Flut sehr schnell hereingekommen war. **8** Zuerst wußten
sie nicht, was sie machen sollten. **9** Nachdem das junge Paar ihre
Rufe (Schreie) gehört hatte, verständigte es die Küstenwacht. **10**
Die Jungen waren erleichtert, als sie den Hubschrauber sahen, der
sie retten sollte.

C 1 'I don't want to go to school at all today,' said Karl. **2** 'Nor
me,' replied Uwe. 'What about skipping school (playing truant/
hookey)?' **3** 'Hurry up, boys, otherwise (or) you'll miss the school
bus!' their mother called. **4** It was the first time that the two boys
had deceived their parents in this way. **5** 'It's half past ten, now,'
said Karl. 'If I had been at school, then I would have been having
history now.' 'And me geography,' added his younger brother. **6**
Suddenly Uwe caught sight of two people in the distance. **7** 'Just
look over there (Look over there, won't you)' he shouted. Take
your shirt off quickly and wave it. Perhaps, they'll see us.' **8**
Although the boys were afraid of what their parents would say, they
enjoyed the flight in the helicopter a lot.

17 In der Jugendherberge (p. 87)

A 1 (Ich glaube), sie hatten sie in ihren Rucksäcken (daß sie sie in
ihren Rucksäcken hatten). **2** Sie würden sie anziehen. **3** Er mußte
sie (nach oben) zum zweiten Stock und in den Schlafsaal führen.
4 Sie sahen sich die Stadt an. **5** Sie halfen ihr, den Tagesraum zu
putzen und aufzuräumen.

B 1 Letztes Wochenende wanderte Georg mit seinem Freund Peter
nach Goslar. **2** Sie zogen ihre festesten Schuhe an und machten sich
mit den Rucksäcken (auf dem Rücken) auf den Weg. **3** Sie hatten

keine Schlafsäcke mit, da sie sie in der Jugendherberge leihen wollten. **4** Wenn es geregnet hätte (Hätte es geregnet), (dann) hätten sie ihre Anoraks angezogen (würden sie ihre Anoraks angezogen haben). **5** Nachdem sie drei Stunden (lang) gewandert waren, setzten sie sich ins Gras (auf eine Wiese), um zu essen. **6** Sie hatten dem Herbergsvater im voraus geschrieben, um zwei Betten zu reservieren. **7** Nachdem der Herbergsvater ihnen ihren Schlafsaal gezeigt hatte, sahen sie sich die Stadt an. **8** Nach dem Abendessen (Abendbrot) gingen sie in den Spielraum, um Tischtennis zu spielen. **9** Die anderen jungen Leute in der Jugendherberge waren sehr freundlich. **10** Während Peter der Herbergsmutter half, den Spielraum zu putzen (sauber zu machen), half Georg dem Herbergsvater, den Tagesraum aufzuräumen.

C 1 'Shall we stop now (Shall we have a break now)?' asked Georg breathlessly. 'No, not yet. I'd rather we covered a few more kilometres.' **2** 'Isn't it marvellous up here on the hill? Just look at the (that) scenery!' said Peter. **3** 'I can't go on (I can't go any further).' said Georg. 'I must rest a moment.' **4** 'I think we have taken a wrong turning (I think we've gone wrong),' said Peter. 'We should have (ought to have) looked at the map earlier.' **5** They turned left and walked uphill through a dense forest (wood). **6** Both the boys (The two boys) preferred to have their supper (evening meal) in the youth hostel instead of going into the snack bar. **7** They fell asleep straight away (immediately) as they were so tired. **8** If the weather had been bad, (then) they would probably have gone (travelled) home by train.

18 Auf dem Campingplatz (p. 89)

A 1 Sie wollten es ausprobieren. **2** Der Bauer (zeigte ihnen, wo sie es aufbauen konnten). **3** Sie aßen ihr Abendbrot (Sie aßen zu Abend.) **4** (Sie fühlten) den Regen (dadurch tropfen). **5** (Sie liefen dahin), nachdem sie ihre Sachen ins Auto gebracht hatten. **6** (Er brachte es dahin), um sich bei dem Verkäufer zu beschweren (weil er sich bei dem Verkäufer beschweren wollte).

B 1 Letzten Montag kehrte Herr Ahrens mit einem neuen Zelt nach Hause zurück. **2** Da seine Familie nie zuvor gezeltet hatte, wollten sie das neue Zelt so bald wie möglich ausprobieren. **3** Letzten Freitagabend erreichten sie den Campingplatz anderthalb Stunden, nachdem sie sich auf den Weg gemacht hatten. **4** Leider war es kein moderner Campingplatz. **5** Nachdem sie das Zelt aufgebaut hatten, aßen sie Abendbrot in dem Zelt, da der Himmel bewölkt war. **6** Sie hatten sich eben (gerade) in ihre Schlafsäcke gelegt, als es zu regnen begann. **7** Plötzlich fühlten sie den Regen durch das Zelt tropfen. **8** Da sie sehr naß wurden, beschlossen sie, zum Bauernhof zu laufen, nachdem sie ihre Sachen ins Auto gebracht hatten. **9** Der freundliche Bauer zeigte ihnen seine Scheune, wo sie übernachten konnten. **10** Am folgenden Montag war Herr Ahrens sehr böse, als er ins Geschäft ging, um sich bei dem Verkäufer zu beschweren.

C 1 'Come with me, children, I've got something interesting for you in the boot,' said Herr Ahrens, when he came home. **2** The two children couldn't imagine at all what their father had bought that morning. **3** As soon as the children saw the tent, they wanted to put it up in the garden straight away. **4** They were only allowed to do that, however, after supper (They could only do that. . .). **5** After the children had gone to bed, their parents looked at the map and decided to go to a camp site in the Black Forest at the weekend, where they could try out the tent properly. **6** Herr Ahrens insisted that the tent had to be waterproof as it was new, but in spite of that, the water dripped through. **7** 'We can't possibly stay in the tent,' said Frau Ahrens. 'Perhaps the farmer can put us up in the farmhouse.' **8** 'You shouldn't have sold me the (this) tent. It's not waterproof at all,' moaned Herr Ahrens.

19 Ein Unfall mit dem Fahrrad (p. 91)

A 1 (Sie wurde) von dem Autofahrer (aufgemacht). **2** Sie (es) fiel zum Boden und verlor das Bewußtsein. (Und sie brach sich das linke Bein). **3** (Er wäre nicht so schnell gekommen), wenn die Frau nicht gleich (sofort) das Krankenhaus angerufen hätte. **4** (Sie wurde) von ihren Eltern (besucht). **5** (Es wäre nicht passiert), wenn der Autofahrer die Autotür nicht aufgemacht hätte (. . .hätte der Autofahrer die Autotür nicht aufgemacht).

B 1 Das blaue Auto (Der blaue Wagen) fuhr die Straße entlang, und dann parkte der Fahrer es (ihn) neben dem kleinen Supermarkt. **2** Das kleine Mädchen war etwa hundert Meter von dem (vom) Supermarkt entfernt, als der Mann sein Auto (seinen Wagen) parkte. **3** Ohne das Mädchen zu sehen, machte der Fahrer die Autotür (die Wagentür) auf. **4** Gerade als der Fahrer aus seinem Auto (Wagen) aussteigen wollte, fuhr Heike gegen die Tür. **5** Nachdem der Fahrer aus dem Auto (Wagen) gesprungen war, sah er Heike auf dem Boden liegen. **6** Sobald die Frau den Unfall gesehen hatte, rief sie das Krankenhaus an (telefonierte sie mit dem Krankenhaus). **7** Zu ihrem großen Entsetzen erfuhren die Eltern des kleinen Mädchens, daß ihre Tochter verletzt war. **8** Glücklicherweise (Zum Glück) war sie wieder zu Bewußtsein gekommen, als sie im Krankenhaus ankamen. **9** Sie aß die Weintrauben, die ihre Eltern ihr gebracht hatten. **10** Sie mußte einige Tage im Krankenhaus bleiben.

C 1 'Oh, good Heavens, what have I done?' thought the motorist as he jumped out of his car. **2** He bent over (leaned over) the injured girl to find out whether she was still breathing. **3** He was afraid that he had killed her. **4** Soon the siren of the ambulance could be heard in the distance (Soon you (they/one) could hear. . .). **5** If the woman hadn't phoned the hospital straight away, the girl could have died. **6** The man was (felt) so sorry for the girl that he visited her daily in hospital. **7** Although she had a headache and looked very pale, Heike was very pleased when she saw her parents coming (walking) into the ward.

20 Der Totoschein (p. 93)

A 1 Er glaubte, daß er im Toto gewonnen hätte (hatte). (Er glaubte, er hätte (hatte) im Toto gewonnen.) **2** (Ich weiß das), weil er immer aufgeregter wurde, und weil er schließlich aufgesprungen war und geschrien hatte, ,,Wir haben gewonnen!'' (. . .und geschrien hatte, daß sie gewonnen hätten.) **3** Er hätte den Schein einwerfen sollen. **4** (Er war dorthin gegangen), weil er seinen Regenmantel hatte holen wollen (um seinen Regenmantel zu holen). **5** (Er hätte gewonnen), wenn Achim nicht vergessen hätte, (wenn Achim sich daran erinnert hätte/wenn Achim daran gedacht hätte) den Schein einzuwerfen.

B 1 Herr Merkl ging ins Wohnzimmer, um fernzusehen. **2** Er wollte die Fußballergebnisse hören. **3** Er hoffte, daß er im Toto gewonnen hatte. **4** Er wurde immer aufgeregter. **5** Achim, der seinem Vater gegenüber saß, errötete plötzlich. **6** Er hatte sich daran erinnert, daß er vergessen hatte, den Schein einzuwerfen. **7** Er war wegen des Regens nach Hause zurückgekehrt. **8** Nachdem er den (seinen) Regenmantel angezogen hatte, steckte er den Schein in die Tasche. **9** Wenn er nicht zur Bushaltestelle gelaufen wäre (Wäre er nicht zur Bushaltestelle gelaufen), (dann) hätte er den Bus verpaßt. **10** Er hätte nicht vergessen sollen, den Schein einzuwerfen!

C 1 Herr Merkl, who was sitting quietly in his armchair filling his pipe, turned to his son and said, 'Achim, turn the television up a little, please.' **2** The family had got used to Sunday afternoons. **3** It was the same every week. Herr Merkl just (simply) had to sit in front of the television (had to sit. . .at all costs) and hear (listen to) the football results. **4** He was always dreaming (He always used to dream) of the day when he would win the pools. 5 He knew exactly what he would do if he were rich. 6 He would go for a cruise around the world and visit exotic countries that up to that time had been mere names to him in the atlas. 7 The more excited his father became, the more embarrassed Achim got. 8 The following week his father would have to fill in a new coupon and try his luck again!

Translation from German

The master Shot (p. 100)

A few friends went hunting together. One of them was a painter, another a teacher, the third was a businessman. They were walking across meadows and fields. Suddenly the teacher stopped in front of a barn and pointed at the large door. Someone had drawn a stag on the door with chalk and someone had apparently been shooting at the stag. He had hit (it) right in the eye.

'A marvellous shot,' said the businessman. 'Right in the eye.'

'Who can that have been? Who can shoot as well (as that)?' the teacher wondered.

'The shot is mine,' said the painter.

The others laughed because they knew that he really couldn't shoot so well.

'You don't have to believe it,' he said, 'but the shot is really mine.'

Then he explained to them how he had done it: 'First I shot, then I drew the stag.'

Modern art (p. 101)

The first thing that Herr Hallfield saw when he came home from work was the picture for it was hanging on the wall opposite the front door. There, where the much smaller Alpine scene had always hung until now. While he was still staring at the picture, his wife came up to him smiling.

'Nice, isn't it? Do you like it?'

You could see clearly from his face that he found it anything but nice.

'Where did you get it from?' he asked.

'A present from my boss. For our silver wedding. Really nice of him, don't you think?'

'Except I'd like to know what the picture is actually about. Is it meant to be a sunset or a tomato on spinach. . .?'

'It's called Nymph in her Bath,' his wife interrupted him.

'You don't say!' he cried in astonishment. 'Can you see the nymph then?'

'Unfortunately I can't either, but my boss says the painter is a young artist of great talent.'

'Hm – I would prefer less talent and more nymph. Does it have to hang just here, then?'

'Yes, my dear, at least until tomorrow morning.'

'How come?' Herr Hallfeld looked at his wife questioningly. 'I've invited my boss and his wife to dinner. Then they ought to see how nicely their present suits our flat. Come on, get changed quickly. Meanwhile I'll make some coffee.'

And as she knew that he couldn't stand her boss, she hurried into the kitchen before he was able to react to her news. He cast another angry look at the picture and grumbled but then went upstairs into the bedroom.

Translation into German

1 (p. 104)

Um halb acht an diesem (*dem*) Abend stieg ein junger Mann aus dem Bus (aus), ging ins Hotel, setzte sich an einen Tisch und bat um eine Tasse Kaffee. Er wartete auf seine Freundin, die ihn dort um acht Uhr treffen sollte.

Nachdem er dort fast (beinahe), eine Stunde gesessen hatte, begann der junge Mann, sich Sorgen zu machen. Er stand auf, ging an die Tür und sah (blickte/schaute) auf die Straße hinaus. Dann ging er zu seinem Platz zurück.

Endlich ging er zu einer Telefonzelle hinüber, die sich in der Eingangshalle befand (die in der E. war), um die Familie des Mädchens anzurufen (um mit der F. des Mädchens zu telefonieren). Aber in *dem* (diesem) Augenblick eilte das Mädchen ins Hotel; sie sah erhitzt und aufgeregt aus. Der junge Mann lief auf sie zu.

„Warum kommst du so spät, Liebling?" rief er. „Was ist (dir) passiert?"

„Zuerst habe ich den Bus verpaßt, dann wollte ich ein Taxi nehmen, aber sie waren alle besetzt. Endlich bekam ich eins (eines), aber es war so viel Verkehr auf den Straßen, daß wir wirklich nicht schnell genug fahren konnten."

„Macht nichts. Endlich bist du hier. Es tut mir leid, daß du eine so schlechte Fahrt gehabt hast," sagte der junge Mann. „Wollen wir ins Restaurant gehen? Du mußt schrecklich hungrig und durstig sein (Du mußt furchtbaren Hunger und Durst haben)! Bestellen wir doch etwas zu essen, und dann entscheiden wir (werden wir entscheiden), was wir nachher machen (werden)."

2 (p. 105)

Fräulein Renate Keller, die eben begonnen hatte, noch einen Brief auf der Maschine zu schreiben (zu tippen), sah auf, als die Tür des Büros sich langsam öffnete, und ein großer junger Mann eintrat.

„Entschuldigen Sie," sagte er höflich. „Ich möchte mit Herrn Hetherington sprechen, bitte."

Renate schüttelte den Kopf. „Ich fürchte; das ist leider ganz unmöglich," sagte sie. „Der Chef ist vor einer Weile weggegangen, um ein paar Kunden zu besuchen und wird erst um halb fünf zurück sein."

„Dann bleibe ich hier (. . .werde ich hier bleiben), bis er kommt, wenn Sie nichts dagegen haben (wenn Ihnen das nichts ausmacht). Heute nachmittag habe ich nichts Besonderes vor." Ohne auf eine Antwort zu warten, setzte sich der Fremde auf einen Stuhl am Fenster und nahm eine Zeitung aus der Tasche seines Regenmantels. Renate bemerkte jedoch, daß er in Wirklichkeit nicht las, sondern die Leute unten auf der Straße zu beobachten schien.

3 (p. 105)

Herr Tate, begleitet von seiner Frau, besuchte gestern abend ihren (gemeinsamen) Arzt, bevor es zu dunkel wurde; denn er war ein älterer Mann, und es war viel Verkehr. Der Arzt war nicht überrascht, sie zu sehen, denn der Ehemann hatte seit langem zu hart gearbeitet. Er war nicht genug spazierengegangen (Er hatte zu wenige Spaziergänge unternommen (gemacht)) und hatte zu viel von dem guten Essen gegessen, das seine Frau ihm gekocht hatte. Es war also leicht für ihn mit den beiden zu sprechen und ihnen gute Ratschläge (guten Rat) zu geben (und sie gut zu beraten), und er vergaß auch nicht eine Flasche der Medizin, die Herr Tate dreimal am Tag (ein-) nehmen sollte. „Machen Sie die Augen zu und stellen Sie sich vor, daß Sie Wein trinken," sagte er mit einem Lächeln, als sie hinausgingen. „Der Geschmack ist fast gleich (derselbe), und ich hoffe, Sie fühlen sich bald besser (daß Sie sich bald besser fühlen (werden)). Wenn Sie sich nach einer Woche noch nicht wohl fühlen, (dann) kommen Sie wieder zurück, oder rufen Sie mich vor halb zehn morgens (am Morgen) an!"

Reading Comprehension (Use of German)

News of examination success (p. 121)

1 (Sie war) von dem (vom) Supermarkt (gekommen). 2 (Sie war dorthin gegangen), um Lebensmittel zu kaufen (weil sie Lebensmittel kaufen wollte/mußte) (damit sie Lebensmittel kaufen konnte). 3 (Sie spielte sich) in der Küche (ab). 4 Sie packten die Lebensmittel aus. 5 (Sie hatten eben gehört), daß sie ihr Staatsexamen bestanden hatte. 6 (Sie hatte es (wohl/wahrscheinlich) in einem Brief/in einer Postkarte gelesen (durch einen Brief/eine Postkarte erfahren). 7 Sie wollte ihre Tochter umarmen. 8 Sie rollten überall hin, zum Beispiel unter den Küchenschrank und hinter den Gasherd.

The watch thieves (p. 121)

9 (Sie lagen versteckt) im hohen Gras. 10 Sie warteten auf die Diebe. 11 (Sie gingen) in eine Turmruine. 12 (Sie waren hierher gekommen), um einen Koffer zu holen (um die Uhren zu holen). 13 Sie hatten sie wohl gestohlen. 14 (Sie waren so erstaunt), weil sie nicht wußten, daß noch jemand da war (weil sie glaubten, daß sie allein waren). 15 Er wurde von dem Kommissar genommen. (Der Kommissar nahm ihn.)

Essays based on a picture series

1 Übung macht den Meister (p. 130)

Eines Tages während der Sommerferien beschlossen Paul und sein Freund Karl, einen Spaziergang am Fluß entlang zu machen. Plötzlich drehte sich Karl um und stieß Paul zum Spaß ins Wasser. Leider wußte Karl nicht, daß sein Freund nicht schwimmen konnte. Paul versuchte vergeblich, allein das Ufer zu erreichen, aber glücklicherweise gelang es Karl, ihn mit einem Rettungsring aus dem Wasser zu ziehen. Paul hatte wirklich Angst gehabt, und nachdem er nach Hause gekommen war, beschloß er, schwimmen zu lernen. Er ging regelmäßig ins Hallenbad und wurde ein sehr guter Schwimmer. Sein Lehrer war sehr stolz auf ihn. Bald begann er viele Wettschwimmen zu gewinnen. Auch konnte er gut tauchen, so daß er sogar die Schulmeisterschaft gewann. Er erhielt einen großen Pokal, und die ganze Schule klatschte ihm Beifall.

2 Ein zerstreutes junges Mädchen (p. 131)

Vor einigen Tagen stand Helga um sechs Uhr auf, weil sie früher als gewöhnlich im Büro sein mußte. Normalerweise fuhr sie mit dem Zug, aber heute beschloß sie, mit der Straßenbahn zu fahren. Als die Straßenbahn an der Haltestelle ankam, stieg sie ein. Leider beachtete sie die Nummer nicht, weil sie noch schläfrig war. Sie setzte sich und begann ein sehr interessantes Buch zu lesen. Zwanzig Minuten später schaute sie zum Fenster hinaus, und es wurde ihr klar, daß sie in der falschen Straßenbahn war. An der nächsten Haltestelle mußte sie aussteigen, und sie begann zu Fuß in Richtung Stadtmitte zurückzugehen. Zum Glück hielt eine Frau in einem kleinen Auto und fuhr sie freundlicherweise gleich zum Büro. Trotzdem kam sie eine halbe Stunde zu spät, und ihr Chef war sehr böse auf sie.

3 Episode im Zug (p. 132)

Eines schönen Sommertages mußte Herr Maier mit dem Zug zur Arbeit fahren, weil sein Wagen kaputt war. Während er auf dem Bahnsteig wartete, las er ein sehr lustiges Buch. Als der Zug ankam, stieg er ein und suchte sich einen Eckplatz. Bald danach setzte sich eine hübsche junge Frau ihm gegenüber. Fünf Minuten später begann er noch einmal über eine lustige Stelle in seinem Buch zu lachen. Leider dachte die Frau, daß herr Maier über sie lachte. Sie wurde so verlegen, daß sie endlich beschloß, in ein anderes Abteil zu gehen. Als sie aufstand, um zu gehen, war er sehr verblüfft. Er konnte nicht verstehen, warum die Frau ihn so böse angesehen hatte.

Answers to the questions on pictures (p. 154)

Bild A

1 Sie findet in einer Stadt/in einer Stadtmitte/in einem Dorf statt. 2 Der eine (Einer) ist Kellner, und der andere ist Straßenfeger. 3 Er hat ein Glas Wein auf den Tisch gestellt./Er hat einem Mann ein Glas Wein gebracht. 4 Er fegt sie mit einem großen Besen. 5 Sie sitzen auf Stühlen an Tischen vor einem Café. 6 Sie sind klein und rund. 7 Sie geht in einen Supermarkt. 8 Sie wird wohl einkaufen./ Sie wird wohl Lebensmittel kaufen. 9 Ich sehe einen Hund und eine Katze. 10 Er jagt die Katze./Er läuft der Katze hinterher. 11 Sie findet am Nachmittag statt. Ich weiß das, weil es fast halb drei ist./weil es fünf vor halb drei ist. 12 Er photographiert eine Frau./

Er nimmt ein Bild (ein Photo) von einer Frau auf./Er knipst eine
Frau. 13 Ich sehe ein Auto (einen Wagen) und ein Motorrad. 14
Man kommt zum Bahnhof. 15 Ich sehe (die) Berge.

Bild B

1 Sie findet in der Küche (eines Hauses) statt. 2 Es ist viertel vor
drei. 3 Er ißt zu Mittag (sein Mittagessen). 4 Nein, sie haben schon
gegessen. 5 Weil er spät nach Hause gekommen ist. 6 Sie schenkt
Kaffee ein. 7 Sie spült ab./Sie wäscht des Geschirr und das Besteck
ab. 8 Sie hilft ihrer Mutter./Sie trocknet das Geschirr und das
Besteck ab. 9 Es ist der vierzehnte Mai. 10 Sie hört Musik. 11 Sie
liegt (ist) unter dem Tisch, und sie schläft. 12 Sie stellt eine Tasse
in den Schrank. 13 Er sitzt auf seinem kleinen Dreirad (Fahrrad).
14 Er sitzt in einem Sessel im Wohnzimmer, er raucht Pfeife und
sieht fern. 15 Man bügelt Kleider.

Bild C

1 Sie findet auf einem Markt statt. 2 Sie verkauft Obst und Gemüse.
3 Sie unterhält sich mit einer Kundin./Sie lächelt./Sie wiegt Obst
(Äpfel vielleicht). 4 Äpfel, Apfelsinen, Pflaumen, Birnen, Bana-
nen, Kirschen und Weintrauben sind Obstsorten. Kartoffeln, Erbsen, Karotten (Mohrrüben), Kohl, Blumenkohl, Rosenkohl, grüne
Bohnen, Zwiebeln und Spinat sind Gemüsesorten. 5 Sie will eben
die Tauben (die Vögel jagen (fangen)./Sie will eben versuchen, eine
Taube (einen Vogel) zu fangen. 6 Sie hat schon Brot gekauft. 7 Es
ist viertel vor elf. 8 Er trägt einen Hut, ein kariertes Hemd und
einen Kittel. 9 Er verkauft Spielzeug/Spielwaren. 10 Er verkauft
Segelboote, Bälle, Lokomotive, Mäuse, Autos, Puppen usw. ...
11 Es zeigt auf eine Puppe. 12 Sie möchte die Puppe haben./Sie
möchte, daß ihre Mutter sie ihr kauft. 13 Man kann Zigaretten,
Zigarren, Pfeifen, Streichhölzer, Feuerzeuge, Aschenbecher usw.
kaufen. 14 Nein, er steigt gerade ein. 15 Er schiebt es wohl, weil
er auf dem Markt nicht fahren darf.

Bild D

1 Sie findet auf einem Campingplatz statt. 2 Ein Mann segelt, zwei
andere Männer rudern, und ein Mann schwimmt. 3 Er ist eben aus
dem Wasser gekommen. 4 Sie reibt einen Mann mit Sonnencreme
ein. 5 Sie macht das, damit der Mann vor der Sonne geschützt ist./
damit der Mann keinen Sonnenbrand bekommt. 6 Er will eben ins
Wasser/in den See springen. 7 Sie hat schon eine Postkarte/einen
Brief geschrieben. 8 Sie schreibt eine zweite Karte/einen zweiten

Brief. **9** Er liest (die/eine) Zeitung und raucht Pfeife, **10** Er trägt sie wohl, damit er besser sehen (lesen) kann. **11** Sie wohnen in Zelten und in Wohnwagen. **12** Es ist zwei Uhr. **13** Er verkauft wohl andere Getränke und Postkarten. **14** Sie winken den Jungen im Ruderboot zu. **15** Das Wetter ist sonnig/herrlich/schön. Ich weiß das, weil viele Leute Badekleidung (Bikinis, Badehosen, Badeanzüge) tragen (anhaben).

Sample dialogue for the role-playing test cards

1 At the dry-cleaner's (p. 166)

Bedienung: Guten Tag. Womit kann ich dienen?

Kundin: Guten Tag. Ich habe einen Rock, einen Mantel und ein Kleid zum Reinigen mitgebracht. Leider ist hier ein Ölfleck auf dem Ärmel des Kleides.

Bedienung: Was für ein Ölfleck ist es denn?

Kundin: Speiseöl, glaub' ich.

Bedienung: Gut. Wahrscheinlich können wir ihn entfernen.

Kundin: Übrigens hat meine Mutter gestern einen Anzug hier abgeholt, aber als sie zu Hause ankam, bemerkte sie, daß er nicht besonders sauber war.

Bedienung: Entschuldigen Sie bitte vielmals. Wir werden ihn natürlich noch einmal reinigen. Wenn Sie den Anzug wieder hierherbringen, dann bringen Sie bitte den Belegzettel mit!

Kundin: Ja, sicher. Bis wann sind die Kleider fertig?

Bedienung: Heute ist Montag. Ihre Kleider sind dann bis Donnerstag fertig.

Kundin: Danke. Übrigens, wann machen Sie zu?

Bedienung: Um sechs. Wir sind auch zwischen eins und zwei geschlossen.

Kundin: Wieviel wird es ungefähr kosten?

Bedienung: Ungefähr 15,00 DM.

Kundin: Schön. Haben Sie recht vielen Dank. Auf Wiedersehen.

Bedienung: Auf Wiedersehen.

2 At a taxi rank (p. 167)

Fahrgast: Guten Tag, sind Sie frei?

Taxifahrer: Ja, wohin kann ich Sie mitnehmen?

Fahrgast: Zum Flughafen, bitte.

Taxifahrer: Das geht.

Fahrgast: Ich muß unbedingt um 16.30 Uhr da sein. Können Sie das schaffen?

Taxifahrer: Ja, keine Sorge; das läßt sich machen.

Fahrgast: Gut, wenn Sie das schaffen, dann bekommen Sie ein gutes Trinkgeld.

Taxifahrer: Ja, ich werde mir Mühe geben. . .Entschuldigen Sie, darf ich fragen, wohin Sie fliegen?

Fahrgast: Nach Hamburg.

Taxifahrer: Geschäftlich, oder machen Sie eine Urlaubsreise?

Fahrgast: Geschäftlich.

Taxifahrer: Wie lange wollen Sie da bleiben?

Fahrgast: Ich muß da heute übernachten, aber morgen fliege ich zurück. Übrigens, fahren Sie oft zum Flughafen?

Taxifahrer: Ja, das ist verschieden. Vielleicht vier- oder fünfmal die Woche.

Fahrgast: Ist hier immer so viel Verkehr?

Taxifahrer: Ja, immer zu dieser Zeit, aber machen Sie sich keine Sorgen. Wir schaffen es schon!

Strong and 'mixed' verbs

(a) For compounds (e.g. *fernsehen, einsteigen, aufstehen*) see the simple forms *sehen, steigen* and *stehen*.

(b) *indicates that the verb is conjugated with *sein*.

Infinitive	3rd person sing. present	3rd person sing. imperfect.	past participle	meaning
befehlen	befiehlt	befahl	befohlen	*to command*
beginnen	beginnt	begann	begonnen	*to begin*
beißen	beißt	biß	gebissen	*to bite*
bergen	birgt	barg	geborgen	*to hide*
biegen	biegt	bog	gebogen	*to bend*
bieten	bietet	bot	geboten	*to offer*
binden	bindet	band	gebunden	*to tie*
bitten	bittet	bat	gebeten	*to ask/request*
bleiben	bleibt	blieb	*geblieben	*to stay/remain*
braten	brät	briet	gebraten	*to roast*
brechen	bricht	brach	gebrochen	*to break*
brennen	brennt	brannte	gebrannt	*to burn*
bringen	bringt	brachte	gebracht	*to bring*
denken	denkt	dachte	gedacht	*to think*
dreschen	drischt	drosch	gedroschen	*to thresh*
dringen	dringt	drang	gedrungen	*to press*
dürfen	darf	durfte	gedurft	*to be allowed*
empfehlen	empfiehlt	empfahl	empfohlen	*to recommend*
erschrecken	erschrickt	erschrak	erschrocken	*to be scared*
essen	ißt	aß	gegessen	*to eat*

fahren	fährt	fuhr	*gefahren	*to go (by vehilce) to drive* (+ haben)
fallen	fällt	fiel	*gefallen	*to fall*
fangen	fängt	fing	gefangen	*to catch*
finden	findet	fand	gefunden	*to find*
fliegen	fliegt	flog	*geflogen	*to fly*
fließen	fließt	floß	*geflossen	*to flow*
fressen	frißt	fraß	gefressen	*to eat (of animals)*
frieren	friert	fror	*gefroren	*to freeze (also + haben)*
geben	gibt	gab	gegeben	*to give*
gehen	geht	ging	*gegangen	*to go*
gelingen	gelingt	gelang	*gelungen	*to succeed (impers.)*
genießen	genießt	genoß	genossen	*to enjoy*
geschehen	geschieht	geschah	*geschehen	*to happen (impers.)*
gewinnen	gewinnt	gewann	gewonnen	*to win*
gießen	gießt	goß	gegossen	*to pour*
graben	gräbt	grub	gegraben	*to dig*
greifen	greift	griff	gegriffen	*to grasp*
haben	hat	hatte	gehabt	*to have*
halten	hält	hielt	*gehalten	*to stop, to hold* (+ haben)
hängen	hängt	hing	gehangen	*to hang*
heben	hebt	hob	gehoben	*to lift*
heißen	heißt	hieß	geheißen	*to be called*
helfen	hilft	half	geholfen	*to help*
kennen	kennt	kannte	gekannt	*to know*
kommen	kommt	kam	*gekommen	*to come*
können	kann	konnte	gekonnt	*to be able*
kriechen	kriecht	kroch	*gekrochen	*to crawl*
laden	lädt	lud	geladen	*to load*
lassen	läßt	ließ	gelassen	*to let/leave*
laufen	läuft	lief	*gelaufen	*tc run*
leiden	leidet	litt	gelitten	*to suffer*
leihen	leiht	lieh	geliehen	*to lend*
lesen	liest	las	gelesen	*to read*
liegen	liegt	lag	gelegen	*to lie/be situated*
meiden	meidet	mied	gemieden	*to avoid*
messen	mißt	maß	gemessen	*to measure*
mögen	mag	mochte	gemocht	*to like*
müssen	muß	mußte	gemußt	*to have to/ must*

nehmen	nimmt	nahm	genommen	*to take*
nennen	nennt	nannte	genannt	*to name*
pfeifen	pfeift	pfiff	gepfiffen	*to whistle*
raten	rät	riet	geraten	*to advise*
reiben	reibt	rieb	gerieben	*to rub*
reißen	reißt	riß	gerissen	*to tear*
reiten	reitet	ritt	*geritten	*to ride (also + haben)*
rennen	rennt	rannte	*gerannt	*to run/race*
riechen	riecht	roch	gerochen	*to smell*
rufen	ruft	rief	gerufen	*to call*
saufen	säuft	soff	gesoffen	*to drink (of animals)*
schaffen	schafft	schuf	geschaffen	*to create*
scheiden	scheidet	schied	*geschieden	*to part (also + haben)*
scheinen	scheint	schien	geschienen	*to shine/seem*
schieben	schiebt	schob	geschoben	*to push*
schießen	schießt	schoß	geschossen	*to shoot*
schlafen	schläft	schlief	geschlafen	*to sleep*
schlagen	schlägt	schlug	geschlagen	*to hit/strike*
schließen	schließt	schloß	geschlossen	*to shut*
schneiden	schneidet	schnitt	geschnitten	*to cut*
schreiben	schreibt	schrieb	geschrieben	*to write*
schreien	schreit	schrie	geschrien	*to shout*
schreiten	schreitet	schritt	*geschritten	*to stride*
schweigen	schweigt	schwieg	geschwiegen	*to be silent*
schwimmen	schwimmt	schwamm	*geschwommen	*to swim*
schwinden	schwindet	schwand	*geschwunden	*to vanish*
sehen	sieht	sah	gesehen	*to see*
sein	ist	war	*gewesen	*to be*
senden	sendet	sandte	gesandt	*to send*
singen	singt	sang	gesungen	*to sing*
sinken	sinkt	sank	*gesunken	*to sink*
sitzen	sitzt	saß	gesessen	*to sit*
sollen	soll	sollte	gesollt	*to owe (ought/should)*
sprechen	spricht	sprach	gesprochen	*to speak*
springen	springt	sprang	*gesprungen	*to jump*
stehen	steht	stand	gestanden	*to stand*
stehlen	stiehlt	stahl	gestohlen	*to steal*
steigen	steigt	stieg	*gestiegen	*to climb*
sterben	stirbt	starb	*gestorben	*to die*
stoßen	stößt	stieß	gestoßen	*to push*
tragen	trägt	trug	getragen	*to wear/carry*
treffen	trifft	traf	getroffen	*to meet/hit*

treiben	treibt	trieb	getrieben	*to drive/go in for*
treten	tritt	trat	*getreten	*to step (also + haben)*
trinken	trinkt	trank	getrunken	*to drink*
tun	tut	tat	getan	*to do*
vergessen	vergißt	vergaß	vergessen	*to forget*
verlieren	verliert	verlor	verloren	*to lose*
wachsen	wächst	wuchs	*gewachsen	*to grow*
waschen	wäscht	wusch	gewaschen	*to wash*
weisen	weist	wies	gewiesen	*to point*
wenden	wendet	wandte	gewandt	*to turn*
werden	wird	wurde	*geworden	*to become*
werfen	wirft	warf	geworfen	*to throw*
wiegen	wiegt	wog	gewogen	*to weigh*
wissen	weiß	wußte	gewußt	*to know*
wollen	will	wollte	gewollt	*to want to*
ziehen	zieht	zog	gezogen	*to pull*
zwingen	zwingt	zwang	gezwungen	*to force*

Weak Verbs

(a) Verbs in this book other than those listed above and their compounds are weak and follow the pattern of kochen, e.g.

kochen   kocht   kochte   gekocht   *to cook*

(b) Verbs ending in -*ieren* omit the *ge-* in the past participle, e.g.

telefonieren   telefoniert   telefonierte   telefoniert *to phone*.

INDEX

R. Warson
Accounts and Book-keeping

The contents of this Study Aid include: profits and stock, profit and loss, the balance sheet, adjustments, the trial balance, final accounts, the journal, banking and petty cash, VAT, control accounts, receipts and payments, income and expenditure, partnership, limited liability.

C. A. Leeds
British Government and Politics

Contents are as follows: basic principles of government, the monarchy, prime minister and cabinet, Parliament, the civil service, the welfare state, political parties, voting and elections, public opinion, trade unions, local government, the legal system, the EEC and Commonwealth, devolution.

N. P. O. Green, J. M. Potter and G. W. Stout
Biology

Contents are as follows: the cell and organization of life, nutrition, respiration, transport, excretion, temperature regulation, coordination, the skeleton and locomotion, reproduction, growth and development, genetics and evolution, ecology, microbiology.

M. J. Denial
Chemistry

Contents are as follows: atomic structure, kinetic theory and bonding, elements, compounds and mixtures, purification, electrochemistry, acids, bases and salts, the air, gases, oxygen and hydrogen, the periodic table, the mole, formulae and equations, metals and their compounds, water, soaps and detergents, analysis, organic chemistry, energy, rates of reaction, the chemical industry.

R. P. Jones and I. Hobday
Commerce

Contents are as follows: the structure of industry and commerce, the retail trade, the wholesale and commodity markets, buying and selling, private enterprise, the public sector, transport and communications, international trade, money and banking, the Stock Exchange, insurance.

D. P. Baron and J. F. Connor
Economics

Contents are as follows: the economic problem and economic systems, organization of economic activity, population, location of industry, production, labour, unemployment, wages and trade unions, demand, supply and price, money and banking, inflation, public finance, national income, international trade, the government and the economy.

P. J. Hills and H. Barlow
Effective Study Skills

Contents are as follows: focusing attention and concentration, reading faster and more efficiently, finding information and using libraries, making notes, essay writing, punctuation and spelling, revision, taking an examination.

L. E. W. Smith
English Language

Contents are as follows: composition, factual writing (including letter writing), summary, comprehension, grammar, direct and indirect speech, figures of speech and idiom, paraphrase, vocabulary, spelling and punctuation.

C. Beswick and P. J. Downes
French

Contents are as follows: revising grammar, revising vocabulary, exam preparation, translation from French, prose composition, comprehension, essay writing, oral tests, dictation, verb tables.

E. W. Young
Geography 1: Physical and Human

Contents are as follows: planet Earth, landscapes and landforms, weather and climate, vegetation regions, fishing, forestry and mining, energy resources, farming, settlement, industry, trade and transport, Ordnance Survey maps.

Geography 2: British Isles, Western Europe, North America

Contents are as follows: British Isles – physical, settlement, agriculture, fishing and forestry, energy resources, industry; Western Europe – structure, climate and settlement, agriculture, energy resources, industry; North America – structure, climate and settlement, agriculture, energy resources, industry; some world problems.

Brian Catchpole
History 1: British

Contents are as follows: British economic and social history 1700–1980 – the beginnings of industrial change, the first industrial nation, from the First World War to the present day; British political history 1760–1980.

History 2: European

Contents are as follows: Europe 1789–1914 – the French Revolution and Napoleon, Europe 1815–1849, creation and consolidation of the nation states to *c.* 1870, major themes 1870–1914; Europe and world history 1914–1980 – the First World War and the peace treaties, the Russian Revolutions, between the wars, the Second World War, European and world history since 1945.

Human Biology

Contents are as follows: living organisms and their relationships, cell structure and function, the skin and temperature regulation, the skeleton, muscles and movement, breathing, the circulatory system, nutrition, digestion, excretion, coordination, perception of stimuli, reproduction and child development, inheritance, prevention of disease.

F. G. J. Norton
Maths

Contents are as follows: arithmetic, units, areas and volume, ratio and percentage, algebra, graphs, set notion, binary operations and groups, relations and functions, statistics, probability, geometry, theorems, loci and constructions, trigonometry, sine and cosine formulae, matrices, vectors, calculus.

M. Nelkon and M. V. Detheridge
Physics

Contents are as follows: dynamics, statics, forces due to fluids, molecules and properties of matter, heat, waves and sound, optics, current electricity, magnetism and electromagnetism, electric charge and the structure of matter.

Derek Utley
Spanish

Contents include: revising grammar, revising vocabulary, exam preparation, translation from Spanish, prose composition, comprehension, essay writing, oral tests, dictation, verb tables.

Reference, language and information

☐	**A Guide to Insurance**	Margaret Allen	£1.95p
☐	**The Story of Language**	C. L. Barber	£1.95p
☐	**North-South**	Brandt Commission	£2.50p
☐	**Manifesto**	Francis Cripps et al	£1.95p
☐	**Save It! The Energy**	Gary Hammond,	
	Consumer's Handbook	Kevin Newport and	
		Carol Russell	£1.25p
☐	**Mathematics for the**		
	Million	L. Hogben	£1.95p
☐	**Militant Islam**	Godfrey Jansen	£1.50p
☐	**The State of the**	Michael Kidron and	
	World Atlas	Ronald Segal	£6.95p
☐	**Practical Statistics**	R. Langley	£1.95p
☐	**A Guide to Speaking in**		
	Public	Robert Seton Lawrence	£1.25p
☐	**How to Study**	H. Maddox	£1.75p
☐	**Dictionary of Life Sciences**	E. A. Martin	£2.95p
☐	**Your Guide to the Law**	ed. Michael Molyneux	£3.50p
☐	**Common Security**	Palme Commission	£1.95p
☐	**The Modern Crossword**		
	Dictionary	Norman Pulsford	£2.25p
☐	**English Proverbs**		
	Explained	James Reeves	£1.75p
☐	**Pan Spelling Dictionary**	Ronald Ridout	£1.50p
☐	**A Guide to Saving**		
	and Investment	James Rowlatt	£2.50p
☐	**Career Choice**	Audrey Segal	£2.95p
☐	**Logic and its Limits**	Patrick Shaw	£2.95p
☐	**Names for Boys and Girls**	L. Sleigh and C. Johnson	£1.50p
☐	**Straight and Crooked**		
	Thinking	R. H. Thouless	£1.50p
☐	**The Best English**	G. H. Vallins	80p
☐	**Money Matters**	Harriet Wilson	£1.25p
☐	**Dictionary of Earth Sciences**		£2.95p
☐	**Dictionary of Economics and Commerce**		£1.50p
☐	**Dictionary of Philosophy**		£2.50p
☐	**Dictionary of Physical Sciences**		£2.95p
☐	**Harrap's New Pocket French and English**		
	Dictionary		£2.50p
☐	**The Limits to Growth**		£1.50p
☐	**Pan Dictionary of Synonyms and Antonyms**		£1.95p
☐	**Pan English Dictionary**		£2.50p

☐ **Pan International Pocket Atlas**		£2.95p
☐ **Universal Encyclopaedia of Mathematics**		£2.95p

Literature guides

☐ **An Introduction to Shakespeare and his Contemporaries**	Marguerite Alexander	£2.95p
☐ **An Introduction to Fifty American Poets**	Peter Jones	£1.75p
☐ **An Introduction to Fifty Modern British Plays**	Benedict Nightingale	£2.95p
☐ **An Introduction to Fifty American Novels**	Ian Ousby	£1.95p
☐ **An Introduction to Fifty British Novels 1600—1900**	Gilbert Phelps	£2.50p
☐ **An Introduction to Fifty Modern European Poets**	John Pilling	£2.25p
☐ **An Introduction to Fifty British Poets 1300—1900**	Michael Schmidt	£1.95p
☐ **An Introduction to Fifty Modern British Poets**		£2.95p
☐ **An Introduction to Fifty European Novels**	Martin Seymour-Smith	£1.95p
☐ **An Introduction to Fifty British Plays 1660—1900**	John Cargill Thompson	£1.95p

All these books are available at your local bookshop or newsagent, or can be ordered direct from the publisher. Indicate the number of copies required and fill in the form below   7

Name_____
(Block letters please)

Address_____

_____

Send to Pan Books (CS Department), Cavaye Place, London SW10 9PG
Please enclose remittance to the value of the cover price plus:
35p for the first book plus 15p per copy for each additional book ordered
to a maximum charge of £1.25 to cover postage and packing
Applicable only in the UK

While every effort is made to keep prices low, it is sometimes necessary to increase prices at short notice. Pan Books reserve the right to show on covers and charge new retail prices which may differ from those advertised in the text or elsewhere